Praise for *Ricko Donovan* and *Sunnyville*

"literate, observational and very entertaining"
- The Muses Muse

"Donovan has a poetic flare for storytelling and artistic descriptions of life."
-Swift Reviews

"In this fantastic debut, Donovan fills a Florida retirement community with a full range of eclectic, unforgettable characters, lifting the veil of the American psyche; the story reveals the breezy- and oftentimes chaotic- world of retirement with some fictional people you may or may not recognize without their filters or hearing aids turned up. This one's a delightful, engaging read that allows you to fully appreciate everything good in your life, body, and soul."
-Nashville Magazine

www.rickodonovan.com

The Broken Promised Land

Ricko Donovan

This book is a work of fiction. The characters, incidents, and dialogue are drawn from the author's imagination and are not to be construed as real. Any resemblance to actual events or persons, living or dead, is entirely coincidental.

The Broken Promised Land. Copyright © 2013 Ricko Donovan. All rights reserved. Printed in the United States of America. No part of this book may be used or reproduced in any manner whatsoever without written permission except in the case of brief quotations embodied in critical articles and reviews.

ISBN-10: 0991188209
ISBN-13: 978-0991188208

Also by Ricko Donovan-

Sunnyville

Acknowledgements

I would like to express my profoundest gratitude to my editors Sherry Wilds and Gail Twine, Wildacres Writers Workshop for providing a foundation for learning the elements of a good story, The Nashville Writers Meetup, both my writing critique and literature tertulia groups in Madrid Spain, to Cosima Knopfel and Jans Schurmanns in Ireland, both of whom provided an idyllic place to work on a good deal of the early drafts of the manuscript all those years ago.

Monday, Her Back To Him

The road was heavily overgrown and they had to stop the trucks a few times on the way in to hack down branches and once to move a felled tree. Now the string of SUVs wind their way back over an old dirt road that is riddled with potholes, hidden by overgrown rhododendrons and sagebrush. Truck wheels trample over brittle sticks, kicking up dust. Branches whack against doors bearing the official DEA seal. The crunch and snap of disruption echoes all over the forest. Inside the last of the trucks are one hundred and twenty six cellophane-wrapped cannabis plants. The dry leaves, stems and flowering tops of hemp plants with the life sucked out of them. Freshly uprooted, neatly stacked and tagged as evidence.

The uniformed men in the trucks speak about yesterday's football games on the jouncing drive along the dirt road and out of the property with a fired intensity that exalts what is merely a simple game to the magnitude of no less than World War Three. A rundown of yesterday's scores on the crackling radio. It is 1991 and there is no hope for Green Bay, the New York or is it Jersey Giants seem sure to repeat, *blah, blah blah*. Madonna has just brought out the racy *Truth or Dare* and one of the men in the trucks wags his head and calls her a fuckin dyke bitch. There is no talk about the seized marijuana plants, because these men aren't interested in marijuana inasmuch as it keeps them in a living and besides their work is done.

An Indian-summer night is long lost to this crystal clear October morning and in the woods cool rushes of air whisper through the branches of pines, the only sound besides the caws of those remaining sparrows and robins who haven't yet packed off for the winter. There are no hunters here, nor ought there be. This is *private property*, marked as such here and there along its one hundred and four acres by weathered signs.

Peace is restored to the forest. A powerful gust of wind blows through a patch of maple trees with just enough vigour to strip a single maple leaf that has lost enough color and life to be taken, its time has come and it glides in the air on a current that leaves it soaring over the heads of the men talking gibberish in the trucks. It will sail just a few miles over pine and chestnut, the fading white wisps of rhododendron, maple, fern, dogwood- it will lilt over the tarmac of two-lane Highway 52, waver and dance in the air way above the white steeple of Rugby's Christ Church Episcopal and come to rest on dying grass at the feet of a man and a woman having just sprung themselves from the gloomy innards of the church. The man will pick it up and hold it before the sunlight to display its arteries the carriers of life, run its barely crinkled singularity through his calloused fingers. *This is the first leaf of fall*, he will announce to she whom he loves and he will hold it tight in his fist and he will kiss her on the mouth, lightly. When he returns the half-dead leaf to the ground at their feet they will understand that this is Fall, the beginning of the end.

*   *   *

She heard him coming. Right in the middle of unloading groceries from the station wagon in the rain. The rear door is still open, bags waiting to be fetched. The sound of car wheels on the gravel drew her to the front door.

A muddy white Ford Taurus bearing the Department of Justice U.S. Federal Marshall Service insignia on its door pulls to an abrupt stop at the front porch. A short pudgy man wiggles out of the car, spitting a loogie on the ground, sniffing at the air with a pug nose and clutching a clipboard.

She pushes the screen door open and then it slams on its hinges behind her as she strides onto the paint-peeled porch.

Can I help you she asks in a tone more impersonal than that of a sales clerk to a loitering customer, with her arms folded tightly. A woman with a wrinkled face and dark hair with streaks of grey tied up in a bun, and fending off mid-life weight gain with a little more success than the federal marshal before her.

Gripping his staple gun he waddles towards her, fixing his gaze over her shoulder on the big oak door behind.

I'm here to serve a notice, mam.

Notice. For what.

He stops for a moment, bringing a hand to his chin as if he can't quite put a finger on what's brought him to this property in the deep woods of the Cumberland Plateau in East Tennessee on a rainy Monday afternoon.

To a reedy voice is injected the command of an official as he places a foot onto the front steps and grips the staple gun in his pudgy fist.

It's all here on the notice, ma'am. I have a copy here for you. I'll just have to post this on your door, he mutters, making a move to pass around her.

But she isn't having any of this, snatching the papers right out of his hands and turning her back to him. Clutching them in both hands and drawing her reading glasses from the pocket of her plaid blouse, scrutinizing the bold headline with a start.

Notice of Forfeiture.

There must be some mistake she says, slapping the papers against her denim skirt.

Strong words of protestation are slow to be conjured out of her bewildered mind as she wiggles the documents under his nose, and he seizes this opportunity to snatch the papers back. From a distance they might be two kids arguing for possession of a toy. With an air of having exhausted all attempts at civility with an unruly child, he places it up against the oak door with his free hand while punching a staple through with the gun.

I'm not here to argue about your case, ma'am. I'm just doing my job, he shrugs. And my job being done I must be going.

My *case!* What the hell is going on here!

She digs a thin heel into the porch's paint-peeled floor. But he's already turned his back to her and shuffles off, with a walk just shy of a jog, back to the Taurus. He chucks the staple gun over the front seat and onto a frazzled map, jabbing the key at the ignition before his ass is situated on the seat, starts the car and bolts away, leaving a trail of gravel dust to drift across the front yard like a storm cloud.

She retreats inside the house and the living room near the picture window, flopping down into an antique loveseat. Clutches the notice in one hand and plants her head in the other.

Regarding the living room as an inappropriate venue for legal analysis, she picks up the copy of the notice and carries it to the dining room. She draws a chair, pulls it in close to the table and places the paper in front of her. Cold analysis. Scrutinizing each word of the document at the dining room table in her house to solve the riddle. Surely the whole thing is a misunderstanding.

One hundred and twenty six marijuana plants growing on a parcel of a 104-acre tract of land. A cash bond must be posted for the lesser of ten percent of the appraised property value or twelve-thousand dollars. Surely this is an administrative blunder, an indolent clerk at the courthouse typed the wrong address on the notice. Some unfortunate quagmire they'll just have to be inconvenienced about. And yet underneath the calm veneer lies a strange sense of foreboding, an intuition that *this is all too real-* that perhaps certain facts might emerge, facts which are unknown to her, but might make themselves known, bearing all their weight down upon her. *Who did this? Who planted this stuff?* Was this one of her husband's cash income sources, one he neglected to tell her about? Or maybe her son- two months home, no job, no indication of getting a job- yes, it could be him. *Why didn't we push the kid more? How could we just let him stay home listless and not contribute to the family? How could I have just let him lay around all day with his girlfriend?* From such thoughts a fury is born.

Oh Sweet Jesus, she thinks, *banish such impropriety from my overcharged mind, this is only a damned accident, a bureaucratic blunder.*

She's possessed by a fresh urge to kick at something, find a target for her fiery rage. Her husband is out working one of his damned cash jobs, and her son's Chevelle is not in the driveway. So, confident of exclusive reign of the house, she rises and dances somewhat salaciously into the kitchen- picks up the aluminum colander and flings it at the wall. The tin hardly makes a sound, not a measure of destruction. She lifts the tall thin glass of iced coffee, chucks it sidearm at the wall. It shatters on impact- coffee splattering in all directions against the wall, dirtying it, sprouting fractals against a serene country motif on the wallpaper.

Yet the rage remains un-satiated. In nearly thirty years of marriage she has never broken a dish in anger, never flung one at the proverbial ducking husband. She snatches up her family heirloom, her best pie dish of decorative cut glass, with its remaining apple pie. She lifts it with both hands and does a sort of overhead slam, shards of glass skip across the linoleum, leaving bits of pie stuck to the floor.

This unbridled tantrum yields to relief, since anger is one emotion she hasn't tapped much lately, despite a few therapeutic approaches she's happened upon in self-help books extolling the virtues of *letting go*. She drums her fists on the kitchen table, spilling all its contents with one broad sweep. They crash to the floor and she stomps up and down in her delicate heels, one lands on some cylindrical object and she feels her weight fall out from underneath her, spills to the floor *on her ass*, sits there stunned as the tiny pink capsules spill over the floor in every direction. Her knees against the cold tile, she retrieves the very cause of her downfall- a tiny brown prescription bottle, its plastic splintered but the white pharmacy label Rx intact. Cupping it in her hands, she reads that which she verifies and re-verifies on a daily basis. *Ellen Griffith, take one tablet by mouth every day with a meal Lovastatin 40 mg tablet, Generic for Mevacor.* Her back aches but she gets up and gathers the other prescription bottles yet intact. *Ellen Griffith, take one tablet by mouth every day, Atorvistatin 20 mg tablet, Generic for Lipitor. Ellen Griffith, take one tablet two times daily, Chlorothiazide 250 mg tablet, Generic for Diuril. Ellen Griffith, take one tablet two times daily, Diazepam 10 mg tablet, Generic for Valium.* Squeezing them, she draws a deep breath, exhaling and returning the spilled pills for cholesterol, blood pressure, anxiety and a few other issues back onto the kitchen table; fetching a sponge from the sink, cleaning up.

*   *   *

Ellen is not alone in the house. Her son Walt is upstairs in his old bedroom, lying naked on his back sucking at a cigarette- the crashing sounds in the kitchen just underneath are somewhat muted by the erratic hum and rumble of a window air conditioner nearing its last breath. Cindy Blum glances over at him, puzzled at the aberrant noises below. Walt Griffith merely shrugs, waves a dismissive hand while exhaling a stream of smoke at the ceiling, wanting to articulate- instead cracking his knuckles and fidgeting with the sheets while she stares impassively at the ceiling.

Are you- he gropes for words contemplatively- were you... I mean...

His utterances trail off- disappear into the dark corners of the bedroom- unkempt corners of castaway unlaundered clothes, dirty ashtrays, cassette cases, and other such clutter- a room kept intact for him throughout collegiate years, as if Mom had intuited his inevitable full-scale return.

Cindy sighs. Hmmm?

He fidgets and the ancient box spring creaks in response. Do I- can I...

Manhood on the line, he squeezes his eyes shut, imagines himself teetering precariously on the clothesline in the backyard of yesteryear, by the creek where his mother hung the laundry out to dry.

Are you satisfied?

With what? Cindy studies her nails.

I just feel like, sometimes you know, you don't, ummm, feel... sometimes, n-not always, but sometimes... it's like you're not feeling anything... I mean...

I like being in bed with you, she says, curling up in the sheets with her back to him. He stubs out the cigarette in the white marble ashtray on the nightstand. The room is an icy haven from the hot and sticky summer just outside. The crashing noises have ceased, he guesses it's just mom returning from shopping and trying to make the Jaycees, or the Lions Club, or the Women of Christ Church Episcopal Tuesday Night Baked Good Club or something.

Walt sits up in bed against the oak headboard and reaches across to the bedside table he'd used in his youth for storing baseball cards. He opens the wooden drawer and pulls out a Florida Sunshine State decorative plate, nestled in it is a curled-up plastic baggie, its green contents spilling decoratively around it like glitter. He takes his time rolling, at last licking shut a tightly packed joint. He positions it between Cindy's lips and strikes a match. He hates lighters. There is something about the striking of a match- the ignition, the spark on sulfur and then the tiny blue flame- something smells of ritual, lends an air of magic to this method of generating flame. They pass the joint back and forth.

He squirms out of bed and fires up the portable TV, and its warm radiant glow soon fills the room. He climbs back into bed, feeling his way through the cold sheets to the warm outline where his body heat still has left its imprint of warmth. It still feels cold underneath the sheets. Her warm feet rub at his chilly calves, embedded in the sensation is the promise of surprise, the hope of some unforeseen and fortunate twist of luck, some uncharted future event, the nibbling of change, the transience of the Winter Solstice, the very mire of life entering his bloodstream, carrying buoyant thoughts to his brain. He starts going on about some band he will form, he's been writing some good songs again, he's gonna get it together, him and Gavin, like old times, he misses the road, misses the spirit of creating wonderful sounds with other people, all that shit. She can't bear hearing him talk about the band, an untenable abstraction- a defunct, bygone yesteryear that was never was as good as he makes it out to be- he sounds like some washed up former jock with burgeoning waistline and lost athletic prowess talking about his high school glory days.

You don't even hang out with Gavin Sharpe anymore, she says to the television.

Well. Doesn't mean we can't be best friends.

It was one damp morning in freezing Cincinnati after a Christmas holiday gig when Walt's oldest friend Gavin decided in no uncertain terms never to pick up a guitar with anything more than a casual predilection, never endeavor to coax money from it. Their band Astroglide had played an all-ages show, the cokehead promoter got ugly and failed to come across with the money at the end of the night, leaving everyone coughing and digging in pockets for gas money that stinging cold Ohio night, like an icy X-ray piercing through to the bones. Scrounging around and searching every pocket to produce a dismal few wads of cash.

Cindy nonetheless lies there beside him in the cold tombs of bygone days- while he theorizes about pulling out and heading for Nashville in search of something other than the nine-to-five deal, something other than another stupid job in a stupid office somewhere, filing and typing and neglecting her degree in Fine Arts. *If things don't work out there baby, we'll go to Santa Fe, I hear there's a killer art scene out there.*

She lets the commentary hang, mulling despondently over Walt's plans. Bored.

On the television another slick Levis commercial. Nubile young things frolicking around the beach with perfectly chiseled torsos, flesh Michelangelos. The commercials promise so much, Cindy thinks, all that Madison Avenue if-you-can-dream-it-you-can-do-it you-go-girl hype that was never, could never ever be a reflection of real life. Real people didn't run along the beach like that. Real life broke you, as your dreams one by one went unrealized, you lost a little, like the aged boxer in the ring, each round taking a little more breath away.

I'm gonna do music as soon's we get to Nashville, baby. Gonna start playing the guitar again. Got the bug.

Yeah, mmm hmm...

I'm gonna bring some demos and walk Music Row until my tired feet can't walk anymore.

You don't even like country music.

Yeah, but I hear there's lots of things happening there right now, it's the place to be, just like Chapel Hill was-

-Yeah, mmm hmm...

I wonder what's taking Reagan with the Chevelle. He said it'd be ready by four.

Walt slumps down on the bed, propping his head on the pillows as some talk show host prepares to flog a dead horse with topics like *Moms Who Date Their Son-In-Laws, Twelve-Year-Olds Who Want To Have Babies, Twelve-Year-Olds Who Want To Get Married, Teenaged Fathers Dodging Child Support, Abortion Opponents Who Regularly Have Abortions, Men of the Cloth Addicted To Sex* and the resultant impassioned confrontation over these topics. Down and out topics.

Life, it seemed, was barreling down like an out-of-control fastball- a wild pitch while everybody looked on eating hotdogs in the grandstand. Or perhaps like the arcing spiral of a pigskin, that graceful coming down to earth of a long pass, the *bomb*, on slow motion NFL highlights- it seemed so many things were spiraling *down* around him. So many people trying to dodge the whirling downward force, only to be sucked into the vortex of distress. Take Jim Ferrer, Walt's old Little League teammate who lived just down the road. He'd gone the way of Wharton Business School, while Walt had stayed relatively local and messed around for five odd years in a clever rendition of a UNC undergraduate degree-seeking student. Jim graduated, got married and went to work for Arthur Anderson P.A. he was his gin-soaked bored-housewife mother's pride and favorite boasting topic. A child began a family and Jim's drinking ended it.

So Jim's back home as well. Broke. Who the hell knows where all the money went, his stranded ex-wife sure as hell would like to know. The only important fact is that Jim is home and he's not very happy. And to sustain a vague sense of responsibility and help a mother pay the twilight of thirty years' mortgage, he works part-time cooking the books for a few self-employed locals. He also mows lawns for The Lawn Stylist, a.k.a. Clyde Simmons, in the hot sun on occasion, much of the same lawns he'd cut as an eager fourteen-year-old.

Then there's Mr. Miller, the Suit- who read from the Holy Scriptures at the podium in a sleepy monotone to Mrs. Griffith and the rest of the congregation at Rugby's Christ Church Episcopal. Mr. Miller had until recently put bread and money on the table via a long-standing employment with DuPont over in Oak Ridge. His twenty-one-year rise up a ladder of offices in that particular ivory tower was terminated on April 18, 1990 in a hostile takeover by a new face in a new suit with a new family and American dreams under his graduate school belt. And so the Suit had packed up all his belongings, including the family portrait of kids with glowing white smiles stood before he and a dutiful wife and mother, her hands resting upon the shoulders of her little future capitalist dreamers. The Suit packed the framed picture in between conference notes and personnel management guideline manuals and then promptly vacated the premises in accordance with written procedures intended to dull the stab of humiliation- he went *down down down* hard, downstairs to the lobby and then to the parking lot in which he'd held extended office conversations that had seemed so utterly critical, so earth-shatteringly important on those twilit nights of the past. Now the blacktop was silent of voices and all he could think of was what the fuck for? His only imprint on human history lay in corporate payroll records. Who would remember whatever the hell he did there for twenty-one malnourished years fending off soul-searching and perhaps some of a universal truth he could only sniff at, choosing instead to spend a lifetime toiling at one determinate task after another for which he was made to believe was so significant. Everyone with their feet planted in companies that were but companies among other companies, an adult extension of little league baseball. Salesmen lying so much they actually believe the lie and what they figure as reality- *Our company delivers! We offer the best products and services*, and *Satisfaction guaranteed. Guaranteed!* and *Our customers are gold, Let our team work for your team* and *Go with a winner* and all the other hyperbole- gluttonous statements emblazoned on company brochures, magazines, and billboards.

Now Mr. Milton Miller was back *down* in Burrville, having fallen from that Ivory Tower in which he'd sweated through promotion announcements. He worked for his brother-in-law as a hack plumber some evenings, liberating clogged drainpipes of hair clumps by means of a plumbing device called the snake. He worked at a corporate-owned supermarket chain as a materials handler. Bagging groceries brought forth much in the way of nice childhood memories but little in the way of compensation.

And the reports kept coming in from the field to Walt, most of the information being disseminated by Mom, the source of all news of the tragedies in other people's lives, at the same time neglectful of those weeds of tragedy in her own little garden- a lackluster son dreaming of a jumpstart, a husband with his own tumble from an estimable management position to odd jobs, their subsequent money problems, and a daughter's marital issues. But Walt's Mom still had her Will, MIT scholar, to buoy her spirits, avoid total collapse into the spiraling nucleus of despair.

And so everybody disrupted everyone else, pulling at one another, spiraling into their web that circled around a black hole of vexation and confusion. Like when Walt dropped in on the Millers last week to borrow a rolling pin for momma. Mrs. Miller had rasped- when Mr. Miller announced he'd seen a flyer posted on the bulletin board by the whirring automatic doors at the supermarket. A meeting of the Native American Culture Society and its offering of healing, building inner life, spiritual enrichment through group transcendence by way of the beating of drums and dance, convening with Mother Earth- *What the hell you wanna do cavorting around some fire with those maladjusted crazy new age people for, when you can stay home and watch Jeopardy and see if my brother has any work for you?-* she talked to him in the manner she used to talk to her teenaged kids. He flopped back down in the recliner- down on things, down on life, down all the days, *down.*

Walt is getting ready to go *down* on Cindy when he hears the pounding of footsteps on the staircase and then right up into the hallway outside the door, causing him to jump out of bed and scamper about in all directions, grabbing his pants here, groping the empty condom package there, stubbing his toe on the bottle of Paul Masson Chardonnay, as Cindy bunches the sheets against her mouth to try and muffle an uncontrollable laughter. Thinking there isn't a chance in hell Mrs. Griffith would barge in on their *tête a tête-* Walt's mother has tried to exude a cool indifference, a begrudged respect for the privacy of an adult living at home *just think of it like an apartment* she smiles, placating, trying to keep everybody happy in a perhaps untenable living situation. All the same, Walt isn't taking any chances.

It's a pretty good idea too, because his mother suspends her privacy concessions, flinging the door wide open before he can pull his pants around his waist, Cindy sitting stark naked, legs flung haphazardly over the bedside and grasping desperately at the sheets, too late.

Ellen shuts the door without admonition or chastisement, shuffling mechanically towards the foot of the stairs in search of some chore to return her to the humdrum of life. She remembers the remainder of the shopping order waiting for her in the station wagon out in front of the house, sprints to the car and returns to the house huffing and puffing with a paper bag of groceries pressed against each bosom. She deftly kicks the door behind her against the heat, drops the bags on the kitchen table, pausing a minute to re-position her bifocals and catch her breath. The clock's tick underscores her heavy breathing. She thinks for a second of asking Walt for a hand, then cancels it out resentfully and returns to the station wagon for the rest of the brown paper bags. Kicks the car door closed and clambers up the back porch and into the kitchen. Fills a glass with tap water and downs two tablets of cholesterol medicine in one gulp. Settles into one of the hard-backed chairs, resting one stockinged foot upon another, determined to enjoy a little solitude after a long day of screaming middle-schoolers and a nagging government official. She's fidgety yet, up and pacing what would constitute the original structure of the Griffith residence, built in the Year of our Lord 1866 by the hands of Seamus Griffin, landlord and farmer of thirty acres of Tennessee land. After obtaining the original deed to the property, Seamus leased parcels to tenant farmers with the abolishment of slavery. The original structure a modest basement, kitchen, living room, a bedroom since converted to a dining room, a front porch now enclosed.

The construction of the three bedrooms upstairs and the extension on the kitchen and the study at the back of the house came to be with a home equity loan. By then a five-member family's cohabitation of a single room was considered a primitive arrangement and privacy became the standard.

In the living room, with the fading sunlight of a dying day spilling through the floor to ceiling windows onto the hardwood floor, she coughs and worries over the possibility of another bout of bronchitis, having just ended thirty years of a steady stream of cigarettes. She imagines dust mites, allergens and then that special vacuum she saw last week that killed all the dangerous micro-organisms living unseen on your home. *How about a vacuum for government officials*, she ponders, studying the old black and white framed photograph of great-great-grandfather Seamus, bearing a musket and a vacant stare in Confederate soldier uniform. More photographs underneath. Seamus's grandchild John Sr. and his wife Elva, John's grandfather and grandmother. In all of these deteriorating black and white photographs the subjects bear only serious countenances. These were the early days of the camera, no one yet had learned how to be silly, or sexy, or conscious of smiling. They bore only the face of life. Life was difficult, why wear a face to suggest otherwise? A black and white of John and his sister Mary perched on a Shetland pony. John plays the serious cowboy, but Mary has a smirk that seems to suggest her own secret inner lens of bemusement at the world around her.

John's grandfather described *his* grandfather as a mostly humorless and serious man who said little, but when he spoke it was generally in nonsensical riddles. He worked tirelessly at cultivating a then-overgrown land. And so the faces of those who began the Griffith lineage in this very house watch Ellen Griffith as she listens to Cindy Blum soft-stepping down the stairs, through the kitchen and out the back door, disappearing without so much as a wave.

Ellen's own lineage unknown. Suffice to say that her Aunt Merry raised her from infancy. Aunt Merry would only say that her mother had gotten herself into some kind of man trouble, but that was it. She could learn nothing more about her mother, and there was no mention of a father. Aunt Merry was responsible for naming her and then raising her. And raise her Merry did, with a most joyless efficiency. Ellen's aunt was a complete antonym of her name- a cheerless tomb of secrecy. She did little else besides command the running of her husband Shoe's general store and pray her Rosary three times daily. There not being any Catholic Church nearby, she held secret masses behind her bedroom door. The pungent scent of incenses and the hushed prayers betrayed these rituals. Ellen inherited an observance of holy days, prayers for the intercession of the Saints, and a well-repeated assertion that the Episcopalian faith was a poor substitute in this place not within striking range of a real Church based upon the ideological foundation of Roman Catholicism.

Aunt Merry's absence at Sunday morning breakfast left Ellen happily free to her own devices in the kitchen, without the pernicious old woman peering over her shoulder with corrections and commands. Ellen would carry water and chicken feed and then gather fresh eggs from the hen house, fry bacon in silence. The smell of heavy grease smothered the kitchen. Shoe would sit disconsolately, hung over from moonshine at the Saturday night bluegrass jamboree. *If you'd keep yer hands on the mandolin and off the whiskey bottle, maybe you'd have the energy for prayer*, Merry would say in the afternoon when she'd concluded her private Sunday mass to find Shoe fast asleep in the couch downstairs like he was most nights. Their marriage was a living arrangement, not a romantic alliance. They had no offspring. Shoe wasn't exactly enamored of children, often leaving the child Ellen to assume the status of dust mite in his presence. Shoe worked every day but Sunday. Every morning he'd be up at the crack of dawn to feed the hens, then prop himself up at the store for business. Every night he'd be down at the tavern, or at the Williams brothers' porch passing the bottle around.

On the fireplace mantle sits a recent family photo of her and John, energetic and eager young parents, hands resting on the shoulders of Barbara, Will, and Walt, all eyes aglow as if gazing into bright futures. A family with an eye on the world beyond. A family five generations fixed to the South, of accents with an odd trace of something else. A family of mainly balanced and healthy diets. A family rooted in dirt and tillers and horses, chicken coops and pigsties trying to grasp Sartre, M. Scott Peck, Bob Dylan, the Beatles, mind-altering substances, product diversity, broad-based marketing strategies, personal computers. A family both gathering and imparting information obtained in the ever-changing world around Burrville, around them.

Still gazing forlorn at the black and white images on the wall, with an agitated sigh she clicks on the 1935 Zenith black dial radio, a tombstone table model, sits among the dead on a re-upholstered couch to catch the five-o'clock news on WSM.

* * *

John Griffith returns a wool-knit hat to one of the pegs on the coat rack in the foyer. Ellen emerges from the kitchen and they nod silent acknowledgement. They don't kiss. He turns his back to her, gazing abstractedly through the window of the heavy oak door onto the driveway and the soft rain. Running his fingers through thinning gray-streaked hair, talking to himself. From her husband's mumbling, Ellen discerns the name of their son Will and wonders what brought this on? Speaking to a lost son as if to a dead spirit? Their son is lost only to Massachusetts Institute of Technology on a full academic scholarship after all.

John, she says. A government man was just here.

What sort of government man?

I think- I think we'd better sit down.

Where's Walt? he wants to know, following her into the dining room, where they sit at a ornately carved table, one of his early restoration projects.

I don't know, she says. Last I saw he was hopping around naked with that girlfriend of his in that- she rolls her eyes at the ceiling- room of his.

Any sign of him since?

I don't know. Off somewhere with Cindy I guess.

At the unfamiliar faltering in her voice, their eyes meet for an awkward moment. They've avoided even the briefest glance in recent years after many years of meeting eyes for long spells. The uncomfortable trance between them is broken by the document she slides over to his side of the table. Then she tells him.

The range of emotions that spill across his face bewilders her, she can't recall witnessing such fierce passion in his soft blue eyes since that grim day five years ago when he'd finally gathered himself to inform her he'd lost his management job at the mill.

At her accounting the afternoon's events, he fidgets in his chair, drumming his fingers on the table. Stiffens at her tenuous probe of his knowledge of the plants. Yeah right. I was just on my way now to tend to the godamn plants.

Ellen blinks at his sarcasm. Well that's not all, she says. If we want to contest it we have to post a twelve-thousand dollar bond with a claim to the property within ten days.

Well that's sure as hell a drop in the bucket right now.

He pounds a fist on the table, springs to his feet. I have to call Clem. I hope he hasn't left the office yet.

In the kitchen he lifts the earpiece from the cradle of an antique wall phone. After three rings, a voice buzzes nasally.

Carter and Associates.

It's Clem's new receptionist Janet. His secretary of fifteen years recently retired, beating him to the finish line.

Is Clem in?

Mr. Carter is with a client at the moment.

Please tell him John Griffith's on the line. An emergency.

One moment please.

The woman at the other end is mildly annoyed. It's five-thirty, she wants to tidy up her desk and go home. Ellen stands in the doorframe off the foyer listening, watching John's back.

Hello Clem… I'm, I got some trouble here... Big trouble, you *know*? Wh-what do you know Clem? On your way home? Yeah…okay, see you over at your place.

The light rain is now a heavy downpour as he retrieves his wool hat in the foyer. Ellen slumps against the wall, arms folded. What's going on?

Clem's waitin on me, he mutters.

Ellen watches as her husband is soaked under the heavy rain as he bolts towards the pickup, hops in the cab and rockets down the gravel driveway.

*   *   *

"Before an individual can be heard to contest a forfeiture claim, he must demonstrate standing through procedures set forth in rule, requiring party to file claim within ten days after process has been executed or within such additional time as may be allowed by court, and to file an answer within twenty days of filing claim."- Supplemental Admiralty and Maritime Claims Rule C (6) 28 U.S.C.A.

Oh Jesus, Clem Carter shakes the forfeiture notice, just when I thought it was time to hang up the late nights and legal documents, go huntin, fishin, sit my fat ass and a six-pack on a canoe in the Big South Fork, you get yourself a full-fledged run-in with the Feds.

Clem peers over bifocals, stroking a thick grey moustache and taking a deep breath from his paunch. Well, he says, your property does anyway.

John sinks into one of a pair of leather chairs across from Clem's big oak desk in the basement office he'd used immediately after law school. Before starting his own practice with an office in downtown Jamestown. There they settle in the basement among bookshelves stacked with Tennessee Code, Federal Code, Case Law, acquired over the years of practice until now meant nothing other than soundproofing for John, now the volumes would have to be gleaned for anything relevant to his case. This room in the basement had been a refuge for two old friends to share whiskey and easy conversation. Now it's become the war planning room.

What's the meaning of this Clem? I've got but two years left on that home improvement loan.

Well, John, I have to tell you the property's at risk.

Just that one tract of land?

I dunno, Clem tempers John's untenable hope. Maybe everything. Including the house.

With his impending retirement, Clem's already begun to let his hair down a little, curly gray hair has reached his collar. He rises to pour whiskey and pushes a glass across the desk at John.

John, you know I cut my teeth on civil matters. Property deeds, estate settlement, registering, incorporating. Y'know that sort of thing. Advising small businesses. So I'm as up on the law as any good lawyer when it comes to property transfer, buying and selling, that kind of thing. Been dealing with it for almost forty years now, as you well know. But property seizure, asset forfeiture? I have to say we're bumpin up against some unfamiliar territory.

John slumps over the desk, folds his arms and buries his head, the desk lamp casting an eerie glow.

Now I'll help you all I can, you know that John.

Sure.

Clem rises and steps out from behind his desk. Just give me a couple of days, I can find out what I can on this. I've only read about it in legal journals. Never actually met it firsthand.

Wish it coulda stayed that way.

So do I, Clem says, patting John's shoulder. But here it is under our noses, and I'm at your service. And don't expect a bill.

John lifts his head from folded arms.

Clem, really-

-You haven't asked a damn thing of me in your life- Clem leans in close enough for John to get a whiff of the whiskey on his breath- or anyone else for that matter.

He retraces his steps and plunks down in the swivel chair behind the desk.

Now, he says, we've got ten days to file a claim defending against the forfeiture proceeding. Then twenty more days to draft a letter exonerating you of any connection to the wrongdoing. So we'll file the claim, then let's get that letter out as soon's we can. I'll have Janet pull anything pertinent to this forfeiture business from the office library. Meanwhile, can you get to Nashville any time soon?

John shakes his head uncomprehendingly.

Vanderbilt, Clem says, has an extensive library on campus there at the law school. You can get plenty of info on this stuff.

But what the hell am I looking for?

Anything and everything you can find on federal asset forfeiture law. But go easy on the case law, John. Just copy down the case citation numbers.

The what?

Every case that comes to court has a reference number. It's how we search for precedent, any cases which have been heard before a judge or jury on the particular body of law we're interested in defending. Or prosecuting, as it were. Meanwhile, I have the latest West library. I have a lot right here- he taps the monitor of his computer- These little babies have sure as hell made my life easier. Less damn paper too.

Clem strikes a match and lights a cigar stub, and the glare accentuates a thick gray moustache. His thick dark brown hair is all but overtaken by light silver. John wonders when his faithful friend's smooth loyalty might yield to the coarseness of betrayal.

I can get all the case law you want, says Clem. These cases are pretty cut and dried. We'll do the best we can, no doubt. I can only promise my best efforts for my best friend.

I know. John taps a cigarette from a full package in his flannel shirt pocket, rolling it through his fingers- it's only been an hour at most since he pulled into the convenience store on the way to Clem and Miriam's house. Left the engine running, ran in and asked at the counter for a pack of that old crutch, something he hadn't done for years. At last, wiping the tears from his eyes, he lights it.

It's just that I can't sit by and promise you a happy ending Clem says, puffing vigorously at his cigar like it's water in the desert. I mean, government doesn't exactly fool around when it comes to asset forfeiture John. I called an old law school buddy of mine after I hung up with you. Fellow by the name of Luther. DEA Legal Advisor in Nashville. He's out of town on federal business. They wouldn't give me a damn phone number where I can reach him. So I called his house. Susan has the number of his hotel. She's not supposed to give it out. But he calls home every night, so she'll tell him to call me here next time they speak. I also have a call in to my pal Meeks, the judge. But just exactly what they can do? Who the hell knows, Clem sighs and stares up at the ceiling. I just don't want you gettin the idea that a few contacts are gonna save your ass, John.

I know.

John coughs his composure back and reaches across the desk for the forfeiture notice. Did you say you know something about what might've brought this on Clem?

Clem lets go a sigh and scrunches his eyebrows, clearly weighing something in his mind. At last he says evenly, Timothy Dawson.

Yeah?

John had coached Eliza Dawson's youngest, Tim, in little league. Her vague, distracted kid whose drunk of a father came and went like the mail.

They got the kid locked up right now, and he can't make bail. Arrested him last Saturday night on the interstate somewhere between here and Nashville. Sheriff said the guy was pretty shook up when they booked him. They really got the goods on him, nearly ten pounds of pot stashed in those hubcaps.

How'd they know to pull him over?

They had him fingered. Had a search warrant.

Who did?

Local authorities.

But the Feds were the ones knocking on my door.

Local authorities working co-operatively with federal law enforcement isn't exactly news John.

What I mean is- how did they pick up on Tim Dawson's activities?

You know how fast word can travel around these parts. Everybody knows Tim's been unemployed for the last year or so.

Doesn't mean a thing, Clem. Lots of unemployed people running around these parts.

John considers Walt, home and unemployed. They don't suspect my son is part of a drug ring do they?

Clem shakes his head and runs a finger around the rim of his glass of whiskey. Somebody must have seen Tim entering and leaving your premises during the week by that old dirt lane off of Lone Tree Road. Anyhow, *somebody* snitched. I don't know all the details yet. They grilled Dawson as to his source, of course they already knew anyway.

That little son of a bitch was using my property-

-Not a word of this to anyone, John. In fact we better leave it at that and let me just advise you off the record as to your civil forfeiture case.

Why?

Because I really ought not to be talking to you about it.

Well, where did you get it from?

DA himself. Last night, at the poker table.

John cocks an eyebrow, stubbing out his cigarette.

Probably, said Clem, ought not be telling you that either.

*   *   *

The '69 Chevelle roars down the county road, the radio blasting Hawkshaw Hawkins' *Rattlesnake Daddy*. The afternoon rain has delivered a chilly night even for October, on the heels of Indian summer days. Walt is jounced along over back roads, the rhythm of the car inducing a surge of good feeling. All the things he had planned fade for the moment- he is glad to be alive here in Fentress County, traversing the back roads with Cindy Blum.

I love driving stoned, he grins at the windshield.

Stop thinking out loud, Cindy says while packing another bowl into the corncob pipe cradled in the lap of her thrift store floral print dress.

Sorry.

He drums his fingers on the steering wheel. The rain has now tapered off to a drizzle as clouds drift across the moon.

A flick of the Bic and the bowl lit, a sweet pungent odor immediately fills the car. He glances sideways at her. Cindy palms the pipe in one hand and twirls her blonde shoulder length bob- she has this tendency that ineffably draws his silent admiration as long as he's known her. It has always enthralled him to lie beside her and smell it, rub his face in it, indulge himself twirling it. Cindy's body has a scent. She leaves it on his bed and it is musky sweet to him, lingering long after she leaves and almost satiating him until her next visit. He knows it will always be him pining after her scent and biting his nails worrying over whether she'll call or not. They've known each other for three years yet he's still surprised she's stuck around. Pushed away in some dark corner of himself is the sense that she's with him only until something better comes along, like some leased automobile, enjoying the ride for as long as it lasts. Always butterflies when he gazes at her this way, watching her gather her straight hair in her fingers and twirl, waiting for her inevitable, *What? What is it Walt?* Then waving a hand in his face to break his love trance. He's quick to jealousy, yes, just last week when she had her heating and cooling system repaired in her apartment and she was home to let the man in, he felt compelled to interrogate- *What did he look like? How long did he stay? Did you talk to him much? Do you remember his name?* He knows she'll tire of his insecurity in time, but still he can't control the feelings that make his emotional state dangling, precarious, like a circus trapeze act on a torn and frayed wire. She will forever be the lion tamer and he the lion in this three ring circus.

It's just before he turns onto Knob Road that he glimpses the headlights behind him in the rear view mirror. First level cautionary paranoia. Reach for the knob, turn down Hawkshaw. The flashing blue lights induce fear and panic. Just knowing you're in trouble, there's no way out, they've got your number. Just pull over and watch your girlfriend attempt to stash the evidence first under the seat and then in her panties, watch her flail her hands at the dashboard and grope the fan knob, try to blow in some fresh air.

He makes a conscious effort to steer the car over to the gravel shoulder in such a manner as not to raise suspicion. Just remain calm, act like everything's normal. But everything is not normal and he knows it.

And just what will he tell his father? *I was just joyriding, joyriding Daddy, joyriding like any other white middle-class kid, any other suburban post-adolescent disaffected, restless guitar-playing dude. Just riding along, catching a buzz with my girlfriend. But I knew it was over, Daddy, just nothing we could do.* He calls his father Daddy only when he is in trouble.

He peers through the glass at his antagonist, a uniformed policeman without a hint of benevolence on his double-chinned face. The cop stares back- it's a frozen moment- Walt sensing that significant events are about to unfold. The cop is crouched with hands on his knees. At last the cop makes a winding gesture with his hand, and Walt rolls down the window.

How long's that taillight been out?

Walt didn't even know it was out.

Before he can respond, the cop leans into the window like a plate umpire preparing for the pitch.

Step out of the car please.

*   *   *

The rain's ended. On the drive home the headlight beams of the pickup cannot cut through the dense fog. John takes the backroads, hoping local law enforcement isn't tailing him because now he is heading to the old dirt road off of Lone Tree Road that allows access to the furthest reaches of his property. He rolls the window down to a rush of air carrying the essence of pine trees strong and rich in the aftermath of a storm, a scent big industry failed to replicate in those pine scent aerosol cans that Ellen's Aunt Merry sprayed liberally at her and Shoe's place. Aunt Merry saved her cleaning for their Sunday afternoon visits- fidgeting about lifting glasses and wiping down surfaces, shuffling around her unfortunate impositions while they sat and watched the football on the Zenith console and listened to Shoe complain about yesterday's UT game. Once the Zenith was begrudgingly admitted into their household, Shoe became a living room fixture, no longer having to drive out to watch the Stevens' console. The television became the main target of Merry's disdain. When John ceased going to church on Sunday morning with Ellen, he also passed on those afternoon visits.

He drives a long stretch of the dirt road dressed on either side with the pink-flowered rhododendrons. The pickup makes that damned curious clicking sound from somewhere underneath the cab. He keeps telling himself it's just a branch caught in the wheel. He slows down when he catches sight of the crooked elm tree on the right side of Lone Pine Road. The last time he'd had occasion to drive this dirt road it was overgrown with thicket. Now he can see clearly to the two lines of dirt where tires had forged a makeshift car trail. He stops the pickup, leaving the headlights on. Here and there along the dirt road branches are disturbed, the surface blemished with several sets of tire tracks. The beams pick up a length of yellow plastic ribbon stretched across the road to serve as a barricade. He kills the engine, retrieves the flashlight from under the front seat and prepares to go the rest of the way on foot.

It's about a mile up the hill to the clearing. The unearthed plants must have been there. Dawson had taken the liberty to use that very spot for illegal activities. Eliza Dawson's kid, the very same Eliza for whom John bore four years of silent admiration. Beautiful Eliza displayed little interest in return, neither advancing nor encouraging conversation. A woman who was drawn instead by unseen forces to a dangerous man who would only go on to hurt and disappoint her the rest of her life. Tim had taken over where his no-good old man had left off. Tim Dawson who John until recently thought about only vaguely, like so many others in the Big South Fork, unconnected as he was with his daily life in any meaningful way. Tim who had dropped in at the Griffiths' New Years' eve party just less than two years ago, an aberration in a series of New Years quiet-night-ins. Tim in all likelihood on that festive night had sneaked out the back door and off to the edge of the woods to smoke a joint like some of the fifty or so others. John is no stranger to marijuana, who isn't in these parts? He and Clem shared many a night themselves joyriding out in the open air, laying on their backs and gazing upon the star-speckled sky after a few hard pulls on a joint.

You smoke when you're young, that's one thing. But after thirty, as a few specks of grey appeared above his sideburns, as the lines made steady progress under his eyes, John quit smoking tobacco and the occasional joint he'd help burn became a distant memory. He wanted to slow the onset of aging, not aid and abet it. These habits could waste one's visage, he'd seen it on the faces of the old farmers who broiled under the hot sun- hardened men who smoked at least a pack of cigarettes a day. He'd also seen it in the younger ones who hung out at the Colonial and got high outside in the parking lot, then drank to the accompaniment of cigarette after cigarette. They'd sure aged quick.

The road is puddle-smeared, fresh tire tracks embedded in the mud. He can't remember the last time he'd been here, maybe over five years ago- then the road was overgrown with weeds and bushes. Now it is clearly disturbed. Just ahead lays the clearing he was figuring on.

The bald spot on the earth is bathed in moonlight, and he stoops down to the freshly upturned soil, running it through his fingers. Nothing there. Clem had said they'd gotten a warrant on the heels of Dawson's arrest, must have been early this morning the DEA came to remove Tim's crops, hard evidence. He tosses the dirt back to the ground. *Of all the remote places, all the secluded and untended woodland in Fentress County, why in God's name here Dawson? Why the hell did you pick my property?*

Tuesday, The Queen of the World

21 U.S.C. section 881(7) (authorizing forfeiture of real property that is "used, in any manner or part, to commit, or to facilitate the commission" of any drug offense).

John's sister Mary had left Burrville at nineteen, the bride of Mike Wells, a military man five years her senior. After the wedding in Jamestown they remained on the army base in San Diego. Not long on the heels of the honeymoon her new husband served two tours of duty in Vietnam. Mary mostly made herself scarce during those days, but years later she would paint a sketch of her life to her brother- a stint as a hairdresser in San Francisco, working for a spell on an organic farm in Montana, hitchhiking all the way to New York, at last getting a job in Boston with a friend from the road, and convincing her returning husband to settle there for a while anyway. When he returned, he commenced medical school on the GI Bill. Inadequate grades forced him to drop out and, disconsolate, he settled on a career in pharmaceutical sales. Ten years and two kids later, he ran off with a twenty-four year old woman for Washington D.C. John's regular checks from Tennessee buffeted alimony and educational grants, and she blitzed through a Masters and then PhD during lean years in a barely livable apartment. She wasted no time to developing a marriage counseling practice while engaging herself as both a patron and volunteer in the arts community, often throwing lavish parties at her condominium.

In Burrville this morning John rubs eyes loose as slinkies, sure there's at least a few more hours sleep in him. Ellen is up already, carrying new linens into the room. He rolls onto his side, giving yesterday's flurry of trials and tribulations a good going over in his mind. First thing yesterday morning he and Ellen had a bitter falling out over some financial matters, particularly what she regarded his irrational urge to dash checks off to their son Will in Boston. He's on a full academic scholarship there at MIT and working part time at a bookstore for pin money. Ellen placed a higher priority on the upcoming payment for their home equity loan for the additions and remodeling of what was for years a modest homestead. She chastised him about the checks to Will in the same way she did when he'd sent checks off to his sister Mary when she went full-time for a master's degree alongside the sole responsibility for the care of two young children. As arguments go, it was not pleasant.

After that another day of swallowing pride in the removal of unsalable junk from the widow Eldrige's six-bedroom home in the service of Frank Lynn. John had enjoyed Frank's company a whole lot more as a friend than he did now as an employer. They toiled alongside the mounting impatience of real estate agent Lura Breckenridge, daughter of real estate tycoon Bill Breckenridge, one of John's old poker cronies. He remembered Lura as a little tyke with pigtails and a rather boisterous and enervating presence. Now she is a woman in stiletto heels and a sharp pinstripe skirt suit, graduated from UT and well-embarked on a preordained career in Fentress County's real estate market. She had *beau coup* appointments to schedule for tomorrow and she needed to keep the ones she'd scheduled today and couldn't they hurry up a little so she could be off in her Lexus and reach Cookeville before three o'clock? He didn't get an opportunity to catch up on old times.

Instead, he and Frank'd hauled the remnants out to the pickup in the rain and mud with an unsettling urgency and at last he took cash from Frank and drove home ruminating over Walt's lackluster performance in the play of life.

The notice of forfeiture. Then returning home from that cursed upturned portion of land. He'd just washed his face and teeth, the mint toothpaste mingling with the whiskey Clem'd poured, readying himself to lay down to collect and erase his thoughts as his wife lay in bed with a self-help paperback. The sound of the phone came with trouble attached.

Walt. How many times had he told his son if you're gonna drink, do it at home, the laws are much more severe than when I was your age, and they'll ruin you in a heartbeat. He never did included marijuana in that warning. It's not as though he and Clem and whoever else tagged along didn't relish those maryjane joy rides of youth. He'd just rather pretend Walt immune to such urges, despite all indications to the contrary.

So he found himself standing in the Jamestown Precinct just after midnight, his thigh-length down jacket zipped to the chin and swishing as he approached the desk. Behind it was a desk sergeant he didn't recognize. Sheriff Sam Williams appeared from the doorway behind him.

Hello John, how ya getting on? Long time no see.

John thought Williams pumped his hand a bit too eagerly, as if he were greeting him at a police fundraiser.

John had stepped into a room that embodied institutional authority and elicited a fearful respect, particularly under the lens of recent events. Where's my son?

He's going to be alright, he's going to be fine- Williams spoke in a tone as if to suggest Walt lay in the intensive care unit- won't be able to drive his car home though.

Well, okay. Fair enough. Where's the girlfriend?

Released of her own recognizance, said the desk sergeant without looking up from his paperwork.

Williams gave him the studied look of a grim undertaker, shook his head and his drooping jowls with it. This always gave him a sort of lost puppy dog look John didn't see as fitting for one in the business of law enforcement. I am however compelled to seize the conveyance as it contained illegal contraband. It was tainted in the eyes of the law.

The conveyance?

Williams gave him a calculating look.

The car, John.

So they wanted the car. And then it'd be up for sale at the Saturday police auction.

Pretty soon you'll take everything I've got, John muttered.

Hmmn? Williams pulled in his face to a double chin.

You heard me. Godamn DEA was all over my place this morning like butter on bread. Pullin up weeds.

John, I'm sorry, but that one's between you and the Feds.

Oh, as if you weren't working with them?

Williams threw his hands up.

That's between you and the Feds now.

But the car isn't, is it Sam?

John drummed his fingers on the sheriff's desk.

Well give me back my son in the meantime, he demanded through clenched teeth.

Williams had him sign the release and then presented the outlaw. John motioned his son towards the door, and just before he crossed the threshold he turned around and actually managed to stifle his rage to accommodate prudence and talk Williams into returning the vehicle after pointing out its trifling selling value.

On the drive home Walt sat stock still and gazing out the passenger window of the pickup as John drove wordlessly. When at last he grumbled the news about the forfeiture notice, Walt swung around sharply, mouth agape.

Are you serious?

I wish to God *you* were more fucking serious.

It was the last thing spoken between them, and it echoes in John's mind now as he rubs his eyes sleepily and teases Ellen.

Good morning miss merry maid. Where's my breakfast?

Ellen is not amused. What are we going to do about that son of yours-

-Son of *ours*.

Right, that son of *ours* doesn't seem to grasp the extra load of trouble he's brought upon this house.

John's feet are moving before he can plant them squarely on the floor, and he just heads straight downstairs for the coffee maker. Welcome back from the world of dreams. There's no way he's going to get in the way of his wife's vacuum cleaning. He badly needs a cup a coffee and some fresh air. The notice of forfeiture lies on the kitchen table, and he studies it as if to verify yesterday's events weren't in fact a dream.

Clem's words come back to him. *Government doesn't fool around when it comes to asset forfeiture.*

Is it a foregone conclusion that the land his family's held for four generations will be turned over to the State? A pang of guilt hits him as he thinks of daddy, grandaddy. The whole of his genealogy. He was negligent, that was it. He should've been more cognizant of his land, that precious gift as neglected as the weeds running wild.

Setting the automatic drip coffee on, he wanders into the living room, studying the framed photographs of Griffin lineage with his hands tucked in pockets, as if idling in a museum. His attention rests on the bright young faces with beaming smiles in stark contrast to the serious countenances of those tarnished by years. Two kids posed on the front porch on a summer's day. The girl in the foreground is enjoying the moment, the lens. The boy standing behind the girl with hands on her shoulders bearing and expression that suggests he has something to attend to immediately after the shutter snaps closed. John would study this photograph many a time after that moment was captured on film. He would stare often at that picture, wondering how this woman with a life of more shuffling about, bad spins and hard luck could be so carefree in every phone call or visit. The photograph would mesmerize Mary at each of her rare visits to her birthplace. She's a long way from Tennessee. So is Will. John doesn't relish the idea of telling Will or Mary about the trouble in Burrville, deciding that for now silence is golden. The coffeemaker knocks and spits, breaks his gaze into the eyes of his carefree sibling of yesteryear.

* * *

As part of the remodeling, a double door was installed at the basement. The doors are wide open to allow fresh air as John probes the scalpel at a delicate potion of wood ornamentation in the 17th century picture frame. Intense track lighting trained on this treasure he brings back to life leaves the rest of the basement in shadows and dark corners. Whittling away, thinking about Walt and the nagging regret once again with the old sting- the listless son camped in his room with that girlfriend of his. Walt's interest in life seemed to have waned while John wasn't paying attention. When the hell is that son of mine going to learn the value of hard work, set his mind to something? At least when he had that damn rock band he had something going on. Now it seems as if the kid is out of gas. *Out of gas*, he thinks, *Christ it took me fifty plus years to run out of gas.* And it started draining away before he lost his job at Imperial.

The basement door cracks open, spilling light down the stairs into which splays Walt's form in silhouette askew, distorted, like a monster film from the thirties.

Daddy, Walt calls loudly, then perches himself on the top steps, just enough space to duck his head under the banister, present his face to John and mutter, I'm so sorry about last night.

That's alright, son.

John keeps his eyes focused on the scalpel and the tiny crevice of the picture frame.

Daddy?

Yeah?

You think they're gonna take the house?

John ceases scraping, doesn't look up.

Hard to say.

He probes his overworked mind to call up all the things he and Clem discussed over the phone this morning. So many details about procedures that lay ahead with the district attorney's office, with his trial and with warrants and court orders. Try as he might, he can't focus his mind to recall the facts, he'd jotted down notes in his daily planner. All he can remember is Clem's voice and attitude. Professional, detached.

How, asks Walt, can they just seize our property?

I don't know Walt.

John looks resignedly at his son. He'd like to flail about in anger at Walt, wants to lay into him again for being so foolish, for picking such a bad time to be driving around smoking dope with his girlfriend, for ever having moved back home in the first place. Looking up at last from the saw-dusted workbench at his son, arms wrapped around his knees, long hair draping over his jeans and shuffling his feet self-consciously on the steps, he imagines the pudgy little kid with a crew-cut watching his father craft wax into candles. Perhaps this lanky loner of the kid grown up is the only person in the world he has right now. He stares at Walt. Shrugs, smiles.

*   *   *

Cindy Blum smiles like the queen of the world, a black headband wrapped around her blonde bob, chewing gum with a sort of calculated seductiveness, draping one finger on the wheel of the little Honda racing along at around seventy miles per hour on a straight stretch of road- her free hand burrowing underneath her black tee shirt to massage her breasts, belly and coarse its way down under her black jeans and she sings freely, her foot shoving up erratically against the accelerator.

More often than not it's Walt coming to her place, but the route is familiar enough for her to know the way the road curves and she has the sensation of being carried along by the car rather than driving it. Her spell is broken and with trepidation she stills her playful hand as a truck appears in her rear view mirror, but it turns off Highway 52 immediately. So she's left alone riding with the window down and moaning into the wind as the car stereo blasts at a new peak in volume. To what extremes she may go today remains to be seen, but she's on her way to a good start.

Walt sits on the front steps staring absently at the ground, raising his head at the sound of her car. He pushes himself from the steps and does a sort of *aw-shucks* dance with his hands in the back pockets of his jeans as she steps out of the car.

Well just look at you- Cindy plucks her pocketbook from the passenger seat- who died?

He mumbles something she can't discern, goes to put an arm around her, and she pulls away. He walks astride her towards the house.

I guess it's just as well we sit on the porch Walt. I've got somethin to tell ya.

Somethin to tell ya, now that can encompass a whole slew of things, running the gamut of possibilities- from gossip-mongering or a silly joke all the way to I'm pregnant. But the manner in which it is spoken reveals what that *special something* is, because it can mean only one thing given the recent awkwardness between them, and when they're seated on the cushioned chairs facing one another on the screened-in portion of the front porch, he goes bug-eyed at the news nonetheless.

I don't believe this. You're breaking up with me?

Let's just say I'm taking a leave of absence.

Leave of absence? I didn't even get an informal request.

I just can't deal with this shit anymore, Walt. I thought we were going to move on, get away from this deadsville geriatric town. Go somewhere.

Yeah well, shit happens. I can't exactly desert my father now. I feel bad enough as it is about what happened.

Yeah, you gotta stick around and sort it out. Not like ole Will up there in Massachusetts. Anybody gonna bother to tell him what's been going on down here recently?

It'd break his heart.

You break mine.

I want us to have a future, just give me time. I gotta help Daddy out of this mess.

You had no real plans before this happened Walt, and I damned sure don't think you'll have any after.

I had plans! We were going to go to Nashville.

Nashville. Pipe dreams. Right now I need specifics. You can never provide specifics. I wanna go back to school. I don't wanna sit around for the next five years waitressing while you try to pitch demos on Music Row, Walt, I want a life. I miss people! Don't you miss being around a lot of people?

Cindy pauses to catch her breath, and for a while there's only silence between them, Walt shaking his head.

I can't believe you're breaking up with me.

This'll be good for you. It'll enable you to work through all your issues with your parents. I've served as a convenient distraction.

I'm twenty-four years old! I don't need to work through anything with my parents!

You moved home. Why'd you decide to move home? To prevent your parents from splitting up? To save their marriage?

Oh Jesus... I believe my motivations were more *financial-*based? Something like coming off the road broke and not getting a penny from our fly-by-night record label?

Now there we have a difference in opinion.

You really believe I had this subconscious desire to save my parents' marriage by moving in and playing the role of dependent again?

This is your narrative, you're talking. I'm just listening.

Oh God Cindy, this takes the cake in your twisted way of looking at things. I mean why do you always have to over-analyze everything?

Well, I was considering about a masters in psychology.

Aren't we being didactic.

Call it what you will.

I call it smug. I can't believe you're breaking up with me.

I need a little space is all.

Sure, *a little space*. That's the beginning of the end. A *little* space turns into a *whole lotta* space. Soon you'll be out of my gravitational force.

You can't force anybody to stay. You can't force anyone to do anything.

C'mon Cindy, you have no idea how much I love you. Restore my faith in relationships, restore my faith in us.

Cut the melodramatic shit, Walt.

Walt rises from the chair.

Where are you going? She asks.

I don't know.

Walt starts for the front door. I just don't know anything anymore.

He pulls the door shut.

*   *   *

John began to run out of gas- he muses amid the strains of Vivaldi from the old vacuum-tube radio on the workbench- probably after his fourth or fifth year of employment at Imperial Textile Mill. When Walt and Will had barely begun to walk, John was finishing his bachelors degree in management at University of Tennessee while working as an orderly at County Hospital. Daddy'd wanted him to keep up the portion of the property that had until then comprised small corn crops and other vegetable produce. Daddy worked odd jobs right up to his dying day and used the small farming operation to supplement his income and help to feed his family of four.

As a young kid growing up in the fifties, working with and watching his father till the soil, plant and then pray for rain, John was keenly interested in the farm. He read the Farmer's Almanac, he studied the Little Farmer Boy books his Uncle Bip bought for him on his birthdays. John Junior revered the tools- the tiller, the shovel, the rake, even rode on the tractor, while Daddy cut back wheat. Junior woke up early even in the summertime when there was no school.

The sixties ushered in sweeping changes and TV brought images of social upheaval to the living room. The seventies came along with cable television, TV dinners, video-cassette recorders, fast food, junk food, modern conveniences and self-help books. John stretched his world beyond planting, harvesting and prayers for rain. By the time he finished his degree the land itself was already overgrown with weeds, begun to blend with the wooded acres, the pines of yesteryear seeded by his grandfather.

Not long after Imperial Textile was snared in a corporate buyout, John was fodder and so like his Daddy before him, came to enter the world of odd jobs for cash. He did everything from gutter cleaning to clearing out the houses of the dead with Frank

Lynn, one of his old high school buddies and poker crony. Frank now operated a marginally profitable Estate Sale management business. *When you die you don't take it with you, so there's Estate Sales*, an oft-repeated pun by this man Lynn as they'd sit sometimes over beers at the Colonial Inn or over a bottle of whiskey at Clem's poker nights. When all of the worldly possessions of the dead had been sold to eager bargain hunters with the hope of good serviceable years in front of them, in would come Frank in his Ford pickup to take possession of the unsold items and ready the house for sale.

The things John'd begun to stockpile in the barn from the remains of the pickings were generally unusable, out of service, dead matter themselves. Antique radios that didn't even light up let alone broadcast, a red wagon with three wheels, furniture that needed re-upholstering, a 63 Ford with the motor missing. Lamps with their AC plugs ripped off, or their shades torn. Mostly wood furniture that he could transform into its original appearance then bring it to the antique market. The dead's unfinished business became his business to finish.

He gleaned contacts from the business of the dead, living folks with good furniture in need of repair at bargain prices. Cash arrived, along with all these useless things. Sometimes unexpected treasures turned good money quickly. Like the baseball card collection John'd gone up to Cincinnati with for a trade show. He came home two thousand dollars richer and told his wife, *Ellen, get y'self dressed we're going to dinner. And I don't mean Hardees.*

John's spirits were buoyed up by these successes, but they were too few and far between.

*   *   *

Barbara

Knoxville 300 miles. If you can drive with just a few short breaks you might make it to Burrville before two am. You tap a cigarette from the pack and touch a lighter to the tip, immediately regretting having done so. The resumption of this old habit is just one day old so you still consider yourself just toying with it. But this makes ten in the three hours since your hasty departure. The sun sinks below the horizon and darkness descends on Highway

81. Drowsiness begins to overcome you, Barbara Griffith. That and a line of questioning, a kind of self-interrogation. Presented once more with the fact that you are *running away from home*, you wonder how long your escape will last. You've been through the reasons why since you left Harrisburg Pennsylvania. Now with signs beginning to appear for Knoxville, you sense the back end of the trip, and along with it the questions shift to the destination. What will you say to your mother? Your father will likely demand no explanations. What are you thinking to do there?

You are the first-born, the eldest child. When you were young, you wore pretty auburn curls in pigtails and flower-print sundresses hand-sewn by your mother. At crafts fairs you would sit and watch with a quiet intensity as Ellen Griffith, your mother, bantered with her customers. Your mother was bordering on skinny back then, her straight auburn hair not yet tainted by grey or perms. By her own hands she made flower baskets of forest twigs and strips of aluminum, as well as napkin holders, magazine baskets and other various household storage devices made entirely of materials gathered in the expanse of Griffith woods. You would tag along, combing the forest floor for fallen branches, twigs, and sticks; you'd join your mother in weaving twigs or tapping in the tiny tack nails that joined them together, sometimes applying a lacquer finish, and then displaying them proudly for the city dwellers. Mama was shadowed by you the pig-tailed daughter throughout the entire process, right up to the money changing hands.

You remember the thrill in the immediacy of commerce, watching your mother take money for that which her own hands created. At that time you'd make believe it was solely this money that provided food on the table and a roof over your heads. You'd prey on those gawkers, cursory glancers, wanderers lurking about for the casual once-over, and induce them to the cash box. A little girl's sales pitch, warming them up to you, proselytizing to them about the aesthetic of the crafts guild, reminding them how precious these hand-made items would look sitting in their home.

You, Barbara Griffith, have grown up and married a man named Bill Fortney. You haven't any daughter of your own yet. You aren't ready. You already feel too confined to take on that responsibility. It all has to do with this recent way of assessing your life. You've decided you've been living in a Box.

The Box is okay, so long as you can deal with the dry predictability of an absolute reality. The confines of a regular schedule hold the comfort of not having to make many decisions. You know where you have to be. You have the steady pace of order. Just remain at a job that provides not a single thread of emotional stimulation, merely a means to pay bills. On payday you have direct deposit so you needn't even bother to march a check to the bank. But you can schedule your timetable weekend- grocery shopping, laundry, bringing the dog to the vet, the post office, prepare the barbecue grille for guests, clean the bathroom, paint the walls in pastel colors, wash the car, dye the hair, buy and hang new houseplants, replace the shower curtain, polish your dress shoes- all of these become weekend routines which squeeze out minutes and result in precious little or no free time.

The thought of having kids terrifies you. Bill wants them, it's an issue, perhaps one of the reasons for getting fucked up when he might have been reading or taking a walk or playing the guitar and singing the way he used to, or gazing at the stars, or perhaps holding you lovingly in his arms.

Bill couldn't avoid promotion to sales manager at the tin cookware company, and so his forty hours of duty turned into as much as sixty. But much of his time is now spent at trade shows, standing around and smiling like a puppet, shuffling his penny loafers and assuring disgruntled retail store managers that never again will the frying pans arrive dented, or their protective coating wear off before the truck delivers it. He'll stand in the convention booth with other sales force personnel and gossip about the people who inhabit the small world of a tin cookware company- any other topic of conversation was merely superficial. A bunch of suits hatched from schools that were just breeding grounds for young little capitalists who dreamed of clambering up to the top of the heap- only they never told you about the scars you'd get along the way, they never told you that you wouldn't actually be able to ascend to the top floor of the enterprise- those rooms *are booked already*- years ago when this elaborate system of contrived reality was constructed by the first wealthy industrial giants, the robber barons, the Rockefellers and DuPonts and their relations.

Well, better than working for some defense contractor, thought Bill. But then the tin cookware company was bought out from under, debt-restructured, asset-reorganized by a behemoth company whose might was built on huge government defense contracts in the electronics sector. Bill was demoralized, he threw his hands up, *I give up running away*, trying to hide from the inevitable, the damned defense contractors are everywhere buying up everything.

You work your job in the system, you hate it but you keep waiting for something else. Surely something better awaits those who work hard weekends on what are now hobbies but one day will be a means of subsistence, even if one has to go from the two-car garage in the suburbs to the cheap rent district, *so long as we can keep a roof over our heads*, as long as we're happy. But alas, happiness dodges and hides around the corner like an elusive masked bandit, it's nearly seven years later and you've still got the itch at another fucking job doing those same fucking things, avoiding promotions because that'd take away from your real love which is, well- for Bill music and for you painting or theater. There you are instead making idle chatter about rosebush pruning methods with the neighbors in your tidy little subdivision. Seven years and your weekend hobbies aren't even hobbies anymore.

Bill would tear into his litany that just because you had a mortgage that you had to pay for thirty fucking years with more interest dollars than the price of the house to some bank that put it with some others in a nice little package and sold it off to some mortgage company didn't mean you owned the land, *the bank did for Chrissake*, you were just a tenant who kept up the property for a spell. A thirty-year spell. So all you had left was what you could create from inside, but Bill doesn't have much to cough up after the sludge accumulated from too many hours in the tight grasp of the system. And so he got pissed off. Well he was always pissed off, feeling robbed of his chances to do music, his college major. At first his anger came out in silent weapons. But now he's begun using his hands for weapons and when the slaps became punches you decided that enough was enough, no more waiting around for Bill the Weekend Artist to climb the next step in Maslow's Hierarchy of Needs.

You called Union Planters Bank, where you worked as a loan officer assisting people in their relocation to new dwellings, the pre-qualification anxiety. You gave the bank verbal notice of your resignation. You gave them two weeks notice before you gave your husband notice, in fact he didn't get any notice, he just woke up one morning with another awful hangover, threw on a wrinkled white-collar shirt, adjusted his necktie and wondered *where the hell is Barbara?*

About a month before getting out of Dodge you, Barbara, retreated to the mountains with Carol your massage therapist, and Janey, an old associate from the bank. Janey quit her post at the bank to work for Social Services, assisting newly-arrived refugees in their resettlement, placing them at jobs in the factories and warehouses of Erie Pennsylvania and the outlying areas. Janey dressed and acted like a throwback to the sixties, and was actually fun to be around, had a knack for making you relax. Cast a spell that imbued you with a strange and new notion that you just may be sweet on another woman.

That weekend you dropped two hits of lysergic acid diethylamide, and the layers of ego were peeled away like the skin and then the pulp of an orange until you got to the juicy inside which was natural and real, the inside you couldn't pretend not to notice, the inside that all at once tore you apart and lifted you up. Not the you that your husband repeatedly put down, the one who never met his expectations, the you he said had scarce acting talent, the you he said couldn't carry a tune on your fiddle, the one he said lacked the self-confidence to get a job promotion at the dismal bank you slaved at.

Under the influence of LSD you glimpsed among other things, the Box. It was then that you saw visions of why just one week later you would give notice to Union Planters Bank and ready yourself to leave your husband Bill. When you tripped you stopped running, you turned and faced the ugly truth which you could not avoid, the monster which roared and told you that you were living in a Box, a prison ready-made for you, guarded by the sentries of your ego and under the cognizance of those on the top floor, in the rooms with no vacancies.

Like a Jack in the Box you would spring out, but everyone knows Jack never really gets out, he just ends up sort of hanging there, jangling around, caught on the same spring that sprung him. The only things that actually get away are those can of nuts gags, the ones where the coiled snake pops out and flies across the room, but even that is gathered up and re-calibrated for the next sight gag on an unsuspecting fellow office worker or in-law.

But perhaps now you've really sprung yourself from Bill and the bank and sleepy suburbia, and there's no going back in the Box.

*   *   *

John

So I'm standing there in line at the supermarket checkout, something I hadn't grown accustomed to until I lost my gainful employment at Imperial Textile Mill due in part to production inefficiencies resulting in three years of losses on the income statement. I've shouldered and re-shouldered that responsibility many times as I'd stood there, waiting. Judged and then pardoned myself, reminded myself that it was indeed a paper loss, resulting largely from the parent company's upgrade of the plant which included significant capital outlays. Significant by our humble standards anyway. These had resulted in a cleaner, safer, and more dependable work environment and process, but also carried a resultant depreciation expense, something new to Imperial, where antique sewing machines and other mechanical apparatuses had chugged away un-replaced year after year. One of the parent company representatives, Mr. Michael Morton, had stood sipping gingerly at his steaming coffee in the conference room one morning after a tour of the plant and he made the comment to us the local management that the plant and its rusting hulks of machinery could pass for a textile museum. We'd all laughed along with him then congenially. Colleagues.

I would think of that joke again and again as I stood in line at the supermarket checkout, slouched and waiting and thinking. Think about how it was really the beginning of the end. Because the truth was, if the plant were to be reckoned a sort of museum of modern industry, then those of us who occupied it were the living dinosaurs within.

After I was removed from the museum and had nowhere to shuffle off to when I woke up in the morning, Ellen had to go from substitute teaching to full-time. She had sort of reorganized things, arranging household duties and chores in a manner which weighed heavily in her favor and on my shoulders, despite the fact that I was some days working longer hours for less money clearing out the houses of the dead or refinishing their furniture with Haverly, who insisted on sanding the more delicate pieces by hand. So there I'd be, rubbing my sore elbows at the checkout, lifting the plastic bags into the pickup bed at seven or eight o'clock at night. I began asking myself a lot of questions.

One night I feebly appealed to Ellen for a re-examination of delegation of duties, after Clem had insinuated in that easy, off-hand manner of his that I just might be getting brow-beaten. She grudgingly relented. I guess when you're in the right you're in the right, no matter how difficult it may be to say so. We began to split the shopping duty, an early battle victory for me in what has become a war.

I'm gripping the cart, eyes glazed over, when I notice Jed Regan standing just one aisle away in the express with a six-pack of beer. He owns a print shop he disdains and a drinking problem he relishes. His grandaddy ran the original printing press for the now-defunct County newspaper. Jed is not known locally as one of the more soft-hearted souls in these parts, and he has never had any more than a begrudging solicitude for his pre-ordained vocation, seems to have stayed on the sidelines with the onset of personal computers and desk-top publishing, struggled along doing things the old way while watching his business drop off. Which suits him just fine, anyway, the old clients still get their church event posters, county fair posters, wedding invitations, business cards printed at Regans- at the same time he hardly has to stomach a new face entering his shop and his world. Tonight he's glaring me down with a scowl more galling than usual. And tonight I return the stare evenly, it may be the first time I've looked him dead in the eyes. At last he breaks the staring contest, muttering to himself incoherently as he turns his gaze to the occupied cashier. He's never exuded what my son Walt would call *good vibes* my way, but given that he's not exactly Fentress County's answer to Mahatma Ghandi, I've never taken much offense. However, I'm not exactly in the mood for this over-indulgent display of spite today. When I'm out in the parking lot, he's just behind me out the door and I can hear him still mumbling but hardly audible. I turn around to find him bullying the cart along in spurts, his gaze seems to go at me and right through me.

Aw, I intimate in mock sympathy. What's the matter there Jed, get up on the wrong side of the bed?

He looks a little taken aback to find this passive body can assume expression in voice.

I got up in the wrong town. I know all about that funny business you got going on over there at your place- he growls admonishingly, scrunching his eyebrows at me.

Well that *funny business* was none of my business. Got that, asshole?

As I turn on my heels, I'm more than a little agitated, perturbed at hearing myself defending my honor to this hapless drunk in a godamned parking lot.

*   *   *

When Seamus Griffin clambered over dead bodies in the hold of a coffin ship and out to fresh air and blue skies above the Hudson River, his heart was filled equally with grief and hope. He'd just fled a land of famine, poverty and war to a place where the streets were paved with gold- it wouldn't take long until he discovered they were paved only with tarmac and he would be enlisted to the cause of paving them for one grueling year until alas came a divided America and he was drafted into the Union Army to fight the Rebels of the Confederate States of America. Not relishing the prospect of another round of bloodletting, he twice deserted. The first time he attributed it to drunken folly and was reinstated at his rank of front line infantry. After he'd marched over the Mason-Dixon line into the South he immediately felt his sympathies leaning on the side of those seeking secession, those looking to break away from the tyrannical economic oppressor, as the Irish Rebel forces had against the British Empire. He believed in the sovereignty of the States and of their right to secede from the Union if they saw fit to do so, as necessary for their self-sufficiency, dignity, destiny. He became impassioned by their zeal. So he deserted again and joined ranks with the Southern boys, a free agent, one of a few men to fight on both sides of the war. The odds were lesser on the Confederate side, but he fought on at Shiloh, the scene of his one and only performance for the Confederacy where legend has it, stripped of his musket, he cracked a whiskey bottle over the head of the same Union soldier he'd shared many a mess hall table with as a former comrade-in-arms. He made it out of the battle in a heroic sprint, a dash to freedom amidst heavy artillery fire and an overwhelming Union penetration of Confederate ranks. He got a good chunk of shrapnel from cannon fire in the leg, but the rest of him was intact. When the dust settled and the Emancipation Proclamation glossed over the real issues of the War Between the States, he came to inherit just over thirty acres of land from a fellow soldier named Jim Armour, whose dying request at Shiloh was for him to make the journey east, to the other side of Tennessee and take up the business of looking after his wife, in the event she'd survived the Union onslaught. He honored that request, dragging his shrapnel-laden legs by night over what was to become the wide state of Tennessee in little over a month. He followed loose instructions from the vague memory of a dying man's blood-laden breath. After the rise in elevation he came upon the Cumberland Plateau, buried in pines and following the Big South Fork of the Cumberland River. Not until that point was he confident he was lost in the right wilderness Armour spoke of so fondly and so often.

*   *   *

After driving his son to fetch the Chevelle, and do a little shopping, John stopped by Clem's and returns with a stack of documents under his arm.

What are you gonna do with all that? Ellen queries from the couch while jabbing a finger between the pages of *You Can Heal Your Life*.

I'm gonna start trying to figure what this nonsense is all about.

She shrugs, flipping a page distractedly.

There's leftover dinner in the oven, she says.

John sits by himself at the table, paging through a bundle of forfeiture case court records Clem's new secretary had printed from the West Law Library. *United States vs. A Parcel of Land in the City of Lucedale, United States vs. Approximately 50 Acres of Real Property, United States vs. A Single Family Residence Located at 900 Rio Vista Blvd., Ft. Lauderdale, United States vs. Certain Lots in Virginia Beach, United States vs. Parcels of Real Property, United States vs. Real Property and Residence, United States vs. 1,960 Bags of Coffee.*

Ellen calls out to John that Clem called. They've passed gradually from lengthy conversations to short sentences. They are now down to monosyllables. They dance around each another, the dance of evasion, skirting around corners, hurrying past each other, Ellen with nose dug in a book, John poring over papers in the study, or in the recliner staring at the TV like a zombie.

The house suddenly seems to her too small, after nearly thirty years of marriage. Even with the family headcount down from five to three at most, too little space. With their thirtieth wedding anniversary just around the corner with its predisposed grandeur and imminent expectations, they cohabitate like ghosts, at the lowest ebb of the whole of those years. Ellen makes herself scarce these days here in this house. Her pivot to the world is Rugby Christ Church Episcopal, and it is there she finds her personal contacts in the form of the Tennessee Preservation Society, the Women's Club, the Choral Society. To these she goes unaccompanied, John's religion motor running on minimum service- restricted to major holidays- Easter or Christmas- smiling at people he knows will shake his hand and ponder his salvation, their own refreshed by his presence. She has to join her husband in pursuing higher education and pays close attention to the news, the rest of the country, the rest of the world. When John returned all of twenty years old from a year of backpacking through France and Spain, his southern accent had become diminished by the Europeans he met and taught and the Yankees he frequently travelled with. His parents were alarmed at the change, she surprised to discover he was local upon meeting him shortly after his year of exile. Her husband and subsequently the voices of northerners, mid-westerners, and mid-atlantics on the books on tape she purchased for her kids at school and at home obviated any diction classes to smooth the effect of Merry and Shoe's accents on her. When she married John and started classes for her teaching degree she set her mind on being broad-minded and worldly in a very local climate. The popular culture, popular psychology of the sixties and seventies was not lost to her in these rolling Baptist church-ridden hills of the Cumberland Plateau. She glimpsed through bifocals at *I'm OK You're OK, The Road Less Traveled*, all manner of Erica Jong. She peered through her wire frames at the dawning of the age of Aquarius ushered in cinematically by dancers in tie-dyed garb. She watched news coverage of the Sex Pistols bolt-out-of-the-blue blitz across Texas and a bible-belted America. There remain only lingering traces of the southern diction of their ancestors in either of their voices.

  Not a day passes in which Ellen doesn't think about the purchase of a wedding anniversary gift, wonder at what surprise John has in store that would only induce guilt at herself besotted with a strange resentment of him- it's an ugly thing, incurable, unavoidable to be unfailingly quick to anger at him. To judgment. How will they act toward one another on that day? Will there be a show for the relatives and friends gathered in their honor, their testament to longevity, to suspending one's personal interests for the good of the team? Would it prompt them to remember with anguish the time when they danced a dance of cohesion, the slow dances of kindred spirits?

Ellen?

She peers up at him over the rim of her glasses as if he were a stranger, the receptionist in the doctor's office summoning her to her appointment. Just looks at him.

Look, this, this not talking, it's... He finds himself immediately emptied of all confidence, losing his lines, his throat is going dry, the way it always is when confronting somebody close to you, you go in with this long speech developed from hours of mulling over the problem, and then you manage to struggle out a few words- it's like holding a piss in until you feel your bladder will burst then managing only a few small drops when you pull your pants down.

I- I can appreciate you're not exactly thrilled with what's going on... on around here. But to let this thing push us apart, make us- believe me, I-I'm not blaming you, or or saying I'm perfect, because I-I'm not. But umm, you have a tendency, ummm, to act, ummm, say ah childish in the face of crisis. Now, I'm not saying-

*Child*ish?

Ellen doesn't raise her voice. She just sits under the pale light of the antique reading lamp, blinking at him as she lays her book on her lap. Perhaps in the distant past, John might have stood around, waiting to see where it went. He can see this isn't going to be pleasant, and it's really almost comical, the way he gesticulates, a sort of wave of the hand as he beats a hasty retreat. To the barn.

The barn has stood through three generations without any renovations or modifications. It is now for the most part unutilized, except the occasional forages for needed implements before giving up and running to the hardware store. The rust-colored paint peels away to the wood underneath, but nobody's bothered enough to fish out the ladders and rollers and brushes and trays. The roof leaks but there are no livestock underneath it to suffer this. The barn just sits, a hulking mass not fifty feet from the house, a relic of the past that harbors within a collection of museum pieces. Wooden pulleys with hemp rope attached, hemp rope strewn about the floor with scattered hay. Pitch forks, rakes, sickles, hay scythes- all rusted and cobwebbed. Larger things also rusted, among them a corn husker machine, hay trolleys, pulleys, cast iron hand well water pump, horse drawn whiffletree, metal tractor seats. Some of the relics gravitated to the house and perpetuated in usefulness- the dairy milk can that serves as an umbrella holder by the front door, the handmade wood candle soap wall box hanging in the bathroom upstairs, the wire metal egg gathering basket that holds the spices over the stove in the kitchen, the old harvest moon thermometer that hangs outside by the back door. John tries the handle on the back door now. It's locked.

*   *   *

When Seamus Griffin crawled out of the bloody pond at Shiloh and pushed northeastward groping for a home, he dropped exhausted at the foot of mighty Appalachia and when he looked around him, he thought of County Cork and the livestock farm his childhood had been spent on. He determined never to attempt to grow a potato crop, the superstition of failure a dark cloud hovering wherever he went. His leg hurt like hell. But he found this wide open land more alluring than industrial Boston with its dirty factories springing up in every direction.

The woman he met at the threshold of what was then a very modest homestead was plain, met him with a face more life-worn than he's expected. She regarded him suspiciously from a crack in the door. When he'd uttered the passwords, the predetermined names of any future boy or girl between Armour and this malnourished woman of grim countenance framed in a raggedy bonnet, he told her of her husband Jim Armour's fate and his dying request and his own arduous journey. She opened the door wide to reveal a woman bearing the complexion of sickness. A single tear fell on a pale cheek, and she nodded invitation at the darkness beyond. She had no food to offer, but he could lie down and rest a while. He limped across the threshold for the first of many times.

*   *   *

Walls, the dividing lines of space. When they'd financed the addition to the house, John had insisted on his nine by eleven foot study. The room offers privacy, a quiet place at the back of the house to read and write- his quiet retreat.

A dormer window affords a good view of the backyard- on the opposite wall are bookshelves that contain dusted-off first editions scavenged from estate clearings, software packages like Lotus 123, Quickbooks, WordPerfect, CD ROM games. There is a neat astronomy package that offers clever simulation of the night sky. John was planning to absorb himself in the study of this star-speckled night sky this summer, out in the open field where he used to toss a baseball or football with the kids. But he merely sighs when he sees this, resigning himself to make use of the study to learn as much as he can about asset forfeiture law before talking with Clem.

On the adjacent wall is a solid oak desk, a PC. He bought computer software for tax and financial planning and preparation for the self-employed life. But it turned out that his cash income had gone largely unreported. He has neither time nor interest for accounting and maintaining financial records for a cash business. He did some writing on the word processor, relished collecting all of the adventure games on the floppy discs- *Avenger, Lock and Load, Flight Simulator*, he had tax preparation software to prepare his under-reported returns. For the money he spent on the thing he wished he used it more, had more reasons to. One Christmas morning not three years ago he stood looking over Will's shoulder while the introverted and science-minded son set up his computer, doing something useful in their inner sanctum on the other side of the wall, the wall filled with R-11 Sound Control insulation preventing sound from escaping the room into the other parts of the house. At the same time holding at bay the sound of Barbara and Bill's marital disagreements that seemed to crop up more and more on the retreats from their high stress city life, blocking the sound of Ellen's monologues on co-dependency, projecting and other pop psychology terms.

The room's paneled walls around the room are dressed with his UT diploma, management awards from twenty years at Imperial, a community service award and two plaques from the Rickman Volunteer Fire Department.

The cordless phone on the desk rings beside John as he sits scrutinizing a document and staring at the pile of documents he returned from Clem's with this afternoon.

It's Clem here. Listen, are you off to Nashville tomorrow?

Yep. Early in the morning.

Well, here's the scoop, and I'd join ya if I could. I just got a call from Mike Luther.

Yeah?

Listen, he's got a flight back to Nashville and he might be in his office tomorrow. In the Federal Building down there on Broadway. DEA is on the fifth floor.

Right.

Now listen, he said he'd be alright with meeting you if you can make it there. Wish I could make it but I've got a deposition first thing in the morning.

Okay, okay Clem.

John wets his lips, drums a pen on the table.

Just play it cool and listen, John. Mike's an old law school buddy of mine. He's as good a contact as anyone.

Sure.

Don't go pullin no country boy bullshit.

Course not.

No bullshit. Just introduce yourself, shut the hell up and listen. I already told him about your situation.

Right Clem. Thanks for-

-Gotta go. Let me know how it goes.

Click. Clem hangs up abruptly, as he so often does in that busy law office, leaving John gazing at the walls. Walls served to maintain the relative tranquility of this sanctuary, a home inside a home. Walls are needed now more than ever.

Wednesday, Housekeeping

John

  I'm dog-tired, my hands draped over the steering wheel as the pickup barrels down Route 40 towards Nashville. There's that damned mysterious clicking sound coming from underneath the truck again. A cursory examination laying on my back against the stabbing gravel this morning at the crack of dawn didn't uncover any trapped branch, wire or other foreign object caught in the wheel. Beyond the windshield lay long stretches of farmland, the same view as in all my life and still my eyes roam to and fro, captivated by that familiar flat landscape. Traffic was slower when we first rolled down this road in Pa's new Ford, a reward for the War years, when government subsidies lined the pockets of many a farmer unaccustomed to a money surplus. Ma sat up front wide-eyed, hissing and drawing a deep breath every time Pa came within ten yards of another of these powerful new machines that bewildered and flustered her. Mary and I in the rumble seat with eyes wide and scanning the new world that our set of wheels was carrying us through, these large stretches of farmland broken up only by patches of forest. We drove over and through mountains rivers, and dales outside of Jamestown, on our way to Nashville and the Grand Ole Opry, because Pa'd decided it just wouldn't do to sit beside the Zenith tombstone another Saturday night to listen, he had to match a voice with a face, had to see what these singing folks looked like. The post-industrial society in the world outside of Burrville tapped into him through the radio and along with the songs brought strange messages, sponsors with products strange and foreign to him, some soap or laxative that didn't line our medicine chest or insurance he could just as well do without. He couldn't reckon what it was the Opry's proud sponsors WSM (We Sell Millions!) actually did, no matter how many times I tried to explain with a nine-year-old's grasp of the rationale for this burgeoning industry. He didn't care to know. He wanted only to drive that shiny Ford to the Opry. Ma wasn't for it, but as with everything else, when the cards were all played and the chips fell, she'd grabbed her shawl and a blanket, adjusted her wool bonnet and fastened it below a chin wagging protest and clambered into the passenger seat next to Pa. Then she sat there without a word, just those cautionary intakes of breath every now and again, for the entire duration of what to us was an odyssey, the longest trip of our lives.

On Interstate 40 I pass the sign for Cookeville, My usual destination on Sunday nights for a favorite part-time occupation-radio host. I've been on the air doing an old timey radio program on WHRS for several years now, and my playlists harken back to the days of WSM old that drew my father regularly to the Zenith.

It seems a long drive, this stretch of highway to Nashville. A trip I don't often make these days. But today is different, I am off and running to Nashville wordlessly, alone but for my own thoughts in the cab of this pickup that seems to be running on its last legs. Now, as back then in that old Ford, I imagine my great-great grandfather Seamus legging out of the battlefields of Shiloh to what is now our homestead on his one good leg, the other wounded and bleeding with only a verbal promise of some wild acreage and a woman who would trust him upon the utterance of a secret word. A story passed down, I remember my father telling it over winter fires, when I'd drop whatever book I was reading and sit in rapt attention to a story that remained essentially the same; dressed up with varying subtle ornamentation, anecdotes, shadings of his own imagination.

I am headed for Nashville with a folder beside me with Clem's legal notes, in that nearly illegible handwriting of his. After we met last night, I didn't want to waste any time getting to the extensive Vanderbilt Law Library to dig up what I could find on federal asset forfeiture law, my task daunting for one afternoon, hence the early jump. It's just after nine o'clock and I'm exiting Route 40 for downtown Nashville, Vanderbilt University. In the ashtray a heap of coins roll around, photocopier money.

* * *

Barbara

In a queen-size bed at the Budget Inn off of Highway 81 in Bristol Virginia you awake somewhat disoriented and groggy from another toss and turn night. Under the starched bed linens you prop your head on the pillows and take in the cigarette-musty paneled room. On the bedside table the clock radio reads 10:45. Fifteen minutes until checkout. You've slept in until half the day is shot, and you're waking up tired all the same. A copy of the Gideon's Bible laying on the shelf underneath the clock radio. The implication that sinners lurk in these cheap lousy places, evil people needing salvation on the heels of a night of infidelity, lust, sloth, gluttony, avarice.

The sun boldly illuminates gaudy seventies orange floral-pattern curtains that hang on thick wooden rungs over a window that affords only a view of the asphalt parking lot.

There's a knock at the door, a voice beyond it.

Housekeeping.

You get up, place an eye to the peephole on the door, see a round face blown up in fisheye view, dark skin and black hair tied in a bun, a stout body attached out of proportion. You open the door upon an unsmiling face.

Housekeeping, the woman repeats with a hand draped on her cart of cleaning implements beside her.

I'll only be a moment, you reply, although you know it'll be at least a half hour.

I'll come back, says the woman evenly as she pushes the cart away.

Shutting the door against the glaring sun, you collapse on the bed, sniffing at your underarms bared by a tank top going on two days wear. You consider calling your folks but decide to stick with surprise-at-the-doorstep. Peeling yourself begrudgingly from the warm bed, you walk barefoot on chilly thin carpeting to a sink just outside the bathroom door. In the mirror you see a drifter in a cheap hotel.

Yesterday you were on the outset of a fresh start, singing to the radio and smoking and feeling bonds untied. Today you begin to pay for this decision, you have nothing in front of you, and you are faced with the unknowable void that lies beyond staying on with your parents for a spell. Arriving in some new city, paying somebody rent. Needing money. Driving your beat-up car to some temp agency that could place you in some sterile office as a temporary employee. A temporary employee didn't have to worry about long-term commitment. It was kind of like dating. If you started liking the people in your temporary work environment, they start liking you in those few months, maybe they'd snatch you up and then you'd be on the more permanent path. Like at the bank in Harrisburg. That one turned into a long-term relationship. Where did those six years go?

Recent phone conversations with your momma centered around your brother back home, her anxiety about his listlessness and inactivity.

I'm with you, Walt, I don't think I want to go down that road again. You haven't even been down it, but you know, you've glimpsed it and said no way. When your untarnished eyes looked at the world, it promised you so much more than a life stuffed away in some office building. So much more than coming home from that confined space and putting kids to bed and falling asleep in front of the TV after chucking down a few beers.

Where did your last six years go? What promise can any largely unplanned out-years possibly contain? Oh well, you might temp for a while, until you're able to figure out exactly what the hell it is you want to do.

*   *   *

A half-day of school today at Jamestown Elementary, but teachers were asked to stay a half hour after lunchtime dismissal for a meeting with the principal. Ellen climbs into the station wagon clutching a few bills and Will's birthday card, stamped and signed *Love Mom and Dad* in the cheeriest cursive she could muster. She draws return address labels from her black leather purse, peeling one off and considering it distractedly. Beside the tiny illustrations of wildlife scenes and printed in black lettering-

> *John & Ellen Griffith*
> *1205 Old Fork Road*
> *Burrville, TN 37298*

Line one, she thinks- what is it that makes two individual souls coupled? Besides the instant rush of passion that fades away with time, is it the familial urge? Is it the fear of growing old and being alone? Staring at the walls and talking to yourself, a habitual caller of radio talk shows, a fanatic of crossword puzzles? No one to rub Ben Gay on your back for your muscle cramps, no one to pick you up if you fell and broke your hip, no one to bring you to the hospital if you collapsed unconscious, no one to assist the nurse in executing an enema? No one to lend a forgiving ear to your litany of complaints?

Seems like the older you get, the harder it is to make new friends and acquaintances. Problem is, she thinks, everybody else gets married and has children, and that becomes the center of their lives. This was most blatantly evidenced every Sunday after services. What is Walt planning to do now that he's back from college? How's Professor Will doing up at MIT? When's Barbara going to grace you both with grandchildren? Never mind about her and John, their marriage was assumed secured and fixed for life, they raised three kids who were out of the house. Walt, six months back home on temporary residence status. Otherwise it was assumed they were making an expected, if arduous voyage into their *golden years*.

What would she have done if she were by herself all these years? Would she have become a swinging single, cruising the run-down honkytonks, backwoods bars looking for... what, friends? Lovers? Would she have gone north to New York or Washington and ended up broke and destitute?

Lines two and three- their nearly full-owned real estate. Soon there were to be no lien holders, no debt attached. In two years when First Tennessee Bank received final payment they were home free, all the more independent of the system, released from debt obligation on the property. Except property taxes- last year in the annual amount of two hundred eighteen dollars thirty two cents. Now the property was being snatched from their grip, seized and possibly forfeited. For what? A few marijuana plants they'd had no idea were growing wildly in a remote and neglected segment of the property?

Ellen had never tried pot before. Well, not publicly. Truth is, one weekend John and Clem took the kids camping up in the Smokies. Ellen begged off, opting for a quiet weekend at home. Barbara was just a sophomore in high school then- the phone rang mostly for her, bringing the solemn voices of haunted male adolescence. Friday night was quiet enough. Ellen fixed herself some ice cream and retired to the living room and the all-in-one Panasonic stereo unit. The turntable now fully available to her, she fished out some of her old records from the rear of the stack in the record cabinet, sitting Indian-style, vinyl spread in front of her like a pirate's loot and examining each LP with the sighs of nostalgia.

She was relaxed enough, there was nowhere to go. No meeting of the craft guild, First Episcopal Church Committee, or embroidery club. No drama rehearsal for Barbara, no science club competitions for Will, nor football practice for Walt. No waiting up for Barbara. That was something she wasn't dealing with too well- the onset of Barbara's frequent weekend night excursions with Clem and Miriam's daughter Lisa, a newly-licensed driver. Or waiting on rides from girls that Ellen would be meeting for the first time. The clandestine aspects of Barbara's life that were begrudgingly conceded caused Ellen bouts of anxiety. She set the 33rpm of Bob Dylan's *Highway 61 Revisited* back on the shelf, then drew out and considered Simon & Garfunkel, all at once stricken with that too-familiar worry plague.

It was in this moment, alone and left to her own devices, in the fading light of day in front of that record player, that Ellen had a sudden compulsion to do something which would only serve to breach an unspoken pact. Something that might make a person well acquainted with modern parenting models grimace.

She executed a room search. Just like that. One moment she's engrossed in a bowl of ice cream and folk music records, then just like that she's bounding the stairs with an inkling she's about to commit a real no-no. She paused there in the doorframe of her daughter's bedroom, more or less an off-limits area since Barbara turned thirteen. She shivered, attempting to conjure up for herself an ostensible motive- a missing blow dryer, a lipstick marketed at teens that might take a few years off her face, a window that needed winter insulating.

Then she went to work. She flipped through loose papers in the desk, extracting and returning with precision the neatly ordered items in the drawers, agonizing over whether to pierce the tiny key into the locked diary she'd given to her daughter. She invaded a teen's privacy. The invasion was premised on maternal concern, that unshakeable urge to protect the child she bore. But no less rooted in fear. Is a mother's fear unjustified? Where's the line between fear and trust? What was she looking for, illegal mind-altering substances, birth control devices? She came up with the former only. This gave her great relief, she'd rather have a stoned daughter than a pregnant one. She had a natural concern when the boys at school started paying attention to Barbara's burgeoning womanhood, had to suppress the impractical measure of tailing Barbara's every move outside of school. Served as a chaperone for the ninth grade cotillions. If only she could be a fly on the wall in the places for which she could not accompany her daughter. After all, Barbara was bright. She had a future, got mostly As, with the occasional B in the less vital subjects like home economics.

She cracked the sealed perforation of the little plastic Ziploc baggie and sniffed. How did they smoke this stuff? Then she spied the EZ Wider rolling papers in that brown packaging she was familiar with, having seen them behind the counters of convenience store franchises just then coming into vogue.

Shoe used to hand roll his cigarettes. One afternoon on the front porch steps, Ellen sat next to him admiring his rolling technique. Aunt Merry chastised her. *Good girls don't do such things, don't you dare let me catch you smokin cigarettes little lady. Next thing we know you'll be runnin around smokin and spillin sweetness on all the boys.*

She remembered enough to allow her to roll herself- what did the kid's call it- a joint, a reefer? No one home, she figured well why not, might as well see what all the fuss is about, what my daughter is visiting upon her bright young mind.

It was a scary experience, an absolute trauma, a disaster Ellen would somehow never be able to shake from her memory. The relaxation, welcomed isolation she felt when the front door closed, leaving her free to her whims was soon a memory. She didn't know what to do, she just froze there on the living room floor for a minute listening to the Carpenters greatest hits Side A, sat stock still on the couch as *Yesterday Once More* faded back into the speaker cabinets. Bob Dylan crooned and his words bit into her and planted thoughts about life that left her anxious. Restless. She tried to distract herself staring at the glowing black dial of the tombstone Zenith radio in its perfect circular numerology. She was surprised when she looked at the clock and saw it wasn't six thirty yet. Time was stretched, ten minutes seemed an eternity.

The phone rang. She was immobilized, deliberating over whether to pick it up. Perhaps her voice might sound different, or she might say something silly or stupid, misunderstand the whole conversation. She let it ring on, wringing her hands. What if it were John? Some family emergency? She didn't like this sense of being out of control, feeling self-conscious though it was only herself in the room. She wondered what it would be like to be in public, trying to hold conversations, trying to not get debilitated with overwhelming self-consciousness.

The answering machine clicked on and she sat stunned at this intermediary she'd forgotten all about, a testimony to her of weakening mental faculties. The voice droned on about the Christmas Pageant at First Episcopal. She decided to walk outside for some fresh air. It was chilly even in her parka but she didn't feel any compulsion to return to dig out a sweater. The night lay in complete stillness, not even the occasional strange night noises in the snow-laden woods just a few hundred feet from the house. All around her lay an alien landscape, the comforting familiarity gone. She gazed upon a clear winter sky for a while, cupping her eyes and seeking out a shooting star. She felt light-headed. She turned her back on the strange black world for the confines of the house. Stood in the hallway, recounting her own adolescence. Shoe's drinking had by then reached a record high- Merry had figured if you can't beat em join em, she guessed, because she began drinking. Except on Sundays, which she still held open for God and the saints. Ellen disappeared.

She remembered one night at Minnie Withers' house. She was only seventeen years old. Her schoolmates were smoking out of Minnie's dad's pipe. She knew what it was. She declined, even after they called her a party pooper. She couldn't understand why they were laughing so uncontrollably they had to squeeze their arms tight around the waist, hugging themselves as if to prevent their sides from splitting. What was so funny?

Then years later, that night on her own, after tapping her daughter's stash. In the bathroom, her eyes darting around taking in every detail- the laundered display towels, the shell soap in the fine china dish, the claw foot tub scrubbed to its perfect white porcelain sheen. Chrome fixtures, a wicker basket holding magazines. The antiseptically treated environs of the Griffith's full bathroom. The crush velvet floral wallpaper she hadn't gotten around to modernizing didn't seem so important now, like so many things, and she didn't like that. She looked at the face in the mirror for a longer spell than her usual daily ablutions would allow- studied the crevices of aging, the tiny scar just off her cheekbone from a childhood fall from a bicycle, considered the freckles splayed on her nose and cheeks, studied her face as one would the surface of the moon, but couldn't endure gazing into those two craters filled with steel blue eyes. Returning to the living room, she switched on the television. A Happy Days rerun, suddenly the Fonz himself took on sinister implications. When even Ritchie Cunningham's affable chuckling suggested ulterior motives, she switched it off. She closed her eyes but couldn't sleep. She began agonizing about Barbara's regularly smoking this stuff.

Now Ellen- lost in such recollections, one leg out of the car at the post office in Jamestown- realizes with consternation she has forgotten to address Will's birthday card, forgotten about the dry cleaning. She glances at her watch. The free afternoon's fast slipping away.

*   *   *

Barbara

Home at last. The driveway is empty. A deer standing still at the edge of the woods, its gentle brown eyes watching you. It takes off like a shot into the woods.

You leave your suitcase in the backseat and make for the front porch to wait, nothing but your own thoughts for company. You think about the deer. You disdain your husband's penchant for hunting. His winter hunting brought an uncomfortable silence while he fished out his thermal outfitting, and then on his return no one to entertain his enthusiasm. The silence rendered the trips much like participation in some occult society's sublime initiation rites. The hunting craze continued despite the resultant spousal discord. It wasn't until the night you yourself became prey that you were set on leaving for keeps.

Hard to believe it was just a few days ago. He had come home very drunk around nine. You regarded him silently, curled up on the couch watching TV in your sweats. He was very talkative. He rambled on and on, came to the well-trodden topic of child-rearing. You said *it ain't gonna happen anytime soon.* He said, *oh yeah we'll just see about that.* Grabbing you by the wrists, he pulled you up the stairs and dragged you along the plush-carpet hall. You tried to bite his hand all the way to the bedroom, he pushed you onto the bed, his eyes glaring like those of a wild boar. He forced himself on his wife. It was that most fertile time of your cycle. He knew it. Even as you cried in a fear he could smell, you screamed at him to get a rubber. He laughed, said he was out of patience and rubbers. You pushed at him, while your eyes darted around the room for a weapon. He didn't notice you raise the shoe he'd just liberated you of. His attention may have been alerted just as you clomped him full on the face with the hard rubber soul, leaving him stunned, pained, and limp-dicked as he tumbled from the bed to the floor. You took this opportunity to bolt downstairs, grab the car keys and drive to the supermarket. You crawled into the backseat and slept a little until the sun and early shoppers woke you. Then you went home, packed a suitcase and left for good.

When your mother's station wagon rolls up into the drive you smile, and your mother's face has the look of bewilderment softening to affection. After she's parked the car and approaches, she beams at you.

Well my oh my, look what the wind blew in! How *are* you honey? What on earth brings you here so sudden?

Locked in your mother's embrace, you whisper in her ear, *Running away*.

*   *   *

It's pushing three o'clock and he's barely scratched the surface. Law students sit hunched over their research, engaged in the theory and conjecture of academia while John Griffith tries to understand the unholy mess his life has been thrown into. Stacks of books lay before him that he cannot check out, and nothing yet photocopied. He pushes them aside, stands up and fishes in the pocket of his wool suit pants for car keys, sliding the chair, leaving a hastily-scribbled note *Be right back* laying on top of the stacks of books. Then he weaves around desks and out the door. On-campus parking was impossible and the walk back across the sprawling campus to 21st Avenue is interminable. He jogs past kids on leisurely strolls, sporting scarves and wool-lined jackets. By the time he reaches the car it's nearly three thirty.

Damn, he mutters, jumping in the pickup, and nearly forgets about oncoming traffic. He's kicking himself for not having called Clem for Luther's number, but he was busy dashing about from the stuffy basement extricating the Federal Agent's Guide To Asset Forfeiture to the top level fetching Case Law. And all manner of books on the subject. Time seemed to move with a distressing speed against such a tranquil, cloistered space. Now he fumbles with his tie in the long line of cars on Broadway, at last knotting it in an unsatisfactory lump. The Federal Building looms tall in the distance among the row of modest-sized buildings that make up downtown Nashville. But the midday traffic in city center is crawling. He repeatedly checks his watch and glances in the rear view mirror with a comb to his hair, in a city he'd never have expected to be just a few days ago on a mission equally unwonted.

His hair, he thinks, ought to be slowly greying at the temples, he should be holding off midriff weight with daily sets of tennis, bearing a more taut skin, healthy teeth and nails. He's supposed to give a warm embrace to his youngest son as he stands with cap and gown on a sunny afternoon, tossing him the keys to the new Jag. Supposed to know the complete lyrics to *As Time Goes By* because he used to sing it, just slightly tainted with booze, to his wife. Supposed to lounge in his recliner with a pipe and exude calmness and utter sage advice to his eldest son to. Supposed to hold a grandchild in his arms, crushed against his cardigan sweater as his daughter flushes at the sight, still daddy's little girl despite her own motherhood. Supposed to write love letters and vignettes to a loving wife. Supposed to hold dignified conversations with politicians and church leaders. Supposed to be bearing interesting anecdotes from life at dinner parties, a pipe in one hand as he swirls the ice around in a tumbler of Stoli with the other. Supposed to say things like *I'm the luckiest guy in the world*.

Instead here he is before the rear-view mirror examining worry-lines, running a comb through a head almost full of grey hairs, running dirty fingernails over teeth that are yellowing. He is a consumer of hygienic products intended to outwit and forestall the aging process. He's trying to keep a sputtering Ford pickup running because a car payment is out of the question. He's like any middle-aged guy who's fallen short of his expectations. The last time he had occasion to wear a suit was over four years ago.

A blue blazer with an emblem sewn on the pocket, white collar shirt with thin striped tie and grey slacks are a safe fashion gamble, such an outfit will never be out of line amongst the ranks of government employees. He shuffles nonetheless self-conscious through the frosted-glass doors laden with bold lettering, Drug Enforcement Agency and its seal. The receptionist, a plump and frizzy-haired young lady wearing a turtleneck sweater beneath a rather nondescript woolen grey dress is in the middle of what is not official business on the telephone but family business, *yeah, right, umm I'm sure he's just trying to do anything to get out of it, that's right, you know my brother, well, sure, right, you tell him I said so, Mom's just gonna flip, right well, listen I gotta go, right, you coming over tonight? Well why shouldn't you? Look I really gotta go,* through this stream of choppy conversation John's empty stomach grumbles as he glances from his watch to the wall clock behind this woman who eyes him standing there foregoing the sofa and magazines.

Good afternoon, he smiles at the young lady after she's replaced the phone and.

Can I help you? Her switches her face to official business.

Yes, John replies, I was hoping to meet with Mike- he meets her quizzical gaze- Mr. Luther?

Did you have an appointment?

Yes. Um, no, not exactly. Sort of left it open. Um, my name is John Griffith. I'm a friend of Clem Carter.

The name Clem Carter doesn't change the blank look and she's making no indication of doing anything on his behalf.

Look, I've come all the way from Jamestown. Could you please see if he'll meet with me.

Just a moment, she replies evenly.

Soon he's pumping hands with a heavyset man with large graying sideburns and blue eyes.

Howdy, he beams.

I hope I'm not catching you at a bad time, John says as Luther snaps the latches of his leather briefcase shut and stands it upright on the top of his mahogany desk.

Actually I was just on my way out.

Luther glances at his watch and clears his throat.

Soccer. My youngest.

John smiles at the floor. Well, Clem thought it might be a good idea if we met while I was here in Nashville today, um, to maybe, ask you a few questions or just maybe you had some information, er ah… maybe some advice?

Clem did mention to me somebody might stop by to visit.

Luther is a little confused, scratching at his close-cropped hair.

Right. It's just this, this...

John draws the forfeiture notice from his breast pocket and hands it to Luther.

Clem sure didn't mention *this*.

Luther nods at the document, clucking his tongue. Have you filed a claim on this?

Yes we have.

I really can't give much advice on this, not knowing the particulars of the case, Mr. um-

-Griffith. But basically, Mr. Luther... Since I had neither knowledge or consent of the plants being grown on my land, isn't this just a matter, well a sort of inconvenience that just needs to be cleared up. You know, a kind of administrative matter?

Luther stares at the wall, licks his lips.

I can't comment, not knowing the particulars of your case sir. But generally these cases... well, I'd say prepare yourself for quite a battle.

But-

-Look, Luther grabs a woolen hat and scarf, I'm already late, now if you'll excuse me please.

John starts for the door. In the hall they shake hands.

Give my regards to Clem, says Luther as he bids farewell to a few DEA agents gathered around the chatty receptionist for their late-in-the-day banter, gossip.

*   *   *

No Bill didn't call the house last night, Ellen tells Barbara as she jiggles the key in the lock and pushes on the oak door to the Griffith household. Barbara casts her eyes to the Honda and again decides against fetching the suitcase from the back.

What brings you home so early? Barbara wants to know, rummaging around her pocketbook for a cigarette, deciding to refrain from smoking in front of Ellen.

Half day, Ellen fusses about with the mail at the kitchen counter, poring over a bill through her bifocals. Are you hungry?

No momma, that's okay.

She'd stopped off at the Waffle House, sitting among the truckers and local contractors with a newspaper and a grease-laden meal in front of her.

Ellen drops the mail into the wall-mounted caddy and draws a chair up next to Barbara, clasps her hand.

What's going on, honey? You wanna talk about it?

Barbara shakes her head.

Can't. Not right now.

Ellen recedes against the back of the chair and regards Barbara with maternal benevolence.

So where's all your stuff?

In the car.

Well it's no good to you sitting out there.

They set about shifting Barbara's gear and transforming what doubles as Ellen's office and a guest room back to what was once Barbara's bedroom.

Barbara pulls a sheet over the day bed. How's Walt?

Oh, you know, Ellen sighs, still doesn't know what he wants to do with his life.

Sounds mighty familiar, Barbara thinks.

He pulled a real winner night before last.

And just what was that?

I don't want to saddle you with all of our problems, Ellen calls from the linen closet in the hallway.

All your problems?

Barbara clutches one end of the bedspread, looks across to the other end at her mother.

Oh, nothing dear, Ellen says dismissively, patting down the bedspread on the mattress of the day bed.

Well just what did ole Walter get up to then?

He got pulled over. Out driving with that girlfriend-

-Cindy?

Ellen nods vehemently, Cindy. Out driving around, with no destination. Smoking *pot*, she barks that word with a decided venom.

Barbara shrugs.

They nearly confiscated the Chevelle. Your poor father had to go down to Jamestown in the middle of the night to fetch him.

Williams still Sheriff?

Ellen nods, smirks. Sure is.

Guess they haven't been able to vote him out yet. So where's Walter now?

Ellen shrugs and waves her hand at the air. Who knows? Probably hanging around at Cindy's.

Walter Griffith is in fact at that moment perched on a stool at the mahogany bar blowing a smoke ring to the ceiling of the Colonial, trying to reassure himself two beers in that Cindy is indeed on a sort of temporary leave-of-absence and she'll wake up and see things in a whole new light soon enough. He lets his mind drift instead to all the wonderful things that might lay ahead of him that do not involve settling down and turning into the corporate robot that the masses aspired to while they looked with disdain and remorse at those outside of the system- the stragglers. Those without the ball and chains of mortgages, car payments, insurance bills, boring PTA meetings, and crazy bosses. Did any of those stragglers give up and enter the system at some point?

* * *

When Seamus Griffin began clawing at the earth with a crude tiller he'd found rusting away in a weed-covered field near the shack that is now the entirety of the Griffith living room, albeit with new walls, ceiling, and floor, he made good on his promise to forego the spud. He was able to clear and till with the one mule he'd managed to restore to working capacity. The first seeds sown were for maize, or corn, a strange white vegetable he's never seen before. Early Higgins in Jamestown sold him the corn seed and it would turn out a good harvest, the first suitable for profit. He got three hens and a rooster from a benevolent soul at a nearby farm.

He guarded his Union Army enlistment papers should the Union present any future challenge to his assuming Dixie land. As a precaution, he changed his name from the Griffin listed on enlistment scrolls to Griffith, lest Union forces should show up raising questions about where his loyalties lay. While a mutual respect grew between himself and his ailing widow-friend over those initial probative days, love did not. So he re-affirmed his love on paper to his northern girl and sent it off by post. She then made the long journey, turning up at his door one rainy night looking white as a sheet. His war face had mellowed to a more sympathetic countenance and he carried her over the threshold into a very rustic bare-bones Griffith residence, boiled tea, and held a cold cloth over her steaming forehead. She healed, but not fast and never fully. She couldn't believe her eyes when she stirred at the first sunny morning to see the land that was theirs; she was from County Kerry in the old country, she thought she'd never see such a wide spread of land again after being cooped up in a New York tenement and adjacent sweat shop. They had the peculiar distinction of being declared man and wife as they lay in their wedding bed. Seamus had run down a wild horse and broke her as he broke horses in his boyhood days in County Cork. Attaching this horse to the buggy left by Jim Armour, he saw fit to take his fiancé to Jamestown. He connected with an old war pal, a preacher named Meryl, who steered him to the only public house. He was introduced to moonshine and drank it with relish. In the throes of drunkenness he suggested to a somewhat bewildered Karan that they might as well not spare any time in sending news of marriage to her obliging but wary brothers in Boston. They booked a room at a modest inn, jumped into the creaky bed in undergarments and continued to drink away with Meryl, who had a whooping cough and would have no business being in a modern-day Infantry. His fellow soldiers steered clear of him in the woods searching out Union ranks. They spoke of binding and gagging him, they often spoke of murdering him in his sleep. But he lived to declare Seamus and Karan man and wife between gulps of moonshine and whooping coughs.

*   *   *

    Can't we at least talk? Even over the phone Barbara can tell Bill's voice is husky with drink.
    I don't know, she says, it's late.
    C'mon Barb.
    I don't want to talk right now. I have nothing to say.
    Alright then. I'm coming to you. This weekend.
    Leave me alone.
    She really wants to end the call there, but can't quite bring herself to return the earpiece of the antique phone to its cradle. She's sure momma's eavesdropping at the top of the stairs.
    You don't know, he rasps, the shit I'm goin through right now. At work. My job's on the line-
    -Your-
    -No, I mean it, Barb. There is serious shit going down at the office. Very *serious shit.*
    I'm sure you'll sort it out.
    Why are you *forever* making light of my problems?
    Barbara sighs into the phone.

Look, he says resignedly, I'll see ya this weekend. Stay put.

Stay *put*? If I feel like going somewhere I'll damn well go somewhere.

She clicks off without a goodbye and goes about putting the kettle on for some of Mom's herbal tea. The front door shuts and Walt bounds into the room, his face flushed with the cold.

Hey Sis! He practically collides into her and she into the counter with his big hug, he gathers her up off her feet and sways her around until laughing, she punches at his arm and he sets her down, looking her straight in the eye. Good to see you.

How long's it been?

Since graduation. Where y'been?

She shrugs, regarding him in a careful studied manner.

What, he says. What's that look for.

Did I hear you been running into trouble with the law?

Not much, he rummages around the fridge, closing the door and coming away with nothing. A little joyriding.

Cindy getting you into trouble?

Naw, he shrugs. Keeps me out of it, mostly. Where's Bill?

Not here.

Walt leans against the counter. Uh huh.

You might as well know, she whispers, I've left him.

No shit. Divorce?

Probably, Barbara mutters, peeking around the doorway to see if her mother is within earshot.

Seen daddy yet, he whispers.

Nope. He's in Nashville.

Oh, that's right. He coming back tonight?

Don't know. It's almost nine o'clock now.

You okay? Walt asks while they both stare at the floor.

Yeah, she nods her head. Better now. *Much* better.

Mom tell you about the notice from the feds?

Yeah.

Whaddya think?

What do I think? I think it's nonsense. Clem will clear it up real fast. Tell them boys to stick it where the sun don't shine. What does Mom think?

I don't know, you know how she worries. I don't think she's too happy with Clem leading the charge though.

Walt bounces on his heels.

63

Hey, you got any whiskey? Barbara asks.

I always have whiskey.

Well be a sport and pour your sister a shot.

A shot? I got half a bottle. Let's get drunk, he suggests, though he's already spent most of the day doing just that.

*   *   *

Barbara

Perhaps it is preordained to be back in your old bedroom, now momma's office and sometimes guestroom. The museum of your youth.

Your memory returns you to that dilapidated old familiar building that housed you in what you often consider to be your last days of freedom. In the rooms of that yellow paint-peeling wreck joints were passed amid the very random and spontaneous conversations. Among the warm buzz of confidences. Deep into the night on its porches came the songs of minstrel balladeers. They sang loud and boldly the song of some obscure folkie artist you were once unfamiliar with, or quietly picked a Simon & Garfunkel song, or created something then and there. Maybe you stretched your arms to the clear night sky as the darkness gave way to the dawn of day, and forgot about exams or auditions.

One semester you focused solely on the songs of Bill Fortney. Bill had long curly hair and restless ideas for himself and his guitar- Bill wanted to head down to Texas, or out west, or one morning after an all-nighter he picked up a bottle of maple syrup from the kitchen table and figured maybe Canada. Bill trucked around campus on a mountain bike with a Sony Walkman playing blues for a sunny day- Robert Johnson, John Lee Hooker and spewing imperatives like *wow man, you just gotta get yer head in this, let it swim around in ya*. He once went a whole month cycling the Grateful Dead tape, he must've played it over a hundred times before stretching it to its death. He often whistled when he walked.

Bill could make you laugh so hard you'd grab for air. He could also make you cry in those early days of your crush when he told you to slow down, those nights when he promised to call and failed to. The phone would ring and it'd turn out to be for

Patty or Renee or Theresa. Long nights when you went to bed and stared at the wall, you'd find out the next day he'd got lost at some party deep in the woods when he turned up at seven caked in mud, or maybe he'd hitched a ride out of town when someone offered him a gig at the last minute.

How the ensuing years have paled in comparison to those halcyon days of innocence. You will press your memory in an effort to locate at what point the tide went out, when was it that waking up in the morning became more and more of a drag?

Memory's a strange thing- on the level of intellect it's the painful memories that we might draw an education from- the pleasant ones are at best a coping mechanism. Tonight is for coping, and you revel in the recollections. The road trip to Myrtle Beach with your group, the drama club people and those on its periphery. That crowd in which you and your best high school friend Patty held court- a nucleus, two electrons darting about haphazardly, attracting other elementary particles. Your gang that began its life in the modest setting of a freshmen dorm and grew into the off-campus house that would become home to what you'd come to know as the One Big Happy Family. It is these days taken as a whole that occupy your thoughts right now. Scattered images of footlights at the front of the stage, the cast parties afterwards there at the house, a reading of lines in the living room with demure and unassuming Renee, her standing in as Stanley Kowalski, your Stella lips meeting hers for a smack, separating quickly as if from static shock. It was the last place you felt at home, a place where anything could happen but it was okay if nothing did. You see their bright faces, the One Big Happy Family- Patty, Renee, Theresa, Bill, Steve and the others. Ghosts now because you moved to Pennsylvania to start a new life. You lost touch. Last year you noticed, with a certain despondency, the drop-off in the Christmas card count.

When you dropped Patty off at the airport for a semester overseas to England you held her as if she were stepping into another dimension. When after graduation she decided to study and then marry and settle down there, you promised to stay in touch. You did at first. But the distance is just too much. Now she's a ghost, with a family of four. Renee lives still in Knoxville, a registered nurse. The Christmas cards come but you haven't bothered to take the hour drive to see her on your annual

Christmas visits home. Renee with the silly multi-colored snowcap, long with a bon-bon which served to hide reefer. Theresa has dropped out of your life and everyone's changing except you. You wonder do they wonder about you? You curse the absence of new friends.

And so the room becomes dark, and the rest of the house with it. The sun has disappeared. You'll break the trance into the past, rise up and mechanically turn on the light switch, dispelling the intimacy of candlelight, and close unfamiliar lace curtains. Mother seems to have replaced so many of the fine details in this house. You lie down and wish you could will the course of your approaching dreams to a destination of your choice. Then you'd relive those days of study and leisure, where everything mattered and yet nothing mattered and there were only better days ahead. Then you could see the faces of Patty, Renee, Theresa. And they would not be ghosts, they'd be real and tell you not to worry, everything will be fine. Perhaps you'd will yourself to dream about a new play in progress for the UT Drama Society, yes that's it, it won't end with *A Midsummer Night's Dream*, that final production for the 1986 season, your swan song, that in which you and Renee overindulged at the opening night's cast party, and paid so dearly for the next night. Indeed, not even Theseus' (Ted) impassioned bidding on the opening curtain- *Stir up the Athenian youth to merriments; Awake the pert and nimble spirit of mirth: Turn melancholy forth to funerals; The pale companion is not for our pomp-* could banish your headache as you waited backstage sparsely dressed as Titania, Queen of the Faeries. Back then it only took a day and a cast party until you could return to the buoyancy of youth. Yet over these last six years try as you might to summon such a spirit, it remains elusive.

You were a natural on the stage and everyone told you so. Right from the very first play in grammar school. There's some of momma's photographs which you dug out from under old report cards in the bottom drawer of the little white desk you used to do homework on. Yourself and Peppermint Patty and Renee locking arms laughing in a snapshot backstage in your Midsummer Night garb. Renee (Helena) and Billy Fielder (Puck) in a scene just after she wakes up in the forest, dramatically lit and frozen in a dramatic moment. You wish you could unfreeze such a moment and breathe life into it, give it action. In your fondest memory is a guy named Bill Fortney, who always had a bit part, having spread himself too thin to give his full attention to a major part in a UT Drama Club production. And here he was as Snout, a tinker, speaking one of his few lines, *Will not the ladies be afeard of the lion?* And then he'd adopted the word afeard into his diction, noting with mirth it fit right into the southern jargon, afeard, like *watchyou afeard of boy?* You want to unfreeze this light-hearted Bill into action in the dreams ahead of you.

But when at last you lay down and climb under the covers to slip through the doors of sleep into dreams you are pursued by Bill. Hunting you like a lion, coming to bring you back to tear you apart. He appears in the middle of Highway 81 in a swaggering stupor and you slam the brakes, then he appears at the grocery as you round an aisle. Only it's the old Bill, the endearing Cowardly Lion, there are no worry lines on his brow, his eyes shine as clear as the day he sang to you on the front porch at the party. Smiling innocently, abstractedly in beat up Doc Martens, multiple earrings in both ears. But still your instinct is to flee. Leave him in the lonesome dead of night in a deserted interstate. Push past him in the aisle of an overcrowded grocery store with the indifference of a complete stranger.

Thursday, Driven on Cash

The colors of autumn are resplendent in the birches and maples aglow in sunlight along the old road. The pickup is jostled by the potholes that blemish Joe Henry Road, and John glances over his shoulder to the dining room server covered in blankets and roped down to the flatbed. Well Barb, he says, really can't say how this mess will turn out. Law can be funny.

Sounds like you've got your work cut out for you.
Didn't get back until after one last night.
Must've been right after I went to bed.
John nods. Well, everything okay?
Yeah. Well... no. Not exactly.
What's up?
Marital problems.
I see.
I wish it were different.
We all do.
Yeah.
Anything your old man can do?
I don't want to talk about it much right now.
Fair enough.

They drive silently a good while, both glancing around in all directions at the autumn colors.

How's the old furniture restoration business?
Ah, you know. I'll never make a fortune.
But you like to tinker around with all this stuff, don't you?
John looks sideways at Barbara. Well, he says, I've sort of grown to like it in a way I guess.
Must be great to like what you do.
Well, it isn't brain surgery or rocket science. Pays the bills.
Yeah I know, but c'mon Daddy, I've seen some of your stuff. There's a good degree of skill to it. Just judging by all those fine tools you got in that workshop of yours, you may as well be a surgeon.

She smiles, looking across the seat at him in his worn brown corduroy flannel lined jacket, saying, a doctor of furniture.

John draws a deep sigh. I just wish I had more patients to operate on.

Don't care much to work for Frank Lynn, do ya?

He was sure okay as a friend, John winces.

Well, why not set your sights beyond Fentress County? I mean I'm sure if we look further, there's a market for what you do. I can help you.

John shrugs, Barbara continues.

Really. I'll help. C'mon daddy, you've got business sense. Take this thing. Grow it into full-time, bring it all above board, taxes and stuff. You've got accounting software, all that stuff on the PC right? And there's the internet.

The what?

The internet.

He stares blankly at her.

It's the wave of the future. On the computer. Everyone's gonna be tied in real soon. By phone lines. It's kind of a shared network, something like that. To advertise your stuff.

I sure wish your mother were talking the way you are.

She still not thrilled about your work?

She thinks it's beneath a man with a college degree.

Everybody's got a college degree now. Nothing special in it anymore.

John looks sharply at his daughter. That's a bit cynical.

Cynical perhaps, but true. And a lot of people don't end up doing what they study anyhow.

I always thought you should have at least gave theatre a shot, Barbara.

Yeah, well I reckon it's not too late.

Never is, he says. Never is.

*   *   *

When Seamus Griffin began to plant his crops along his thirty acres, the woman whom he'd met at the door of the modest homestead bearing nothing but bad news when she'd implored of him 'Well, what is it?' fell weak to pneumonia from a brutal winter, her frail frame spending too many long hours foraging about in the frozen forest for wood to burn. She handed him the deed to the property on her deathbed and told him to live a good life, as his newlywed Karan looked on pityingly with a nagging cough, grateful herself of the good fortune of an arduous but manageable journey south as winter gave way to spring. He kissed the widow on the forehead, handed his

69

wife a shovel and together they buried the widow under the pines in a pine box he'd set about fashioning two weeks prior. They carried the pine box and its near weightless contents deep into the woods with the help of a neighboring farmer. There the widow lies, in a lonely meadow where the earth hadn't been raised until a few days ago. And perhaps it's a good thing they didn't disturb the ground any further than to excavate plants.

* * *

It's almost noon and Walt's just getting up. He descends the stairs with a headache accentuated with every step, saunters into the kitchen, knowing beyond all doubt there will be no post-it note saying Cindy called. Finding a table of empty chairs and coffee cups, he pours himself a bowl of corn flakes and returns to his room. Fires up the television to catch the local news at noon. Half paying attention, mulling over the fact that his net worth is fast approaching zero. That credit card would soon be put to use. At least everything in the music business was driven on cash, cash was taken and cash was sometimes given- it was one of the last standing remnants of what for him was innocence growing up in rural Tennessee. Childhood and cash. Those were the days before ATMs and credit cards and debit cards - back when money was everything, it bought your groceries at the Safeway, you got it for cutting lawns, Mom sent you on errands with it. He used to love playing with it, fanning it through his fingers- he loved the old singles, the dark ones that were soiled and soft as silk to the touch. Now paper is out and plastic in- the credit card- laying at the ready in Walt's wallet.

Walter Griffith had no interest in school from the first grade. In rural Tennessee there were enough distractions to pull him away from Jamestown Elementary School. Baseball, baseball cards, Strat-o-matic baseball games, bashing fireflies with wiffle ball bats, playing spin the bottle with five boys and one older girl named Ellie Ward, with whom he one night conducted a post-game show with, she let him put his hands under her T-shirt, but quickly snared his wrist in a vice-grip when he placed his palm on her belly and slid his fingertips down behind her jeans button.

Walt wanted to dive into anything creative and there was music, he started playing guitar, learned all the popular songs in a few days, forgot them just as fast, and instead started doodling around with garage bands. By senior year of high school he found himself each day in the renovated barn at his best friend Gavin Sharpe's house. The sonic experiments there on those afternoons and evenings back then in high school evolved through personnel changes into Astroglide. And then Astroglide migrated from Burrville to University of North Carolina Chapel Hill campus-spiraling with a kindly twist of fate into one of the hottest alternative music scenes in the nineties. The band fizzled after their first ramshackle tour, nothing but the clichéd pitfalls of rock n roll in the dawn of their demise -substance abuse, related ego problems, problematic club-owners, sleazy promoters, almost-got-signings- laying aside for bands like Velocity Girl, The Connells, and The Minutemen.

 Walt has ceased talking about his future prospects and the house has grown silent. Will's gone north to Boston and MIT, switching his major from molecular biology to computer-assisted cosmology. From the study of the infinitesimal to the infinitely immense. Will's room across the hall, with his science magazines, microscope, chemistry set and the glow-in-the-dark planetarium on the ceiling. Will knew the names, shapes and locations of the planets and constellations, Walt just thought it looked cool. Will the boy scientist with his ant colonies in aquariums. Walt came to regard himself and his brother as polar opposites while growing up together, like two worlds neighboring each other with vastly different landscapes and chemical composition. Walt well-built and dark-haired, Will lanky and fair-haired- they didn't even look like each other.

 After a degree in Mass Communications threw him at the mercy of generality with few contacts, he oddly sprung an interest in physics and the laws of science, at first out of a philosophical impulse, but then from what he felt to be a genuine scientific curiosity. Will's room still holds his bookcase filled with Scientific American, old high school texts, and Dungeons and Dragons, among other testaments to an inquisitive if somewhat introverted childhood and adolescence.

 Walt's room never had a bookcase. It had instead a chest of drawers where he kept baseball cards, Strat-o-matic baseball, Rover Boy readers, and underneath a pile of baseball uniforms copies of Hustler, Playboy, and Penthouse.

Last week he paid a visit Will's room in the dead of night. From the huge bookcase he withdrew Stephen Hawking's *A Brief History of Time* with the mathematical expressions of theoretical physics broken down and explained in layman's terms. It seemed to articulate the inspirations from those moments of cannabis elucidation. He became convinced that while there was a First Cause, there was no subsequent divine order to the universe, and therefore no reason for his mother or anybody else to show up at Christ Church Episcopal or any other house of worship on Sundays. Science allowed no room for myths, whether popular or unpopular. Even generally accepted myths like Christianity couldn't provide durable answers for such elusive questions; *When was the beginning of time, what happened before the beginning? Is there an end to space? Time? Does it end on itself? Do the laws of science break down at the Big Bang? What lies on the other side of Black Holes? Why are we here? Who's out there?* Science, he felt, served to answer these plaguing questions as part of the evolutionary process. So he's started cheering his brother on, squirreled away like a monk among the libraries at MIT dedicating his life to this mission, rather than at some religious seminary dedicating his life to some overplayed myth.

Because as different as he was from Will growing up, it wasn't as if they didn't get along. They rarely argued or shouted at each other, he could recall only one occasion in his life that he actually came to blows with his brother, and whatever ignited the rage was negligible enough to be lost to memory. Beyond their differences, two years in age separated them. Barbara's age made her a distant planet to Walt and Will's solar system. Barbara was pretty and popular as a high school student, Walt and Will were not. Barbara believed in the angels that decked the walls in Mrs. Griffith's Christ Church Episcopal Church and the saints and apostles that decked the walls of her hidden Catholic heart, Walt and Will did not. Barbara attended most every highs school social gathering that happened in Jamestown, Walt and Will did not. Barbara liked having her bedroom in perfect order, Walt and Will thrived among mess. Barbara liked writing long letters to pen pals in other parts of the world, Walt and Will wrote very little and only when necessary. Barbara hung out with athletes and was a founding member of the Jamestown Young Democrats, Walt and Will hated jocks and had little interest in politics. Barbara spent much of her childhood at crafts fairs, Walt and Will spent a good chunk of theirs in front of the television. Barbara had several boyfriends and went through each of them with an innocent aloofness, Will never had girlfriends and Walt always got roped in for the long haul- five years with Christine Porter, then three years on and off with Cindy.

Just then the power cuts and the television blinks off, flashing to a white dot and becoming a dark mirror in which he sees himself, the soles of his feet disproportionately huge in the foreground, he on the bed alone- and suddenly such abstractions like black holes *become black holes*, folding in on themselves and opening onto a universe of Cindy Blums.

*   *   *

Cookeville lies just west of the Big South Fork. John is on the way for his Thursday Night Old-Time Jamboree on WHRS. In a netherworld of division between the time zones, he crosses the border of Eastern Standard Time to Central Standard Time. One hour given on the way to town, then taken back on the way home. It'll take longer tonight, the winding mountain roads need to be handled with care even by familiar locals in this messy weather. He clenches the wheel, a severe thunderstorm outside the heated pickup pounding areas of Fentress and Scott County with gale force. A good night for folks to tune in the dial and take a trip down memory lanes of lost love, heartache, good hard country livin. As part of a programming re-shuffle, his show was switched from Wednesday to Thursday night last month.

WHRS is the only station that transmits classical music through the airwaves of the Cumberland Plateau. A local affiliate of the National Public Radio Network, it broadcasts from the premises of the Cookeville Public Library. With just under a thousand watts of power, catching the signal can be a hit or miss through the mountains of the Big South Fork. Steve Meigs, the chain-smoking program manager is a likeable thirty-something with the onset of gray at the temples, a disarming dimpled smile and a penchant for flannel shirts and jeans. John Griffith holds rank as the exclusive old-timey music deejay.

John fixes a cup of coffee in the office just outside the broadcast booth, trying to put himself in the broadcasting mind, simulate a Thursday night like any other. Conjuring up his usual unfettered deejay chat seems like a sham tonight. He flips through the shelved vinyl with a waning interest in changing over 78s, 45s and re-mastered CDs. He flops down at the broadcast desk and picks up a CD, a very austere cover design, just a black background and in the foreground a profile in silhouette of an old woman. The combination makes for an image of grieving, loss. He thumbs through the cover, thoughtfully reading the liner notes about the exodus of Jews from Poland during World War II. He removes the disc and drops it into the CD machine, drops the tray on the desk, looks at the clock. Dennis the engineer is running a short taped program of local news interest on Historic Rugby, having just cut away from nationally syndicated *All Things Considered*.

John leans against the back of the chair and rests his feet up against the table. There won't be any Louvin Brothers for old Breckenridge or anybody else tonight. Instead it'll be Gorecki's Symphony No. 3, with a total running time of 63 minutes and 42 seconds.

It was Bip Sanders who got John his deejay gig at WXPN Jamestown. Old Bip, who headed the co-op in Jamestown. The station's programming featured mostly old-time gospel and some bluegrass. In the early days, John was in night school, and ran the Sunday night show that featured some local crooners plus some Bill Monroe and Uncle Dave Macon. Some of the employees at the mill listened to his show and made their requests known to him at lunch hour, or stuck their head in his office at the end of their shift and told him they'd really like to hear Bill Monroe or Doc Watson, or the Carter Family.

Now it's Gorecki's Symphony No. 3, the low approaching rumble of bass violas was now joined by cellos and violins, as John waves goodbye to Dennis through the glass- the broadcast booth all the world to him now, him the only man in the world.

He blows smoke rings that waft through the table lamp's beam of light and disappear into the darkness. The red LED light of the request line blinks and he ignores it. He spots an ashtray laying on the Formica table on which the shelving rested. Steve Meigs's cigarette butts are piled within, and a crumpled Marlboro package beside it. Steve smokes more than cigarettes. He'd left a joint for John one night shortly after he started the Saturday night program. But John refused. It wasn't as if he were being prudish. A few joyrides with Clem and whomever else cared to jump in for the cool mountain air, after those prayer meetings with the youth group at the church. Smoking dope was always meant for fun out here in the middle of Tennessee. The social revolutions in the big cities met with mild interest in Fentress County. People smoked grass because their parents and their grandparents did, when it was legal and you could grow it for the fiber. It was just a fun thing to do. John didn't care much for it after high school, with his college scholarship and its attendant responsibilities. But his father loved to smoke grass on occasion, it was like his fine wine. Back before it was officially illegalized. Most every night after a long day of farming, while the farm animals and family slept, John's dad would sit out on the porch and look at the stars that appeared on the dome of sky above the outline of his trees- wife and two children inside what was then a cabin by today's standards. He'd strike a match to his corncob pipe as John peered through the front window of the bedroom.

And now Tim Dawson sat in jail for selling the very same substance. John couldn't even speak to him, he knew nothing of the kid's intentions. Anyway, the burden of proof was on John Griffith to demonstrate he collected no rent for the use of his land. Given the unreported cash income, his chances looked slim. John hadn't any occasion to read the Bill of Rights since grammar school, but yesterday he read and re-read the Preamble and the rest of the inland tributary to that river of freedom embodied in the Constitution. The Fourth Amendment, cruel and unusual punishment. Was the forfeiture of the land and a house thereon, at an estimated value of over $200,000 a fair price to pay for some wild weeds growing unbeknownst to the man whose name was on the property deed? John spent a good part of the morning in the study poring over documents, reading up on some recent forfeiture cases, and the proceeds the federal government realized from forfeitures. Still stinging in his mind is a July 1990 U.S. Department of Justice bulletin sent to all U.S. Attorneys, calling for an increase in forfeiture "production" to a $470 million projection, and going on to say that failure to do so would expose the department's forfeiture program to criticism and undermine confidence in its budget predictions. It went on to state that every effort must be made to increase forfeiture income in the three remaining months of the department's fiscal year.

Such thoughts plague him while the softly straining violas and weeping violins lay a bed of melancholy for the soprano's lamentation of loss. By the time the final strains of the first movement of Henryk Gorecki's plodding composition exhaust themselves in the dim and windowless room, John Griffith sits in what might appear to be calm repose, legs still crossed on the table. Yet inside of him inner turmoil had given over to rage. He stubs out his cigarette, snares the desk microphone and a long stretch of dead air is broken:

Miles away, old widow Cotter drops her sewing needles into her lap at the fireside as an ominous silence is broken by a heavy-hearted voice crackling from the old Emerson vacuum-tube radio on the mantle.

My faithful listeners, usually at this time I read you my playlist and tell you what we've just listened to. Perhaps read a few PSAs about what's going on in your community. Well here's a piece of news about something that's going on in your community. A man stands to lose his property to the federal government for no good reason. In fact, there are no formal charges against the man, but a case against the property itself. Now when I say lose his property I mean everything. House, barn, land, little pond, the very pine trees great grandaddy planted... Sorry...Sorry friends, it's just that it's been one hell of a week. The U.S. Marshal Service notified me on Monday that forfeiture proceedings are underway concerning the land that's been in my family for five generations. I have ten days to file a claim to the land, and twenty days to file an answer to their notice. I have no idea- wait, let me back up- the DEA found marijuana plants growing on a remote piece of my one hundred and four-acre property. Growing without my knowing anything about it or giving permission. I had nothing to do with their being planted there. My wife is beside herself. I won't tell you all of the grief I have suffered as a result of this intrusion on my life. I know everyone has their own cross to bear. I only want to tell you what is happening to me within the legal system currently in place. The DEA, the Justice Department, the Tennessee Bureau of Investigation, all of these government agencies refuse to let me explain myself in a human manner. I have the right to file an answer with my claim to the land, in writing. But these agencies which I, like the rest of you pay for in my taxes all my life, want to take everything I've got and they won't even give me the time of day when I call them! Soon the Circuit Courts will most likely move for summary judgment for the forfeiture of my property. I'm not even entitled to a trial by jury!

I'm using this forum because it's in my power to do so right now. Please when you see me walking into the market in Jamestown, or driving around in my truck trying to make a living, don't avert your eyes or look down upon me with scorn. I've done nothing wrong, and if you alienate me you are just playing right into the hands of an unjust and evil greedy money-makin government. Indeed, friends the scales of justice are not in balance in this system of law where every day something is being declared illegal, and the laws and punitive effects therein are being piled onto us humble citizens with complete disregard for the Constitution.

I declare publicly what is happening to me unconstitutional. Tonight I give a public record of breach of four Constitutional Amendments. That's the Bill of Rights folks. That's our bill to the people who are charged with safeguarding democracy. They've done and are continuing to do a terrible job. Oh well, here goes, got this Constitution of ours stuffed in my jeans here somewhere, okay, okay, Fifth Amendment, No person shall be deprived of life, liberty, or property, without due process of law; nor shall private property be taken for public use without just compensation. Now word has it that plans are in the making to construct a route 40 bypass to Historic Rugby that may require use of what is now my property. Local authorities worked with federal authorities in seizing the strange plants and initiating seizure of my land. Folks, my great grandaddy fought in the bloody War Between the States and I'm beginning to wish more and more that he'd won the cause. Our nation is diseased folks, it's got a sickness in its heart what amounts to fascism. When folks can lose their land over acts they're not even responsible for, there's contamination in democracy. I'm tellin you what my great-grandaddy fought for was the same thing the thirteen original colonies fought for in the Revolution. Freedom. Both wars fought on American soil were for sovereignty. I'm beginning to wish the South would've won. The Confederacy would've drawn up its own Constitution and maybe stuck by it. The Union sure hasn't. Thanks for your time. I don't think you'll be hearing from me any more after this broadcast becomes public record, the station has its limits, I know, this is public radio programming after all, but I just couldn't help it. Couldn't sit here with such uneasy thoughts and not speak em. If that makes me a criminal, then so be it. I don't have to tell y'all Patrick Henry's famous words, ya oughtta know em. But the hell with it here goes anyways, give me liberty or give me death. Now y'all know the phone number here, two four eight nine six nine seven if you don't, please call in and tell me if you don't think this is wrong. Use your head when they tell you they're passing laws to protect you. Look a little deeper for the ulterior motive. Wake up! Wake up.

John switches off the microphone. He thinks for a second about shutting the transmitter down, but decides against it, not wanting to violate station policy and FCC standards for signing off. He sits in the dead air state, thinking about Beth coming in for the news and then the overnight shift, two hours away. Most of his listeners gave up within the first half hour of Gorecki's symphony. Oh my word, says old widow Cotter to the cat as the voice breaks up and there is nothing but dead air. The cat plays with the ball of yarn at her feet while she returns to her sewing.

This bastion of culture and refinement was unchanged to his eyes- a little haven which has remained unfinished for almost ten years for lack of funding, the voice of the media, a sanctuary for the playing of old gospel hymns or high-lonesome or ancient mountain music to little old ladies poring over fabrics and sewing needles, or spacy new-age music to graduate students working on their thesis, or on the next shift Janet might induce lovers to lay coiled in embrace with piano music of the Romantics, or young co-eds to lose their virginity with the Rites of Spring.

He lopes with a sense of obligation to the tall shelves and goes straight for a CD of patriotic songs - America The Beautiful, The 1812 Overture, The National Anthem. They'd used it every year he's been here on the 4th of July and he would leave the CD on repeat and let it run until Janet shows up. It sure is gonna be a hot time on the old town tonight.

The station phone rings. He picks it up, cradles it in the crook of his shoulder. It's a little old lady from Black Creek who regularly calls in requests. Just as she starts to offer a few words of support and comfort, Steve Meigs stands in the doorway. He clears his throat. John spins in his seat.

John.
Steve.
He doesn't look surprised.
Gonna have to ask you to leave John. Dammit, you gotta know I sure don't want to do this.
How'd you hear, so fast?
I heard you. On the radio. Over dinner. Sitting there and wondering where in the hell is the old-timey music?

John imagines Steve at home settling in to a quiet evening in his modest cabin home bordering Pickett State Park, listening to the station. Sprawled on the couch and smoking a joint before the old Zenith tube radio, furrowing his brow in confusion at the onset of John's speech. Steve smokes pot just like a lot of other people. Steve likes John. Steve has a job to protect, John can't say he'd do any different than Steve right then.

When did you get here?

I've been standing here for ten minutes. I thought I'd let you finish.

Thanks. Thanks Steve.

Look John, you know as well as I-

John holds up his hand, shakes his head.

If I see you on the street, I'll treat you no differently than I always have. Just promise me you'll do the same to me.

Steve nods and clasps both of John's hands. John feels twenty years slipping away in the handshake. Slinging his jacket over his shoulder, just a dark silhouette to Steve as he calls over his shoulder.

We got freedom of speech Steve. Freedom of speech, just watch what you say.

Friday, Stuck on the Other Side of You

Barbara

You went to sleep last night to the pitter-patter of rain on the roof. It had the effect of pulling you away from the ghosts in the photographs and left you in the moment. You woke up to an empty house. You've just stepped out of the shower when the phone starts ringing. You instinctively wrap a towel around you, even though you know the house is all yours. Darting across the hall, you think for a moment that it's Bill, and that would be his timing, *ring when I'm at my most vulnerable- naked and shivering wet.* But a familiar female voice greets you on the phone line.

Renee. Oh my God you say to her, mom said you called. I was gonna call you today.

Bill, she says, rang my phone twice last night.

Well I guess you know the score then.

I don't know. Are you alright?

Yeah. Just a little tired. I was digging through some old photos from our plays the other night. So you could say I've seen you recently.

Listen, I have the day free. Let's hook up.

You're a dear. Give me directions to your house and I'll shove off from here soon.

I was thinking of coming out to see you, actually. I sure could use the change of scenery.

Sounds great. See you in a little while.

You hang up the phone, pat yourself dry with the towel and stare in the mirror, searching your face for wrinkles.

*   *   *

An end of the week lunch date at the Jamestown Diner is fairly regular between Ellen Griffith and Miriam Carter. They seat themselves over a checked tablecloth while the waitresses flitter about, plunking down silverware in preparation for the lunchtime rush.

You okay? Miriam removes her gloves and frowns over folded hands.

Ellen shrugs, plucking a menu from the holder. As well as can be expected I guess.

How's school?

Frightening.

Miriam fiddles with her place setting.

You've seemed rather... I don't know... distracted lately.

Well there's a lot to distract me at the moment.

No. I mean even before this mess.

Miriam fishes about in her purse and shakes her head. Oh look Ellen, Clem will get to the bottom of this, don't worry yourself too much over it.

With all due respect Miriam, I think this matter is out of his... range of expertise.

What makes you say that?

Oh c'mon Miriam. He knows civil law good enough. Real estate, contracts, wills and estates. But dealing with the DEA? I really appreciate his willingness to help. Only natural he'd-

-Do you honestly think he'd want to represent you if he didn't think he could do the job?

Well he may think he can, but...

Miriam leans in and whispers through pursed lips. Well, at least give him a chance. There's a lot of things Clem isn't, but a fool's not one of them. If he thought for a second he was in over his head he'd get on the phone in an instant to somebody who wasn't.

Ellen folds her napkin, coughs. Can we drop this? For a little while anyway?

As you wish, says Miriam, clenching her lips, shifting her attention to the waitress who's arrived at their table, clutching pen and pad and smiling expectantly.

How's Barb, Miriam asks after they've placed their orders.

Confused, says Ellen, shaking her head slowly.

She home for a while?

I don't know. We haven't talked any about it.

Lord, Bill seemed like a right nice kid.

He's not a kid.

Well you know, to us they all are. I guess you never know what goes on under other folks' roofs, Miriam says wistfully gazing into space.

No, says Ellen, you sure don't.

* * *

I was thinking, Barbara says, pulling the refrigerator door open and examining its contents. We don't have to go out for lunch. There's leftover chicken, bread, salad. How about a nice long walk and a picnic?

They assemble their picnic morsel by morsel, right down to the wicker basket replete with red and white paper napkins, foregoing the kitchen table for woods that seemed boundless to Barbara as a child. She slings the knapsack over her shoulder and they walk to where the back yard meets the darkness of the thick woods. They trudge on as the sun shines intermittently through passing clouds, making their way amid the shadowy pine forest, leaves crunching beneath their feet. The sweet summer fragrances of honeysuckle and azalea have long given way to the muskiness of damp pinewood. A beam of sunlight spills through a gap in the trees and spotlights a creek bed and a moss-backed log that's just enough dried to sit on. They pause a moment, dropping the picnic basket and knapsack.

Neither of them has mentioned Bill, and it's probably just as well, it would seem a disruption to their reminiscences about the undergraduate years that seem like another lifetime.

Why didn't we ring each other up more over these last six years, talk like this, says Renee as she hands Barbara the basket and steps tentatively on a rock to cross the wide creek.

Dunno, guess sometimes it takes something bad to bring people together- she picks abstractedly at a dandelion- or maybe just changing situations. New beginnings.

Amen to that Renee says, lobbing sticks at the creek bed.

Barbara nudges the ground with her feet. I'm not sure I'll ever get married again.

I don't guess I ever will. Renee's soft words seem more directed to the green crush velvet seat of moss-laden wood as she runs her hand along its sheen.

After almost an hour walking the dense forest they meet a grassy meadow bathed in sunlight. They spread the blanket in the tall grass and the two of them lie on their backs watching puffy clouds drift over a bright blue sky. Renee sips at the Chardonnay she brought. Barbara digs the chicken sandwiches and salad from the basket and after a welcome repast Renee lies down on the blanket and soon drifts off to sleep. Barbara removes her sweater to make a pillow of it, feeling her energy beginning to wane, laying back and propping herself up on her elbows, glancing across to the side of the meadow opposite the forest from which they entered. There's a thin line of birch trees beyond which lies another clearing. Something catches her eye, a movement in a thicket of bushes at the far edge of that next clearing beyond the birches. At first she thinks it's a deer, but when she shields her eyes from the bright sun to get a better look she's certain there's someone crouched in that thicket of bushes. Someone in a red jacket. The figure quickly jumps into the thicket with the sound of crumpling branches.

Renee, she whispers. *Renee!*

Renee's eyes flutter open to a sky that has darkened to an ominous grey. Wow, she says, looks like a downpour any minute.

Ssshh.

Barbara's panic-stricken eyes pan along the thicket of bushes that can't be more than fifty yards away.

What is it? Renee whispers urgently as she stands up.

Thought I saw someone. Right over there. Barbara points towards the small opening in the thicket where the red jacket disappeared just moments before. I'm going to have a look.

Barbara sprints across the meadow, Renee in tow.

When they reach the birches at the edge and look beyond, Barbara gasps at the sight in front of her. The ground has been turned up in every inch of the meadow, heaps of dirt in a clearing of what must be almost an acre. She shivers beneath her sweater and long-sleeve tee shirt. From the other side of the clearing comes the sound of something crashing through the thicket, sticks and branches crunch under running feet.

Let's get outta here, Renee urges in a hoarse voice.

Barbara is already past her, bolting back to the tall grass and the blanket. She snares it, gathers it into a ball and throws it to Renee, taking the basket and her sweater under one arm and leaving the wine bottle standing in the tall grass. They sprint as fast as their legs will carry them. The sky breaks and the drizzle quickly turns to a downpour as they dodge this way and that through a darkened forest of pine trees, never once stopping to look back.

* * *

Barbara

The both of you didn't stop running until you pulled the back door closed behind you, panting, drenched and holding the picnic implements. Renee started laughing and then you, perhaps as a catharsis after the high anxiety or because you'd behaved like schoolgirls back there, tearing through the woods. Now, as your laugh turns to a cough, you feel the effect of all those cigarettes you've started back on. The two of you soaked from head to toe- Renee's hair so immersed you can see her scalp and the blond roots and you just stand there dripping, giggling like schoolgirls. *C'mon*, you say at last, *let's get out of these wet clothes*, while removing your shoes. Dripping wet, you dash upstairs to the bathroom, its linoleum floor peculiarly warm on your chilled-to-the-bone feet. You remove your flannel shirt and heave it on the floor. Renee is struggling with a clinging silk blouse, she's managed only to pull it as far as her shoulders, now it's bunched up around her head- her muffled voice between giggles says *I'm stuck* into the fabric and you tug at the back of the blouse. Telling her to hold still, you pull and pull- *ouch!* she laughs, *my earring!!* At last her head emerges, her hair flopping completely over her eyes and she tosses it back, in this moment your eyes meet, they can't help but meet with your proximity, and you are transfixed by those soft baby blue eyes. All at once your mouth is upon hers, there you are pressing your lips to hers and a sort of soft laugh escapes through her nose you think maybe this kiss is merely a stolen kiss, but as you begin to draw back she mirrors the strange hunger, her tongue darting at your lips provokingly and you're crushing your mouth against hers and before you know it you're helping her out of her Levis and she out of yours. Without a word you stand with mouths locked as your hands move up underneath her shirt and you feel her fingers running down the middle of your back and soon you are stumbling toward your bedroom, stopping a few times in the hallway, forgetting where you are as you close the door behind you. You remove what little is left of Renee's and she yours. When you collapse naked on top of her and feel your own rigid nipples rubbing against her own and it doesn't matter where you are, who you are. For the moment, nothing matters.

     *   *   *

John

We used to have regular company picnics out at Pickett State Park. We'd pack the kids up in the station wagon. We'd fill the Coleman cooler with ice and cokes and a six-pack of beer. I can remember it like it was yesterday. We packed hotdogs and hamburger patties into the cooler and we had those brown paper grocery bags filled with buns and chips and marshmallows to roast on the fire when the sun went down and everybody retired from the pick-up softball game. Walt and Will loved those softball games almost as much as they did little league baseball. I'd usually do the underhand pitching for my side and I had pretty good accuracy. When it was our turn to bat I'd sprawl out in the high grass on the hill behind the third baseline and watch Ellen talk to the wives and Patty, my floor supervisor. We'd tell Barbara not to stray too far into the woods on her nature hikes with the other girls. Everyone seemed to get along. My employees looked up to me. I guess I figured myself just one of them with a management degree. When the corporate forces came down to buy us out and impose their new culture and expectations on us, I guess I was forced to make a choice. My natural inclinations were to those I had come up with, those who had been loyal to me through many lean years, those with whom I'd played softball and picnicked. The corporation had the interests of its shareholders to serve. I resisted. I ultimately paid the price for that. But I like to think about the picnics we had before Imperial was acquired. Those long lazy Saturday afternoons out at Pickett. Back then it seemed those days went slow and you could savor the picnic outing from morning to long afternoon and into early evening when at last you'd have some leftovers from lunch and watch the fireflies light up the night. Then you knew it would soon be time to roll up, tired as you were. We'd load the station wagon and drive out of the park, headlights piercing the darkness of those pine-covered narrow roads. From the back seat the kids would drill me with questions and listen intently at my responses.

Back then Ellen and I didn't fuss so much over things, didn't argue so much.

*   *   *

Barbara

The sound of a door slamming shut downstairs as you wake up nestled in Renee's arms. You sit bolt upright and Renee stirs. A hard rain on the roof. The sound of drawers opening and shutting in the kitchen downstairs. You pull a big tee shirt over yourself and dash to the bathroom to gather up wet clothes. Carrying them back to the bedroom, you watch Renee fidgeting under a sheet. Here, you say, you can borrow some dry clothes. And it's easily done, as Renee is only one size smaller. After both of you have dressed more awkwardly than you'd undressed, you realize you don't have a pair of shoes for Renee's tiny feet. On the way downstairs, you meet your brother holding a plate with a sandwich. When you're fetching Renee's shoes at the backdoor you spy it, hanging there on the coat rack. Walt's red fleece jacket.

*   *   *

John sits at a long table in the conference room adjacent to the waiting area that is part of Janet's domain- legal documents arriving and departing for typing and revision among the three separate offices of Carter & Associates. He's spent the better part of an afternoon scouring legal journals as Clem helped a young couple sort out a modest inheritance. By the time the young heir and heiress shuffle out of his office it's heading for four o'clock and Clem's in a Friday state of mind, sending Janet home early, waving John into his office, leaning back rocking in the hardback leather chair with fingers locked at the base of his neck.

So Luther wasn't much help. Dadgummit. Well I guess he's about stuck on the other side of you. Running down drug dealers and stuff. Raids, seizures. Pushes these forfeiture cases pretty hard too, from what he told me.

Other side of me?

Sure, he's prosecuting forfeiture cases, not defending them- Clem taps his temple lightly with a finger- military man, thinks in terms of lines, clearness, sides. You walk in there, even if you're a friend of ole Clem Carter's he's gonna clam up some. I might have thought.

Yeah, you might have.

Well, what *did* he say?

Not much. Said get ready for a long battle, something to that effect.

Don't get discouraged. Not all these forfeiture cases come up guilty. Luther did tell me they've been expediting these cases pretty quick here lately. We gotta get that claim filed.

What about the bond?

Yeah, the bond. Twelve thousand.

Clem pushes himself out of the chair and at the window he parts the blinds to look down onto Main Street, Jamestown. You need money? he asks with his back to John, watching people shuffle along the street.

John sighs. Maybe.

Done, Clem says. You just let me know how much.

He turns from the window and walks around his desk to lay a hand on John's shoulder. Why not come by tonight, have a few shots and play some poker? I'll call Breckenridge and some of the others. Take your mind off things.

I gotta keep my mind *on* things. Gotta start looking at some of the stuff I copied at Vanderbilt. Organizing it.

John pictures himself in the cloistered walls of his study at the back of the house, designing a game plan for the filing of the letter of response against the forfeiture.

John, says Clem, fitting his fedora over his skull, bag it for tonight. Pull the mess out over the weekend, we'll look at it first thing Monday. C'mon over to the house tonight and take the edge off.

Really Clem, I-.

-See you at eight. C'mon, I gotta lock the place up.

Where's the rest of the gang around here?

Fishing, says Clem, jiggling keys. Like any old fool with a damn bit of sense on a sunny Friday afternoon. Fishin.

* * *

Barbara has a modest dinner in progress, a simple country stew- potatoes and carrots and a roast brewing slowly in a large pot over a low flame. She shakes spices into the pot and stirs it.

I'm gonna have to do you a real dinner soon as we do a proper shopping. Whadda you guys do, eat frozen dinners every night?

Ellen looks up absently from the dog-eared pages of *You Can Heal Your Life*. I don't have the luxury of time I used to, dear.

Daddy, she knocks on the door to the study, you hungry?

Yes, a weak voice replies from the other side of the abyss. John grimaces at his desk, he's barely glossed over the court transcripts of the nightmare of Delmar Puryear. Puryear owns a thirty-seven acre farm in Kentucky that the government moved to seize when five hundred marijuana plants were found growing somewhere on the land that the disabled retiree could not farm. The jury apparently hadn't lost all sense of reason, they acquitted him. Even so, the feds wouldn't drop the charges until Puryear agreed to pay $12,500. He replaces the document back into the heap on his desk.

At the dinner table, they are all sat and after Ellen says the grace, John glances at each of them in turn.

Well, he says, isn't this just like old times. Maybe if we just ring Will and have him catch a Greyhound, we'll have the whole family back intact.

Ellen shakes her head slowly. Damn that old oil burner blowing a fuse and breaking down. Gonna get cold soon.

Walt spoons his father some potatoes. I didn't know what the hell happened to that TV.

You're hopeless Walt, says Barbara. Damn, the first place you look is the godamn fuse box.

Ellen glances up sharply. Can we please refrain from the foul language?

After an uncomfortable silence Ellen turns to John. Just when do you reckon they can come and look at the furnace?

John shrugs. I'll see Frank over at Clem's tonight. I'll ask him when Jones can come round and look at it.

Conversation resumes without any further expletives or blown fuses. When they've finished, Barbara wags a finger at her brother and says, Walter clean your plate.

Let me help you clean up, says John, wiping his mouth and watching Ellen gather dishes. That's a lot of pots and pans.

He pushes in his chair, rolls up his sleeves and begins to scrub with a sponge.

You didn't have to put so much liquid detergent in the sink Ellen says, peering over John's shoulder.

Why do you have to fuss over everything?

It's not fussing.

Yes it is.

Well only if you choose to see it that way.

I see it for what it is. Fussing.

He flings the sponge at the water and beats a hasty retreat to his study.

*   *   *

Deal me in, John announces to the table in the Carters' den- what could be the lounge of a hunting lodge, its log walls decked out with all manner of outdoor sport oil paintings, Miriam standing behind him with his jacket draped over her arm.

Didn't think you were gonna turn up Griffith, rasps Bill Breckenridge between puffs at a cigar.

The lounge is smothered in cigar smoke, one thing John doesn't care for at these poker nights. What's soothing is the light banter that's exchanged between hands.

What the hell took you so long? Clem rises to put another log on an already blazing fire.

Oh, you know, John shrugs.

Oh, you know, Clem mimics, I got these two jarheads poundin on me, and nobody to dump shit on.

Clem, says Miriam reproachfully.

Woman, will you leave us world-weary men to our foul ways? Drinkin, cussin, fartin, belchin, all manner of bad manners?

Nine thirty tomorrow morning for Ed and Sheila's party. John, you and Ellen coming?

John looks quizzically at Clem.

Baptism, their little squirt. Didn't want to you to bother about it- he says with a glance to his wife- He's got other fish to fry.

I'll call Ellen, Miriam says. Maybe she'll want to tag along with us.

Good idea, says Clem. Now can we get back to this poker game?

John becomes the player for Clem to dump shit on, along with Breckenridge and Frank Lynn. He doesn't care much for the hands dealt to him, he makes blunders along the way, he looks from Frank to Bill and wonders who knows what and what all he should tell them. Clem's silence about the forfeiture impels his own muteness on the matter, in fact he's pretty mute altogether.

What's eatin you John? Bill Breckenridge says with a grimace after a full shot of his whiskey.

Frank here's workin him too hard. Bastard, Clem grins.

That or my daughter, Breckenridge sighs. How's that old radio show goin?

He plays the best damn music in the Cumberland Plateau, boasts Frank.

I won't argue you there says John, meeting Frank's raised whiskey glass with his own.

Heard ya last night, Breckenridge glances conspiratorially at John. The music wasn't exactly on fire but you sure's hell were.

Thought it was Wednesday night, says Frank.

They moved me to Thursdays.

Oh hell, says Frank. No wonder I ain't heard it in a month of Sundays. Request?

John grins, Yeah sure, go ahead.

Louvin Brothers. The Devil is Real.

I just played that last week.

Well godammit, play it again Sam.

You gonna be able to, John? Breckenridge shoots him a knowing glance.

Not to worry, John says, losing another hand and cashing in his chips.

Saturday, The More Grounded Road of Supposition

As utopian ideas often will, Rugby fell apart at the seams. The wee colony was founded in 1880, an experiment in a design for living when a handful of English prospectors for perfection burrowed themselves deep in a wooded plateau at the foot of Appalachia in East Tennessee. The community was founded by Thomas Hughes, a British social reformer and author at whose hand *Tom Brown's Schooldays* was born. For ten years they planted, schooled, debated, nursed, danced, suffered, sang and harvested together. They idled, they drank, they begat, they were flooded and fired out of their modest homesteads, all the while regarding their earthly surroundings as Utopia with an unshakeable faith. There's no telling exactly when and where the cancer sprouted that set the ideal on its path of debasement and decay, but some've reckoned it the night the Tabard Inn burned to the ground in 1890. Is it eternal fate that all paradigms masterminded by a collective of idealists that promote a pure mission for the well-being of all are eternally doomed to that foul curse of greed- is humankind infected with an unavoidable primary self-oriented drive? Whatever the cause, Rugby *fell apart at the seams.* By the 1890s many of the original colonists had vacated. By the turn of the century, English investors had sold out to American interests.

What remains is Historic Rugby, a tiny village with a scattered few surviving buildings- the Thomas Hughes Library which houses a collection of more than seven thousand works of literature, Christ Church Episcopal with the original pipe organ, the Schoolhouse Visitor Center, The Founder's residence, the residence of Hughes' mother, a two-story General Store stocked to the rafters with perishables of the home-made jam variety and other such country crafts. The center of attraction for the tourist trade however is not deep in history, swelled with literary tomes or liturgical music. The Harrow Road Cafe, reconstructed after a fire consumed the original structure, serves food regularly in the summer season. These architectural ingredients now incorporated as a place of historical significance in this stark, remote region of the Cumberland Plateau. A monument, a museum- a reminder that such collective ideal lifestyles, later manifested in the hippie commune experiments of the sixties, eventually succumb to those nagging imperfections of the broader society they'd aspired to disentangle themselves from.

John's just finished yet another estate clearance job with Frank near Iron Mountain and heads east on Highway 52 towards Rugby- he parks by the cemetery and heads down the old trail to the Gentleman's Swimming Hole. Trees of changing colors aglow above, sunshine shooting through them and resolving in split rays over the floor of dead leaves that crunch underfoot. The usual sense of comfort and ease in such idyllic surroundings is elusive, his mind restless after a night of tossing and turning, advancing Ellen's argument for twin beds. Along the river lays a trail he's tread many a time before. Lit by sunlight the moss-covered tree stumps and fallen branches glisten like precious jewels set in green velvet. To the immediate right along the trail stands a towering rock formation. On the other side of the cliffs is the river, twisting here and there. He reaches the meeting of the rivers. At this fork is a sort of natural rock platform, the scene of former family swimming outings where shouting kids would leap off the natural shelf exuberantly. Everyone except Will with his awful fear of the water. He'd seemed to John more like an adult on those afternoons, dismissing Walt's goading and burying his face into his science fiction novel or Popular Science magazine.

He lies on his back in this former refuge that now fails to provide any consolation. He is restless, grunts at he lifts himself from the rock bed, grunts on the whole hike back to the pickup, grunts as he settles into the cab. He makes the drive home with a reluctance that has recently become all too common, pulling into the driveway and sitting a good while before killing the engine.

When at last he enters the house, Ellen is in the kitchen doorway in an apron holding a wooden cooking spoon.

Where have you been, she asks.

I was at Cawleys' doing some finishing.

I called over there an hour ago and they said you'd left at two thirty.

I had a few things to pick up from the store, he lies while watching her gaze fall to his empty hands.

From the hardware store he says, hoping she won't check the bed of the pickup as he turns around and walks aimlessly out the door he just entered.

He kicks at the air, cursing himself for his careless lie, curses *having* to lie. Again a sense of shame at his lack of industry, hiding the fact of having spent the afternoon doing what?

He spits at the ground.

Ellen calls out to him. Coming in for supper?

Ever since he'd lost the job at Imperial Textile, his wife had come to view any activity without income as wasted time and spare time came under her vigilant scrutiny.

Right after college John roamed the world unburdened, backpacking around Europe. One evening in a bodega after a long day trekking through the Pyrenees in the north of Spain, an unshaven young man clapped him on the back and mussed his hair, said *you Americans live to work, we Spaniards work to live*. He wonders whether he should have stayed there forever. Because here his livelihood dogged him all his days it seemed, and now it was reduced to odd jobs, and Ellen hovered over him like a dark cloud. Son of a farmer gone off to college, and then done wrong by it. You shall be punished for the rest of your days. Rest ye shall never know. Just toil the rest of your days after just enough money to pay for your financed home additions, your foolish idea to build a rich man's house from a poor man's house.

Ellen hollers up to Walt and Barbara from the foot of the stairs. They spill into the kitchen and supper commences on the solid oak table upon which has been served the meals of four generations of Griffiths. John had stripped and re-finished it the week after he lost the job at the mill. They talk about Will and his doings, gleaned from his few letters home. They embellish these to suit their tastes. The lab partner in Microbiology has surely by now become the object of his desire according to Barbara, his experiment in quantum physics would result in a ground-breaking new discovery in scientific research and lead to a Nobel Prize according to Walt. As John pitches his rejoinders with an affected laughter, his wife remains silent and expressionless. Against such indulgences of the imagination she's always preferred the more grounded road of supposition.

After an awkward silence, Barbara shakes her head and looks from one to the other. So, she says, I guess we're the topic of many a dinner conversation now. I can just hear Mrs. Miller, 'I just knew there was somethin fishy about those Griffiths'-

-Barbara, please.

Ellen rises from the table, lifting her plate and taking it to the sink, her footsteps falling like a judge's gavel. How's our case coming along John, she says with her back to them.

I don't think it's a good idea to discuss it in front of the kids, he says while tapping his fork against the table.

No? Her voice pitches up as she calls over her shoulder, busied in the sink. Why not?

I'd just as soon the adults discussed it themselves first.

We're all adults here, she waves her fork at the table.

Walt scoots his chair out and heads for his room, Barbara heads outside for some fresh air- the screen door slamming on its hinges behind her, leaving her father alone at the table massaging his temples and speaking with chin buried in his chest.

Why not just say it? You don't like it one bit do ya? Clem handling this case.

Oh I see, is that what he's doing? Handling our case? I'd have never noticed.

Kill the sarcasm, sister. He's doing the best he can. I have complete faith in him. He's my friend for chrissakes.

John this-

-My *best* friend, he thumps the table with his fist.

John, this is not a friendly matter.

How dare you question my own good sense!

Really John- she flings a dishrag at the counter.

No Ellen, listen to me for once. I worked, by the sweat of my brow I provided for this family, those were some of the best years of my life. And then things go sour at Imperial and you, you change you entire opinion of me-

-You said-

-yeah that's right, you're mad as hell cause life dealt you an unexpected blow. It was none of my fault-

-John, you said yourself, maybe if you'd been less of a softee, giving slack on production deadlines, giving Dora days off for kids with sniffles-

-Godammit, he slams his fist on the solid oak table. When are you gonna drop this grudge. The job's gone! Four years now and just look at you! Who the hell made you God anyway!

Oh here it is, you can take the boy out of the country, but you can't take the country out of the boy.

He mimics the last bit in unison with her, and adds, S'far as I can see we're still in the damned country. But you, you sure as hell bring out the worst in me. Such a sophisticate, Miss new-age intellectual with your slew of self-help books. Tell me Ellen, just how exactly have they helped? Huh?

I thought this argument was about Clem Carter, she says. Seems to have strayed.

Strayed, eh? I think it's high time this country boy strayed.

His voice bears a tone of resignation alien to her. After he strides out she hears the front door latch click and she wonders whether this were intended as a mock-country voice summoned up by her husband on the spot or a voice deep inside himself, one he'd buried and forgotten about. She dabs her eyes with the dishtowel.

* * *

Barbara

So you're off for a walk in the woods in the same manner as when you were a teenager after the family dinner- as if seeking answers in nature, enamored of the breadth of plant and animal life. Or maybe seeking amelioration of the imperfect human soul that'd fail time and again to protect your mother, your father, your brother. Yourself. You came home a mess. How can one mess aid in fixing another mess?

You turn your back on the fading rays of sunlight, leaving the woods behind you- gliding through the kitchen and taking the stairs two at a time. Once a little girl bolted down these very steps two at a time to a kitchen brimming with welcome smells, sights and sounds. Tonight you've fled an unhappy kitchen. In your old bedroom you lean against the closed door and drop your head in your hands.

You are a woman of thirty years who has seen the passing of time accelerating in a vortex. One month ago you had specific events that gobbled time, lent it sensibility and order. You gaze absently into the framed photograph on the wall of you and your best friend Patty at your college graduation- your smile is genuine enough to mock you now. Your wedding picture hangs beside this. That photograph marks the end of an era that included people who've faded away like the sun does now outside your window.

More than six years since that Kodak moment you stare into now. And what occurred in that span of time, what occupied those moments? Upon cursory review, on paper it would seem a lot. Marriage, semblance of a social work career, graduate level coursework. These formalities, the peripheral distinctions, bullets in the resume of life are references for folks far away, the scanty information they receive to keep up with you. But beyond these facts fixed in time, you have the dullness of the day-to-day. For you, the years have flown by too fast. And unlike the years that preceded them, memory is hard-pressed to recall any days filled with charged feelings. A mere collection of ephemeral moments. Like those afternoons you got out of work early and didn't know what to do with yourself. Stepping lively about the paved lot towards your car, feeling as if the world was your oyster. Hitting the public library under the pretense of gathering source material for your post-graduate coursework. Instead, browsing the fiction rack- or periodicals, or reference, or world history, or the occult sciences, or the catalogue of CDs. Over an hour would pass- you were unbridled and unfocused, scatter-brained, reckless with your time. You went to the supermarket for a gallon of milk and ended up drifting around the entire shopping complex for a full hour, the aimless consumer, wandering around like a zombie. What was it that kept you off the beaten path, made you late for classes, meetings, work, returns home? What was it that accounted for all of this down time? In your youth through adolescence and into college years no record exists of such long stretches of banal distractions. Analysis of these empty periods came fiercely to the forefront of your consciousness under the influence of LSD. A painful realization.

More painful yet the incompatibility with your husband, the person for whom you sacrificed, relinquished a part of yourself at the altar. Nonetheless related because at the core of these 'killing-times' there lay a restlessness, an incapacity to face the significant fact of your insignificant little world.

* * *

The light is on in Clem's basement office at this late hour. It casts a short beam across the well-crafted lawn and its environs of decorative flora. Moonlight slices through the black wrought-iron fence, casting eerie patterns on the dewy lawn, frosted blades of grass give the illusion of a diamond-sprinkled coat of velvet.

John makes footprints in the dew, tapping on the tiny basement window. He circles back and opens the gate at the end of the drive and walks the path of rounded sandstone alongside the house. The light comes on at the backdoor and then Clem peers between lace curtains, bringing a finger to his lips.

The Carters had their kitchen gutted out and redone. All installations are varnished knotty pine, from the kitchen cabinets to the floors and walls. As part of the architectural facelift, they'd had a glass-encased sun porch built adjacent to the kitchen, where they now stand. John glimpses the neatly arranged décor right out of the pages of Better Homes and Gardens.

Wanna beer?

Yeah, sure.

Here, gimme that jacket.

Their whispers reverberate against the porch's glass walls. It's plenty warm in this room, in full view of a cold wet night. Still he feels exposed sitting in the glare of track lighting, prefers the cozy environs of Clem's basement.

The kitchen's wall recesses contain the many country craft decor items from Miriam's collection she hawked regularly at flea market booths. The Carters' world- the motif extends from the tiny knick-knacks on the wall shelves to the coat rack with mirror that Clem hangs John's ragged old split-leather jacket on- to the napkin holder, paper towel holder, straw wreaths, woven-straw plant holders, framed embroidery of plaid bordering, plate ware with cozy country winter scenes.

Let's go down to the office, Clem whispers.

Downstairs, Clem settles himself behind his big oak desk- elbows planted, fingers interlocked under his developing double chin, eyes peering out from wire-framed glasses. John paces and rubs his hands together.

Clem, he says at last- flopping into one of the leather chairs in front of the big oak desk- Ellen and I- you're maybe thinking it's the case I come to talk about- but well...

Spill it, John.

We're... damn... this...

His syntax is all jumbled up. He can hear himself trying to find a voice, somehow detached, unable to scare up words.

Pull yourself together, says Clem.

We're havin some... real problems.

John's throat stiffens, he's blubbering and wonders how much longer he can go to Clem with all of this. How long before Clem's reserves are tapped and their relationship evaporates into brief civil exchanges, polite greetings upon crossing each other's paths?

Truth is, John says, it's been rapidly getting worse. Since Will left.

He wipes a shirtsleeve at his eyes. You know how bad things have got from around the time Walt left for college, I lost my job, all that shit.

What've y'all bickerin about lately?

Everything under the sun.

Well I mean, you know, we've talked about this stuff before eh? Huntin, fishin, or just havin a few drinks, he gazes abstractedly, Women...

This is different. It's gotten way outta hand.

Ellen isn't too keen on me advising y'all is she?

How'd you know that?

Clem leans back in his chair palms behind head, shrugs his shoulders. He says, not hard to imagine.

John heaves a sigh. It isn't personal, you know that. You know Ellen thinks the world of you. And Miriam. Ellen just feels that maybe we're swimmin in too deep of water here.

Clem adjusts his glasses and looks back to John. Let's cut to the chase and look at the facts. You have a serious federal case on your hands.

John nods and slumps deep into the chair.

I mean, Clem says, these forfeiture cases. I have hardly a lick of experience in them, except peripherally. But I have to say they're pretty cut and dried, not much room for legal wrangling. But Ellen's not far off the mark. There are plenty of law firms in Knoxville with more experience of court proceedings, building a defense, some expertise in guiding you-

-But Clem-

-Now hold on a sec. You can go that route, pay their fees. Personally I don't think it'd make one damn bit of difference. But do what you think is right. No hard feelings. We've been friends too long- yourself, Ellen, Miriam, myself, our families. And Ellen knows that. No offense taken.

Clem, I've told you before and I'll say it again. I think we can handle this case. Together. Look, I've been reading up a lot on this stuff. We can work together, right?

Clem lets out a soft chuckle, his folded hands bounce on his belly. You're beginning to sound like one of those cons who sits in jail building his own case. Y'know they sometimes end up ex-cons and legal experts.

I am in jail, Clem. I'm in goddamned jail already.

*   *   *

He's worked up his nerve and is burning to speak to her. *Damnit, Clem's our lawyer, it's my decision and that's that. I'm taking this thing into my own hands as well, don't need no fancy big-city lawyer to run me around and leave my phone calls unanswered or talk to me in a deprecating manner. Patronize me, give me a distant reassurance. I can read. I can get my hands on Federal Law, can look at precedent, I'm a college man after all goddamnit. Maybe both of our names are on the title to this property, but that's something I conceded in good faith when we were married. Something my father didn't concede to my mother, nor any other Griffith man before. It's my family, goddamnit. It's my decision. If you don't like it, there's the door and don't let it hit you in the ass on the way out.*

He's cruising downhill approaching a bend with his foot off the gas and picking up speed when a deer scampers out of the woods and into the path of his headlights. It freezes in the road as the headlights hit its timid transfixed eyes. He reflexively slams on the brakes, sure he's going to hit it, bracing himself for the crumple of metal against flesh and bone. The pickup jerks and bounces to a stop and he's just sitting there still in the middle of Highway 52. The deer runs over the ditch by the side of the road and with his window rolled down he can hear only the tread of its hooves over sticks and dry leaves. Draws a heavy breath, his heart thumping rapidly. *She had the expression of a deer caught in the headlights.* Who'd said that and who had they been referring to?

Then he remembers. Eliza Dawson. It was Dora Wallace who described Eliza as such. It was one day in the lunchroom at the plant amid the gossip he'd sometimes come across, standing there like a lieutenant with his GIs knowing the minute he left their turf such palaver would almost immediately shift to him. Dora had said she'd run into her old friend at the Safeway and Eliza *had the look of a deer caught in the headlights* and turned away with nary a word. He had to suppress a desire to defend Eliza back then, Eliza who'd after all fallen victim to dire circumstances with two kids and a no-account drunk of a husband. Eliza who'd then just been diagnosed with a terminal illness. Eliza for whom life must have seemed unbearable, kids in and out of trouble. Eliza whom he last saw sunning herself- face sunken, arm like a stick, waving at him. Eliza whom he kissed on that oppressively hot summer evening after a cotillion in a summer when the air was still and the crickets sang.

He turns the pickup into the circular gravel drive. The air is chilly, the vapor from his breath when he climbs out of the cab makes it all the more apparent his heart rate is up. The surprise encounter with the deer seemed to take the wind out of his sails for a rehearsed encounter with his wife. He stands at the door of a dark house and takes a few deep breaths, resting a hand on the doorknob while he tries to compose himself. He turns the door handle. It's locked.

Now, they have never been in the habit of locking doors. Who'd there ever been to fear, thieves? Was someone thinking the Feds might come to raid them in the middle of night?

He sticks a seldom-used key in the lock. The hall is in darkness. He cases the first floor- switching on lights, glancing over each room like the night watchman in a museum. Climbs the stairs, faintly lit by the tiny lamp at the end of the hall. All at once hoping and dreading evidence of Ellen in the bathroom of the master bedroom. She was usually good for near a half hour in there- bath, cold cream, nocturnal preparations. But she's already in bed, lightly snoring. He thinks for a second to wake her, dismissing the thought just as fast.

Sunday, Door's Always Open

Barbara knew he was coming. In the guest bed half-asleep she's probing her consciousness to recapture an elusive waking dream about her husband. When her eyes blink awake she just knows he's coming. Propping herself up on one elbow, a glimpse at the ceramic country-garden motif clock of momma's shows it's just after ten o'clock and both her body and mind are fatigued, even after all these recent late risings.

Downstairs by all appearances it's just another Sunday morning in the kitchen. Ellen's finishing a cup of coffee and readying herself for noon service at Christ Church Episcopal, that understudy she'd tolerated all these years as a substitute for her Catholicism. Today she would pad her usual petitions to present a new and challenging task for the almighty- divine intervention in the nightmarish legal dilemma that they are mired in.

John has just broached the subject of Clem's earthly intervention in the matter, but with less conviction than the fervor with which ideas were hatched last night, a troubled sleep having put the edge on. He mutters away, hasn't even mentioned the locked door, making loose intimations to induce an argument that fall wide of the target. Not a single word of last night's script winds its way into this morning's sparse conversation.

Ellen flips through the pages of *You Can Heal Your Life* distracted, unfocused. Settling at last on The List, where the text runs vertically, turning the book at a right angle to accommodate, *I am healthy, whole and complete.* She scans a list of physical ailments, their probable cause, and a new thought pattern for the afflicted. Phlebitis. Probable cause- Anger and frustration. Blaming others for the limitation and lack of joy in life. New Thought Pattern- *Joy now flows freely within me, and I am at peace with life.*

Well, she says. I've got to start for Church.

Just when John's prepared to broach the subject of last night's locked front door, the sound of wheels on gravel. A new reflexive fear seizes him and then he reproaches himself- each unexpected guest could be any number of friends and neighbors, not the D.E.A. or the U.S. Marshal or the Sheriff or perhaps some federal agency. They sit frozen. Ellen drops her book on the table in front of her.

She walks to the hall for a peek at the visitor- immediately overcome with relief when she sees the familiar sleek silver and black jeep of her son-in-law. Oh how hard she's prayed on her knees for this reconciliation and restoration of marital vows. The durable jeep sits in contrast to its driver's own fragile state belied in his comportment as he clambers out of it. And now she'll miss the opportunity to witness the answering of her silent prayers.

Why Bill, of all times, did you have to pick my Sunday morning to show up?

And the worst of it is she'd wanted to get up and moving early, as she customarily did for the eight o'clock service. But last night John had wakened her, arriving in the middle of night, and she'd spent what seemed an eternity feigning sleep until at last she dozed. She'd woken up at six thirty, rolled over on her side and glumly resigned herself to the noon service.

Now as she paces the floor at just ten thirty with her son-in-law about to knock on their door, she considers asking God for a special exemption due to extenuating circumstances- her aid in preserving the sacred sacrament of marriage. She hates the idea of leaving Bill to John, whom she imagines will be indifferent or even slightly rude. At least she's here to greet Bill with a smile and reassuring hug, let him know in no uncertain terms that at least she, the matriarch of the Griffiths, is rooting for him.

Having already announced her intention of leaving to her husband, she fishes in her purse for the keys. Should she decide to stick around, decide against church, her intentions at meddling would surely be transparent to her husband. Ellen never misses a Sunday service.

Bill lingers in the driveway. His dark curly hair is mussed, eyes sunken. Ellen watches through the glass as he stoops down and sticks his head into the cab of the jeep groping around for something, at last drawing a punished blue Navy-style wool overcoat.

Ellen doesn't wait for him to reach the door. She lifts the latch, primping her floral-print Sunday dress, and swings it open. For a moment nothing is out of order and lives are suspended in their perfect unblemished space, immune from complications on the ground. Bill just has that effect on you- calamity and disaster aside, everything's going to be just fine. She strides out onto the porch, smiles and clutches Bill in a hug at the foot of the stairs. She can sense her husband's presence from behind, an imposition on her euphoric glee. She grips Bill's arms and fixes him in front of her as if to verify he's not merely an apparition. You look tired, Bill. Are you hungry? C'mon in, we'll fix you something.

John leans against the doorframe with a strange sort of bemused expression.

Bill, how are you.

His son-in-law has a vice grip, it strikes John as he pumps Bill's hand and looks straight into his swollen eyes. Beneath the folded brim of a wool knit hat his eyes are underscored with dark rings, but the blue irises still glow with magnetism. *Kid's missed his calling, should've been a politician*, John remembers Clem having once said. John politely nods toward the house behind him as Bill pumps his hand like a well lever. C'mon in son. Door's always open around here says John, with a significant glance at Ellen.

Ole Griffith household. Same as I left it.

Bill removes his hat and wipes his feet on the doormat.

Not quite, John mutters while Ellen hangs his tattered coat. He draws a chair in the familiar old kitchen where in the distant past Bill had asked John for Barbara's hand. On the night of this nuptial announcement the Cumberland Plateau was in the throes of one hell of a storm- residents rushed home to drag in firewood after drawing down the local market's insufficient supplies of milk and kerosene, on Route 52 power lines thrashed and fell as over-eager young drivers skidded to crashes. The storm lent an atmosphere to the occasion, two men seated across from one another at the table, tumblers of whiskey twinkling in the glow of kerosene lamps and candles. Bill'd had the feeling that it was more an announcement than a request- he'd just always relished giving significant events an extra dramatic flair. Then it had been so convivial, so familiar- the two of them in a slow and easy discourse, honoring one of the ancient betrothal rituals there in the dead of winter. The wedding was planned for springtime and John's imagination ran to exotic and panoramic images of sunshine, fresh flowers, tuxedoes and formalities. Well-wishers from family, friends and work. The two of them emptied a bottle of Kentucky bourbon, John refreshing the kitchen hearth at intervals with seasoned firewood. They spoke in hushed tones while upstairs the others slept serenely under blankets manifold.

John shook his head sagely, recalling memories of family life, inter-splicing these with tidbits of marital advice. The sacrifices, how he'd returned from Europe with such ideas for idyllic marital union, but then got broken in to the fine art of compromise. Mrs. Griffith was a different sort of creature than him in many ways, *but hey* he'd chuckled, *you have to compromise to complement. Yep Bill, that's what I always say. We have our occasional squabble but hey, who doesn't?*

    This morning there's this uncomfortable silence, just the drip of the percolator as Ellen excuses herself respectfully to her Sunday obligations. He fidgets with the paper while rummaging a mental portfolio of things to say but it's all empty cards. He has no idea of the exact circumstances that have brought his son-in-law to his doorstep an unwanted guest. Just what are the issues, the infractions- a drinking problem, a gambling problem, marital infidelity, mere suspicion of marital infidelity? On whose part? He realizes with a measure of self-indignation that he hasn't a clue. No preparatory facts, no briefing, no known grounds for a show of either resentment or support. He has no conversation opener. He keeps his mouth shut.

    Bill's eyes dart nervously as if taking in new surroundings. I remember the first time I sat in this kitchen, he cups his hands together and blows into them. Had to be what, eight years ago?

    Yep, John pushes himself up from the chair to draw coffees. You had your guitar. Sang us a few Osborne Brothers songs. Won my heart.

    From beyond the kitchen doorway they hear the sound of feet padding down the stairs and they look over to the doorway expectantly. Bill braces himself but it's just Walt- sluggish, clad in torn jeans and a UT tee shirt, a once brilliant orange now washed out and faded.

    Hey there Bill.

    He lumbers over and high-fives Bill. You just get here?

    Yeah, not five minutes ago.

    Walt pours himself coffee, topping up Bill's cup.

    Barb up yet? asks John, rising from his chair.

    Don't know, says Walt, patting his father's shoulder. I'll go and see.

    The Sunday paper is sprawled across the table in sections.

Help yourself, John fans the front pages. Excuse me, I've got a few things to do in the office.

He grabs his coffee and retreats to the back room with a calculated casualness. *A few things to do in the office*, like read up on civil forfeiture law and try and to make some sense out of the godamned mess he's up to his ears in. Build a defensive argument to present the powers that be to prevent them from destroying him. And of course keep a vigilant ear to the goings-on nearby. Be ready to react if... if what? If he should catch the sound of noises which hint at violence? Be ready to protect his daughter.

Bill thumbs the front pages, unable to concentrate beyond the headlines. He picks up the local news section and gleans a story about a kid busted for dealing pot. Arraigned on charges for possession of marijuana with intent to distribute. He squints at a high school yearbook photo. He's sure he recognizes the face but where from?

There's the tread of footsteps on the stairs and once again it's just Walt in the doorway. She'll be right down, he says.

Say Walt, this Dawson guy in the papers. Didn't he come to that New Year's Eve party here a few years back?

Oh I dunno, could be, Walt shrugs his shoulders as he gets a refill at the counter.

Hmn. I just can't help but remember a face when I see one, he says as Walt scans the room- still the restless, disaffected youth that Bill remembers.

Anyway, says here they picked him up this week on drug charges. Seems he had a little operation going between Knoxville and Nashville. Right here. See?

Walt turns his attention from the sports page and glances somewhat deferentially over Bill's shoulder at Dawson's picture, the same as the one in his Jamestown High School yearbook on the bookshelf upstairs.

Interesting, he mutters and then beats a hasty retreat with the dog to the chilly morning air outside the door.

Bill is restless. He scoots out his chair and walks to the hallway, to the left of the front door is the living room which he enters now feeling uneasy as if he's taking liberties. Light streams in through the long white lace curtains that have hung there for ages. He wonders abstractedly how one washes lace curtains. Scratches at unwashed hair.

Late morning light spills onto the original oak log walls, upon the portraits of the Griffith ancestry that line the wall in the living room, the origin of the house. He trundles over to the Persian rug in front of the hearth. Over the mantle is a framed photograph yellowing with age. Seamus Griffin posed at the front door, his stern countenance framed by long grey hair, a wispy moustache and beard. Bill's always marveled at the capacity in this household for preserving its history. This room, which was once just a humble log cabin in the East Tennessee hills, houses some of the oldest photographs in the world. Preserved behind glass and hanging on the original logs with the clay in between plastered over. He's passed by them countless times, but keeps forgetting to ask Barbara about them, perhaps it's now too late. Both her and John have given him the names and little anecdotes associated with these portraits, but he's forgotten the facts. He does recognize a young John, stood next to his father who rests an elbow on a shovel in a cabbage patch.

Bill always looked forward to any visit to his in-laws. He allowed himself only the utmost respectful thoughts concerning his father-in-law, never seeming to have passed much beyond that stage of the tenuous, warily treading new boyfriend. They'd had discussions around nagging existential questions, subjects bordering on the arcane- throughout which Bill had an unfailing tendency to play sidekick, nod agreement and at best supply addendum to John's remarks. But they weren't exactly polarized in viewpoints. Both were men of high ideals struggling or having struggled in a corporate culture that snuffed ideals. John the libertarian, less government and more honest work. Bill willing to go along with that. Nonetheless Barbara sometimes wondered why there couldn't be occasional disagreements. What had happened to the usual cocksure Bill, the devil's advocate in social circles, with professors, in drama rehearsal? Where was the former voice of reason, the antagonist, setting everybody straight when they needed setting straight?

Bill immediately considered Barbara's parents an ideal model for marriage.

C,mon Bill, Barbara would say, *they're not perfect people. They argue like everybody else.*

I've never seen them argue.

They won't, not in front of you.

Just look at how they are with each other. The caring. The respect. They're on their best behavior when we're here.

Of course. Same as us. I just don't sense any tension beneath the surface.

Whatever. She'd twirl her hair and assume that look of indifference that kept him forever chasing. Waiting.

He rubs sweaty hands together and glances at his watch. He's been here for twenty minutes and it feels like two hours. Ten hours driving and the six-pack are catching up with him fast, the blood's rushing to his head and he flops down on the ancient re-upholstered love seat. An interminable wait and he wishes he didn't have to be here. He reckons maybe the loveseat isn't the best place to sit with its implication of courting and pursuit, he tries to stand but senses his knees are too weak for the effort.

She's been absent for thousands of minutes but the last twenty are the most poignant because she knows he's here and yet she remains upstairs. Disconnected thoughts flash randomly like a B movie montage. He has no idea whatsoever about what he's going to say, thinking she should be the one to do the talking, but knowing she'll leave that to him.

Soft footsteps from the hall and then she's leaning against the doorframe with arms folded, her mussed auburn hair glinting in the sunlight. Studying him, drawing a colorful beaded necklace from the neckline of a well-worn maroon tee shirt. Well, she says. What do you want?

I want us to be together again.

Not going to happen, she says distractedly.

He presses on nonetheless, appearing not to have heard. I know I haven't been good to you. I just want another chance. We can work this thing out.

I can't.

How do you know?

He bears the face of a child, wiping at moist eyes with a sleeve, his pained voice sounding affected even to his ears.

Barbara draws a deep breath and wonders if anybody's in earshot. We've got an incompatibility problem is all, she shrugs as if she's at a bank meeting analyzing a bug in the computer system.

Bill says, that's an oversimplification of things.

She leans against the doorframe. Are you happy?

I could be.

So could I. With the right person.

Bill shakes his head. Y'know, the grass is always greener on the other side. You seem to think there's a Mister Perfect just waiting around the corner for you.

Well, momma always said I was cursed with an overactive imagination.

Bill springs up with a raised hand and Barbara backpedals into the hallway.

Look, he says, can we go for a walk or something? We need to talk.

There's really nothing to talk about, she mumbles.

Oh great, nothing to talk about. *Nothing to talk-* he catches himself just as his voice is rising to a shout, gaping at his clenched fists. Dammit Barb, don't give up on us.

I need space, she says. Don't you get it? Ya think it's real fucking... what? *Noble?* Showing up here like this?

You just *split-* his jaw drops and his head shakes- I think I'm due some explanation.

Maybe you oughtta search inside yourself for one.

Bill's dizzy and feeling feverish when he rises and walks toward her. She moves aside to clear a path to the front door.

This isn't the end Barb. Sorry, but I'm not giving up. Not that easy.

She steps back to let him pass and nods at the door. He fidgets with his wool hat and mutters something about staying at his parents nearby in Johnson City and that he'll be back, but his feeble tone betrays that he has lost steam. He shuffles over the porch to the driveway- head lowered, kicking at the gravel. He turns around for one last glimpse of her at the big oak door, but she's already closed it quietly behind her.

John is leaning against the counter, thumbs hitched in the pockets of his jeans. He looks on as his daughter steadies herself with one hand on a chair and buries her face in the other hand, unkempt hair flopping around delicate fingers. She starts blindly towards her father, crushes her face to the soft flannel shirt and a soothing hand rubs at her back. Wordlessly, gently rocking on his heels, John thinks *the last time I held a crying daughter in my arms she was just a baby.*

* * *

"The most persistent and the core rationale for civil forfeiture laws, however, rests on a personification theory under which inanimate objects are imbued with a personality and are then held accountable for "their" violation of applicable federal laws.(14) As a result of this fiction, courts have historically disregarded the owner's innocence; the forfeiture action has been deemed an action against the res, or thing, not against its owner."- Terrence G. Reed, American Forfeiture Law: Property Owners Meet The Prosecutor

Conjure up from imagination a full body image of Marilyn Monroe. Shouldn't be too arduous a task. If one may be indulged to describe the Griffiths' parcel of land so as to draw analogy to a movie star, one might take the liberty to go with Marilyn Monroe. The body of land is curvaceous, due in large part to its two main creeks, which serve as twisting and turning property boundaries on both sides. A hilly land of folds where fawns nestle with their mothers on chilly nights. Platinum blonde cottonwoods abundant at the northern extreme, intelligent life tucked beneath white tufts of the new siding on the family residence, which is surrounded by sprouts of white azalea. The sweet smell of honeysuckle perfumes warm summer evenings.

This body of land's protective warmth and alluring nature draws you into its obliqueness, its mysterious forces of darkness that lay in the still of the night. It has taken in all kinds of night creatures, held them sensuously in its cavities and soothed them in its creek beds. It is captivating and tragic. One might imagine a young James Dean with slumped shoulders and a thumb hitched in the pocket of his jeans at the edge of the property, agonizing over a rapidly sinking sun and the ensuing surreptitious midnight rendezvous with the farmer's daughter. Or one might imagine him under one of the elms just off Old John Henry Road, in the same denim jeans and white tee shirt, staring sulkily at a fertile ground where seeds may take root, but never birth a single plant that is not tainted by sin.

Over these voluptuous curves and hilly ground John now paces. October is John's favorite month. Things tend to slow down, and many a night he'd sit with Clem around the fire ring out back to chat about all manner of subject- politics, civil war history, old-timey music, and maybe the kids over pints of John's home brew. Nights when the air would just be turning cold, the days were crystal clear sunlit spectacles that turned one's wistful nature and nostalgic tendency full on. Things were dying, yes; but at the time of their choosing, and retaining dignity in the process.

John's reminiscing over some past football games played on the makeshift field through the woods behind the house with the boys, Clem and his son Tommy. The Griffiths vs. the Carters. Clem muttering about home-field advantage each time John hit Walt on the numbers in the end zone.

Clem's voice breaks uncannily through his daydreaming. Hey pardner. Wanna toss some ball?

It is Clem in the flesh, standing under the shadows of an elm, shuttling the pigskin between hands like a tossed salad. He stares at John, and it isn't hard to guess at his friend's feelings of anxiety, or his own of concern and protectiveness. But John Griffith didn't invite protection, never suggested he required it. Back when Clem stayed on at UT for an advanced degree, John sweated it out as a young supervisor in the heat of the textile factory. All the years in that modest company, staying on when those Yankee mavericks from Massachusetts gobbled it up and in the ensuing re-organization agreed to retain him as Operations Manager. It'd been tenacious Clem who'd finagled what was at best a tenuous agreement of a probationary nature. Then they brought in a fresh face and John was gone. Now Clem was here, still on the path he chose long ago, preparing to get off and see America in a Winnebago with Miriam, live on a fixed income, sit at the kitchen table and do crosswords.

They begin spiraling the pigskin back and forth to each other, gradually widening the gap as stiff arms come unglued.

I stayed up late last night looking at some case law John, says Clem. You know there's something truly amazes me.

What's that?

Just how much the government rakes in on the forfeiture cases. The Drug Enforcement Act of 1970 was meant to target the rich drug cartels, the kingpins, you see. Now, here's an amazing fact. Of the billions of dollars taken in by the feds from forfeited property, the amount taken from big operators has been steadily decreasing against that taken from the small guy. They intended to put the hurt on the kingpins, and instead more and more they're hurtin the little guy.

Well I guess that's me. Clem, I'm worried.

No shit.

No I mean I'm worried about something new.

Yeah? What now?

What if they drag the IRS into this? You know I haven't reported these last bunch of years. Or at least, I've taken a lot of cash that doesn't show up on my 1040. What're the chances of one government agency tipping off another?

Clem pauses, football pawed in one beefy hand. I dunno. Mebbe so. One of the things the Marshal Service is gonna do is look for you to substantiate your claim to the property. I-I mean beyond the deed, how did you pay your note? See what I'm gettin at? Right now they're running with the notion you made some good money off of Tim's dope business.

John felt his blood rise.

God, I'd kill to have five minutes with that sonofabitch.

John, I'm gonna try like hell to get you off on this thing based on Tim's testimony. He may be your only chance. Don't ruffle his feathers and ruin it.

John lofted one high, a perfect spiral. Whaddya mean?

Look, the burden of proof's on you right?

Right.

That you had neither knowledge or consent of the illegal substance growing on your property.

Right.

Well, maybe if Tim can testify on your behalf that he never made it known to you, planted without your permission, there's a chance, just a chance, that your name and therefore your land will be cleared of all charges.

John hurls one over Clem's head. Sorry.

Clem hustles after it, calling over his shoulder,

Hey why don't you and me take a road trip to the UT game next Saturday? Watchin some football or maybe just some young girls in orange mini-skirts might be the best thing for you right now.

I-I don't know Clem, I got things I gotta do. Lotta chores and stuff. Not to mention preparing the answer, and for the trial.

Leave the trial up to me. Nothings gonna happen for a few months at least anyway. Lets go watch UT whip Florida's ass.

So my life's on hold for some indeterminate time measured in months, thinks John, *and he wants me to pick up and enjoy a damn football game.*

Look Clem, why don't you take Walt to the game? He's been moping around in that room since Cindy stopped gracing us with her presence.

Just then, as if summoned out of the wilderness, Walt comes breaking through the woods in a sprint and out on the makeshift football field.

Throw some ball? Clem hollers.

Lemme punt one, Walt hollers back.

You wanna take a ride to the UT game with me next weekend? I got an extra ticket.

Sure.

*   *   *

"When forfeiture statute is invoked by the Government, it embraces all of the unitary tract although only part is being used illegally."- 21 U.S.C.A. S881(a)(7)

In the Griffith living room, three glum faces glance from one to the other. A fire blazes in the hearth, the crackle and pop of moist wood punctuating the silence. This somewhat premature use of wood is owing to the fact that the gas furnace that drives the central heat has given out. Twenty-four hours later it remains inoperable, no arrangements made for a repair. Because there's an intuitive sense of an impending *cash flow crisis*, but something *had to be done*, and so it was that John earlier this morning had come to be at the tarp-covered woodpile next to the barn, extracting the dried pieces.

Well, says Clem, here's the claim to the property. I had Janet type it up this afternoon. Got a check to go with it?

Yep, says John, getting up to fan the flames.

You need any money?

No.

He pulls the check from his papers and hands it over to Clem. A twelve-thousand dollar check for the cost bond. After a few thousand from Clem, they'd had to empty out their savings.

John returns his gaze to the framed portrait of great great-grandfather Seamus, whose frozen expression that once conveyed a sort of vigilant serenity has now become for him the ominous apparition of accusation and condemnation. Next to this guardian ghost, the grandfather clock chimes four o'clock. John fidgets through the stack of papers containing case law that Clem had dropped in his lap, as if in some manner to appease the ancestors present on the walls surrounding him.

Clem paws at his greying moustache, ruminating over the summons he holds in his free hand, at last breaking the stillness with his gravelly voice. He looks squarely upon Ellen. Now as I told John, it's officially the United States versus the property.

But John said the house... Her voice trails off as Clem nods gravely with head bowed, the nod shifting to a slow shake as if he's listening to a woeful gospel song.

The house is an appurtenance, and as such is treated as part of the proceeds from the crime.

Appurtenance? Ellen squints at Clem as John continues rummaging through the stack of papers.

An appurtenance is part of a piece of property. Like an accessory. Like you have your land here, and its appurtenances. One of which is the barn, for example. Or the greenhouse.

Or the house.

Or the house, Clem echoes.

They just lump everything together, John sighs heavily.

But my God, how can a house commit a crime? she asks.

How can *land* commit a crime, for that matter?

Ellen looks away as if to some distant fixed point beyond the picture window, kneading her knuckles.

The *logic*, says Clem, is an assumption that the proceeds from the illegal activity were used to pay for houses, mortgages- he raises a finger at her bewildered and anxious look- thing is, we're not here to agree or disagree with the law, we have to live with it. And then we have to *deal* with it, best we can.

Ellen sits upright. How can the government just, just- *rob* us of our land, our house, on- on not even circumstantial evidence? For something- and here she locks eyes with John and drops her tone a pitch- *something we didn't even know about.*

Nobody has an answer to this and she sighs. I'd like to get a second opinion.

Yes Ellen, of course you do says Clem, standing up with pipe in hand and fidgeting for his tobacco pouch. And I've got the second, and *third* opinions. I'm still waiting on the fourth. And as many more as I can gather. I immediately consulted an old buddy of mine, works for the DEA. He's to be trusted, and it's as good advice as any, straight from the horse's mouth.

Ellen, John starts- but Clem halts him with a palm to the air.

Ellen, I know what you're thinking.

This is nothing personal Clem, she says, eyes glistening and voice trembling as she tries to push a smile through.

Ellen, by God, you know damned well I don't need this case. *I don't want it.* I'm fixin to pack it in. I mean it. This, this business is the last- he grimaces- *godamn* thing I could wish to face right now. But this here, you here, you people- he indicates both of them with a sweep of the hand- you're about the closest we got, me and Miriam, once I shut my door for good and pull down the sign. I wanna go fishin with him- he nods at John- I want he and I to go down to the local and toss back a few beers in our old age and talk what-all. I want all of us, you, me, John, Miriam to pack a wagon and head for Florida, California, hell, anywhere we get our sights on. Together.

He sighs, shakes his head at the ceiling. I've been thinking about it all year, I've refused some twenty new cases since July. And this may very well be my last legal effort. And it's very personal. And there's not more I can do but advise, because to be honest our hands are tied, tied pretty tight.

He crouches near the fire and empties the ash from his pipe. I'm prepared to fight the good fight though.

The room is silent except for the hiss of wet wood as the sparks alight to the chimney.

John's hollow voice seems as if far away. I am too, Clem.

Ellen springs suddenly from the chair to John's side- her hand grabbing and squeezing that of his own surprises him- it is warm and bonier than he remembers, and the wedding ring crushes against his knuckle.

We are too, Clem.

      *   *   *

There's a meadow- just a slice of ground presenting itself as a break from the tall pines and the darkness they harbor, it lies basked in the light of a near full moon on this night. Walt shivers a bit in the early autumn cool- crouching, cupping his hand to light a cigarette. A gust of wind extinguishes the flame, but not before it burns his finger.

Shit, he mumbles, sucking at his finger before giving it another shot. It catches and he pulls hard, the lit end glowing brightly. In haphazard disarray on the ground around him lay fallen branches. Clouds pass in front of the moon and he watches their shadows drift along the ground over the branches.

On an ordinary night, he'd be caught mesmerized, he'd be *daydreaming*, he'd relax, light a joint and nothing would matter. On an ordinary night, there'd not be such cold harsh reality staring him so forcibly in the face- there'd be just Cindy on the phone, Cindy in his room, Cindy riding shotgun in the Chevelle, Cindy complaining to or laughing at him and him *just taking it*. Cindy of the subtle perfume and hair-twirling aloofness, Cindy of the Moon, Cindy of the Stars, Cindy of the Angels, singing her tenderness to him, singing that song she sang once in a while, that sweet and gentle song... he could hear the melody, but what were the words again?

Callin on angels, callin on angels,

He can hear her soft voice, feel her soft breath on his ear. *Callin all angels.*

He rubs his ears as if to shake the memory from inside his head. A crack of thunder in the distance and then a raindrop hits him square on the nose, more of a splash really, and the scent of pine reaches his nostrils as he realizes the rain has picked up and he must seek shelter pretty quick because the sky has just been pierced by lightning and he is on his feet running and coughing, *running and coughing*, bolting for the house- dodging pines all the way, in and out of the shadows and then it hits him as he nears the back steps bathed in porch light, soaked to the skin.

When it rains it pours.

Monday, Wood and Blankets

John kissed his wife goodnight for the first time in years last night. Ellen is sleeping soundly this morning, head pressed against his shoulder. Carefully extricating himself so as not to wake her, he plunges cold feet into socks and slippers and tiptoes across the hardwood floor to the window. He peers through the blinds at a dismal dreary day. Columbus Day. Ellen can sleep in.

He is the first one up. There's the morning routine- fetch the Tennessean, let the dog out for a piss, get the coffee brewing. In all the weekend's commotion they've run out of coffee grinds, inside the aluminum drum lays only the plastic scoop and perhaps enough to pinch for one cup. He scratches abstractedly at his ass and returns the tin to the cupboard shelf.

Good morning daddy.

He nearly jumps out of his slippers.

Oh, good morning, Barb.

She saunters into the kitchen. I didn't mean to scare you.

She pulls a chair out from under the table and unfolds the newspaper, massaging her arms. The kitchen is freezing cold. He considers the wood-burning stove in the corner, then the long dormant fireplace on the wall opposite the oven and fridge.

How did you sleep? John starts towards the door of the living room to fetch firewood.

Oh alright, she replies vaguely.

There's no firewood in the living room and he remembers placing the last piece in after Ellen had gone to bed.

Standing at the back door in his pajamas, he shakes the slippers loose and slides warm feet into the cold encrusted insoles of ancient work boots. Out the door he meets the sharp sting of wind, cups his hands and starts for the barn and the woodpile.

It's going to be a slow week for the odd jobs business. Frank has three days lined up at best. Dwindling cash. There's basic necessities to be fetched on top of the coffee. In fact they're not far away from a full-fledged shopping order. Since he began working for cash two years ago he's not been in the habit of drawing down on savings. He has been trying and succeeding at living on largely a cash basis and its attendant frugality.

Lifting the tarp, surveying the freshly split wood. Damn, he thinks, this will need a good month until it's ready to burn. Best to enlist Walt's help for a day to scout the woods for old fallen trees with good dry wood. Walking back toward the house with arms loaded, dismissing the notion of having the gas furnace repaired. For the time being, he muses, they can get by heating the house the old-fashioned way. Wood and blankets.

Barbara holds the door for him, and steadying himself on the mantle, he drops wood on the hearth of the kitchen fireplace.

You want me to put the coffee on? Barbara rifles through the cabinets.

We've run out, he mutters disgustedly.

Well, I'll go pick some up.

You're a dear, he grunts, crouched on all fours with his head twisted around to afford a view of the flue of the chimney.

Need anything else?

That's okay honey.

Too many things to mention he thinks, laying there on his back and catching soot in the face.

Suit yourself. I'm going to make a stir-fry for dinner.

Oh wait, he says, let me get you some money.

Starting to get up and realizing at the same time there is no money at hand for the fetching.

Daddy really, let me pay this time.

Alright I guess, he grunts, pushing on the unyielding flue. We may need cream or milk too.

I'll be back in a jiffy, she snatches her jacket and keys.

Barb?

Yeah?

Thanks.

Laying on his back looking up at the impenetrable flue, he wipes at dust in his eyes. He beats a palm at the flue. It gives.

*   *   *

Walt is a no-show for the morning coffee session. A night of tossing and turning, passing in and out of wakefulness. Upon entering the house last night rain-drenched and shivering, squish-squashing in Converse high-tops he'd overheard his father from beyond the door to the study, his voice tinged with concern, then

Clem's own voice- typically gentle and reassuring yet betraying a kind of uncertainty. Walt couldn't make out the words but he didn't need to. He'd bent over, removing one foot and then the other from the soggy shoes, balled up the wet socks and made a beeline on tip-toe for the doorway at the opposite end of the kitchen and out into the dark hall among the shadows. Still dripping, he'd pranced up the stairs gingerly but two at a time and hesitated at the sound of a door, *sneaking around his own house*.

Entering his room, he'd flung his wet things on the floor, where they remain this morning- balled-up socks and Converse high tops laying underneath a pile of damp clothes, effecting a mildewy smell to a room which already has the smell of neglect- dirty laundry, dirty ashtray, dust matted on furniture and carpet.

He'd lain awake most of the night, listening to the pitter- patter of the rain on the roof. And there he is now, blinds drawn, staring in semi-darkness seeming like 8mm vagueness penetrated only slightly by the green glow of a digital clock that he doesn't even bother to look at.

*   *   *

John sits at the kitchen table in front of the warm blaze of fire from the hearth, gathering his thoughts. He shakes a cigarette loose from Barbara's pack, turns it in front of him, considering, sniffing at it, replaces it. While his thoughts revolve around the *situation* at hand, there's the hollow feeling of not having much to do, nothing to distract him. The *situation* is a mental parasite, demanding to be fed by his thoughts. Still, the feeling that there is little that can be done to help the *situation*. Then he remembers the pile of case law Clem left him with last night. The stack of papers lay neatly assembled on the desk in his study. He imagines them spread all over the place very soon. *Sure, today would be the right time to look it all over, find out what I'm up against. I have free time, I'll use it to full advantage.*

But what will an examination of federal law, statutes, case law, precedent offer besides an understanding of the *situation*? All at once the sting of helplessness, the feeling that nothing he will do before the sun sets will actually improve anything.

But there's a response to draft. Surely an understanding of the situation is required in order to draft a credible response. He remembers Clem's words yesterday afternoon,

Our hands are tied pretty tight.

The sound of footsteps on the stairs draw him out of his revelry. Ellen shuffles into the kitchen, halts and stares fixedly at the fire in the hearth as one would at an unwelcome guest.

Have you called anyone about the furnace? she asks icily.

No.

Shall *I*?

I thought we'd make do without it. For now.

He drums his fingers along the empty coffee tin and has the sense of having tested cold water with his feet. She responds with no more than a grunt filled with more disapproval than any amount of words might convey. He rises with an effort, wearily rubbing her sagging shoulders from behind.

Look he says, just for now. I won't have you freeze. It gets too cold we can call Jones Service.

Alright then.

Walt can help gather some dead wood. It'll be romantic. Fun.

He turns her to face him and she clearly has not warmed up to his idea of fun.

We can-

-Alright, John.

What are you going to do today, he asks.

Oh, I thought I'd have a real day off.

She rubs at puffy eyes beset with crow's feet wrinkles.

Do some reading, maybe take a drive with Barbara. Did you make the coffee?

We ran out. Barb said she'd pick some up at the market.

What are *you* going to do today, she says.

Thought I'd start on that case law Clem left last night. I wanna organize my thoughts for this defense, Ellen. I wanna do the best job possible.

Just what response is it he expects- a pat on the shoulder, a cheer? *Rah-rah*, at least some indication of support-instead she's slumped at the kitchen table, one arm raised and head resting in the crook of her elbow.

* * *

Barbara

For the first time since you arrived, it almost feels good to be home- as much trouble as the family has been thrown into, it was reassuring to see Uncle Clem last night and you listened, after daddy said they had to get down to business, crouched there just outside the closed living room door, eavesdropping.

This morning when you returned with the groceries your mother and father were sitting down talking to one another. Not exactly clapping one another on the back laughing but talking. You looked on quizzically and then daddy said, your mother and I were just remembering when we used to have to heat the house by wood. Until... yes, I think we were still wood burning for a few years after you were born. Do you remember?

Do you remember? Do you remember two young ebullient parents who lived neighbor-less in the country and heated their modest home by wood and flame? Do you remember the warming fire- were you afraid of it, its potential for danger? Did you ever try to play with it, had you ever burned a precious little finger from it?

Seeing your parents caught in the spell of nostalgia leaves you just a tad bit confused at seeing their marriage fail to deliver that nasty tension you've recently come to expect. For a moment you are reminded that people sometimes stay together anyway. And then the coffee is brewed and mom pours the cups like you remember and it's just like a Maxwell House commercial- a happy morning picture of nuptial bliss with one happy family seated at the breakfast table. Just a few days ago, half asleep half dressed, you drove away your husband. He promised again he'd change. No matter how many times this promise had been made and unmade, the fact is this was the first time he had to follow you across state lines, the first time you really ran away from home.

You knock back another cup of coffee, watching daddy placate momma with recollections of fantastic days you wish you could re-invent. A little girl with Barbie dollhouses, beauty salon toy play kits, the land of make-believe. Staying up late with your cousins Tommy and Lisa, Uncle Clem's and Aunty Miriam's kids, to watch *The Wizard of Oz*. Momma gathers your empty cup from under you and starts for the kitchen sink to do the washing up, but your father is walking over to the cold terra cotta tile in front of the kitchen sink insisting he'll do the washing up, as you've already mentioned your intention to take your mother for a drive to browse the local flea markets and general stores in search of a birthday present, because you forgot her birthday last month. You said you were sorry about that, but you'd had so much on your mind and of course momma nodded and waved dismissively and told you not to bother, presumably because now more than ever momma is worried about money, worried about money as we all worry about money, we're either trying to get it or keep it. Now more than ever your mother could use a gift though she may not realize it. You want to plunk down the credit card to buy something nice for her because she's been through a little too much lately, just a little too much and it's beginning to show.

*   *   *

Barbara's eyes are glued to Highway 52 as the windshield is sprinkled with rain. But clouds have shifted, giving way to the bright shoots of light that pierce autumn foliage, reaching out to illuminate and clarify nature. As much as Barbara would like to fancy this a simile for her own life, she is unable to. She tries all the same to enjoy the sun as she listens to her mother fill her in on the latest at Jamestown Elementary School.

Kids just aren't what they used to be, Ellen says, shaking her head while pulling on the visor mirror to apply lipstick. What I mean is... the level of respect has gone way down. You've got to *command* these kids to do their work, she sighs. I'm really getting tired of having to raise my voice. Every day.

Much different than when we were kids, Barbara switches off the wipers.

Oh, Ellen waves a hand dismissively, you wouldn't believe it. Just last week I had to break up another fight. I mean, a *vicious* fight. Broken nose, blood spilled all over the hallway. In all my years of teaching, nothing more than a minor disagreement.

The rain lets up and Barbara switches off the windshield wipers as the sun glares on the blacktop. She reaches for her Ray Bans but they've slid all the way to the passenger side of the dashboard and Ellen hands them to her.

Not enough, she continues, we have to break up fights. I can hardly turn my back without somebody disrupting the class. It's tougher today as a regular teacher than it was as a substitute.

So, Barbara says, the rest of the world has caught up with our little haven in Fentress County.

Fentress County- a region of towns with single-lane roads that wind through the mountain passes, home of modest little firehouses and police stations, country fairs, Italian ice and little league baseball, one of a few remaining bastions for mom & pop businesses, small town gossip.

Ellen says she's willing to bet even a few of the seventh graders are smoking pot, and just like that they both reminded of *the situation*, this mere mention in passing invites back that which they've just fled- as if materialized from thin air like a phantom. They've just passed the *Welcome to Historic Rugby* sign on Highway 52. Barb flicks her wrist over to glance at her watch. Tell you what- she drums her fingers on the dashboard- let's go to the Harrow Road Cafe. For lunch. My treat, of course.

The café is open and they order coffee. The Harrow Road Cafe is rustic in decor, its oak-paneled walls are bedecked with landscape paintings, its windows dressed in lace-embroidered curtains. A well-prepared fire blazes in the giant hearth at the far end of the room, it has a not-too-intrusive stereo system with speakers hidden high above held in hanging fishing nets in the tall A-frame ceiling. Through these modest-looking speakers wafts soothing authentic Appalachian music played on the hammered dulcimer, dulcimer having its linguistic origins in the Latin word dulce which means sweet- sweet is how it sounds and sweet is how Barbara feels at the moment, watching her mother smile and dab her mouth with a red and white checkered napkin. Noticing a few more gray streaks in her mother's auburn hair.

Ellen says, it's been a long time since anyone took me to lunch.

Guess I haven't been coming back home enough. Things have been kind of um, crazy.

How did it go with Bill?

Ellen sips at her coffee and replaces the cup to its saucer. If you don't mind me asking.

The same.

Ellen glances furtively over her shoulder and then leans in confidentially.

What's happened dear? I —I know you had your troubles. Is it really all that bad, honey?

Barbara bites her bottom lip and draws her knuckles to her mouth.

Sorry, Ellen reaches a hand across the table but Barbara has already placed her hands on the coffee mug.

No, Mom, it's really okay-

-Barbara, really. I'll wait until you're ready to talk about it.

Wait, Barbara is struck immediately presumption in the statement that she'll one day soon have to bear all of her marital business to Mom. Pressured thus, her anger mounts but she'll not give in to it, she'll not spoil this lunch.

I need a lot of space right now, she says evenly.

I know, I know. Of course you do.

Ellen sighs, fishes for a new topic- as one might search a catalogue, plucking out and discarding ideas- realizing at the same time the effort necessary to evade the difficult ones. She settles at last on the time-tested path of nostalgia. Nostalgia, after all, can harbor happy memories, storing them like fuel to use as needed. *Do you remember...* and she'll just wing it from there, see where that road will take them.

It works its magic on Barbara and she smiles. How could she forget the two week cross-country trip in a rented Winnebago with Uncle Clem, Aunt Miriam, Lisa and Tommy? Walt had to have been just four years old, her and Lisa having just hit their teens. Tommy somewhere in between- always too old for Walt but too young for her. That summer she received her first kiss, during a silly game of truth or dare on the periphery of the perilous Grand Canyon. The shy blonde boy whose name is plied to her memory as all first-kissers are. Greg. Greg whats-his-name and his family from California, traveling from the other direction with another itinerary, they and the Griffiths bidding goodbye after two days of a shared campground experience. Letter writing promises that would go unfulfilled.

And when you and Lisa got lost that afternoon in the lake in- where was it now? Utah, I reckon.

You mean on the inflatable raft?

That's right. Your father and I were so worried. He and Clem were just fixin to fetch the park rangers when, I'll never forget, you two appeared out of nowhere. It must've been eight o'clock. Carrying that raft like nothing happened! Just laughing and... you know Barbara, you weren't exactly *trouble*, don't get me wrong. But your father and I always found it difficult to discipline you- she smiles and tilts her head- you always had your head in the clouds, you did.

I was a bit of a space cadet.

Oh well.

Still am, I suppose.

Well, that's not such a bad thing really, says Ellen while fussing with her napkin.

It's hard on other people sometimes.

I'm just happy to have my space cadet back to home base, Ellen reaches across the table and takes Barbara's hand in both of hers, massaging and warming.

And just how are things on home base Mom. If you don't mind me asking.

Well. Ellen plays with the napkin.

A waitress sidles up next to their table with pen and pad and the innocent smile of a teenager. After they've ordered salad and entrees, Barbara looks at her mother inquisitively.

So you were saying?

Ellen draws a deep sigh, fidgets the napkin in her lap.

Oh Barb, she clucks her tongue, I don't know. Ever since your father lost his job, it's been... her voice trails off and Barbara considers it's essential for momma to refer her husband as *your father*, it grants a certain impersonal latitude in confidences.

Your father, he has these... oh, bouts of depression. Poor man, I know I haven't been easy on him. But he's not easy to live with, *you* know.

I'm afraid I don't.

Oh, Barb. You haven't been home for such a while. It's changed. So different from when you left. So much happened. What can I say? Your mother is growing and your father remains- her face freezes up- remains the *same* person.

And what's so bad about that? Dad's always been a... a pretty damned nice guy.

Mmm, *simple*. I-I don't know. I just can't talk to him anymore. Nothing in common. He works these menial cash jobs, works with people who are far less educated than him. And he's, I don't know, becoming like them.

He could've given up when the mill closed. I don't know that there's much opportunity in these parts for a fifty-four-year-old man with general management experience in one place.

You don't understand.

Ellen rolls her eyes, taps the fork on the table.

Mom be realistic.

Realistic. This coming from a space cadet.

I'm just saying it's not all his fault. I mean about the layoff. At least he's still up and running. He, he's taking that computer course, he still has his interests, the radio show-

-He's a depressive personality. You know- Ellen taps her nails on the table- I was just reading last week about such people as your father. *Pathway to Clarity*, it was-

Are you still reading that junk?

It is not *junk*. Ellen purses her lips in defiance. Barbara throws up her hands and glances around to see if the waitress or the guests at the far end are picking any of this up. Lunch is turning out to be not so sweet after all.

Mom, stay with me here a minute. These books you read are written by people, human beings with their own hang-ups and-

-No one obtains a PhD in psychology, religion or what have you without having obtained a certain degree of authority on the subject.

Which subject?

Whichever one they're writing about. Now you take M. Scott Peck for example-

-Okay. Look momma, I don't want to argue, okay?

Ellen stops tapping her fork on the table, points it at Barb. You'll never understand. Nobody will.

A woman enters with a young girl clutching her hand, trailing them is an eager-looking guy with close-cropped hair, a neatly-trimmed beard and a receding hairline backs into the door and hefts a stroller over the threshold. Bill had become urgent in his demands to start a family while Barbara continued to plead *just not ready yet*. And that became an issue, she felt simultaneously guilty and annoyed, what a horrible mixture of feelings. But now she spots these two and their two little ones- she'll bet anything they're younger than her and they both appear so calm and well-adjusted- he appears to love his work and to be not prone to extended bouts of melancholy nor quickness to anger, unlike her Bill- so feckless as to be enmeshed in the couch, indeed she can't peel him from the couch to take her to dinner for godsakes, and that's dysfunctional enough to dismiss the notion to read books written by any number of PhDs .

Lunch commences and Barbara determines to steer things back in the right direction, maintaining a steady stream of polite conversation around Jamestown Elementary, short of related problems with illegal substances.

The sun beckons and their spirits are lifted at the prospect of having an afternoon free of all encumbrances and the dictates of responsibility. It's a lucky and uncanny phenomenon about families that the tone must be reset to civilized and slowly work its way back to a mutual peace. You can't stay pissed off at your mother when you have an afternoon to pass together- bad vibes pass like a moving weather system.

You remember all them flea markets, momma? All them Saturdays. You and me at the fairs, Barbara says between bites.

You must've been the youngest merchant, Ellen's laugh is polite if a bit forced.

Oh, let's go and see one.

That's for weekends.

I know. Maybe next weekend.

Whadda we do now.

Let's go to Knoxville.

Knoxville?

Yeah, why not?

What for?

Barbara wraps her hair around her fingers. I don't know, go shopping, walk around Old Town. Get you a birthday present.

You don't have to buy me anything Barb.

No really Mom-

-Barb that was a lovely lunch, just having your presence is enough for me, really.

Then let's just go and window shop.

But that's nearly an hour and a half from here Barb. Your father will worry.

We can call him, she says and at the same time recalls the fresh vegetables and her stir fry for tonight. Hey, I know what we can do. Let's go up to Pickett, it's such a nice day for a walk.

Ellen smiles, slaps the table. Now you're talking.

Barbara thinks what a nice way to spend an afternoon, wandering the trails of Pickett State Park and talking about everything under the sun. Everything of course except husbands, sexual orientation, illegal substances, legal problems and broken dreams.

*   *   *

"Once Government shows probable cause that property is subject to forfeiture, burden shifts to claimant to prove by preponderance of evidence that factual predicates for forfeiture have not been met; claimant must prove that property was not unlawfully used or that he did not know about or consent to illegal use, and, if claimant cannot produce any such evidence, summary judgment is properly granted to Government based upon its showing of probable cause."- Comprehensive Drug Abuse Prevention and Control Act of 1970, 21 U.S.C.A. S881(a)(4,6,7)

So what you're saying is that forfeiture is subject to just an administrative review, right?

That's right, John, Clem leans forward, folding his hands in front of him on the desk. Summary judgment.

No trial, no jury?

Just like you said on the air the other night night.

So what the hell do we do, sit around and wait for some government nitwits to make a decision?

John rolls his eyes and begins to pace the floor of Clem's office.

John, go home. Busy yourself in that furniture restoration. It'll take your mind off things, help you focus on something other than this. I've been telling my clients for years, worrying doesn't help one godamn bit.

How can I not worry? I stand to lose everything.
No you don't.
No I don't?
No you don't.
And just what the hell makes you say that?
This is a case of the government versus a piece of the earth. A piece of the earth you happen to live on now. A civil case. Nobody's trying to put you in jail, there is not a single criminal charge against you.
But I lose that property, I lose everything.
I never knew you to give up. Lost your godamn job at the mill, you picked yourself right the hell up and kept going these last four years. You'll pick yourself up again no matter where it has to be and do it again because that's the stuff you're made of. A resiliency that's still a mystery to me.
I don't know if I've got enough wind in me for this shit.
Course you don't, that's why you're leaving it to me. Any and all correspondence is going through this office. I'll keep you abreast of anything significant.
John heaves a deep sigh, shakes his head slowly.
Get yourself down to your workshop. Pick up your tools. Turn something ugly into something beautiful.

*   *   *

What better way to focus the mind than the culinary arts, thinks Barbara. With perfect attention she makes precision slices of green peppers, carrots are lacerated to bits, onions impaled and lanced on the cutting board, fillet of chicken chopped to bits and bathing in a tub of teriyaki sauce.
Need any help? John looks like a kid who showed up at the wrong game, this diversion from a steady diet of frozen pizza, hamburgers or microwave dinners.
No.
Sure?
She turns and glares, clutching the cleaver.
I work best alone.
Okay, he throws his palms up and backs away.
Bill used to take offense to her territorial nature in the kitchen- cooking is a form of meditation to her, she'll sometimes

dance about while cutting and it's hell for anyone getting in the way. How can cooking be such a *personal* thing Bill had asked and she'd replied, I guess you can't understand it until you've tried.

Barbara fetches the unused wok, an old Christmas present she'd given to her mother when Ellen took a shine to an oriental cookbook. As with many other books the novelty lost its sheen along with the wok- it lay buried in the cabinet next to the oven underneath a puzzle of cookware- pots, pans, lid covers, rice steamers, colanders.

Ellen's apple pie bakes while she lies on the bed upstairs, unable to nap. The timer dings, leaving Barbara searching about for a potholder in an unfamiliar kitchen. As she's rifling through the silverware drawer, then down the drawers in succession, Walt strolls in and sits at the table rubbing his eyes.

Thought you'd died, says Barbara, once again feeling her working space invaded.

Watcha lookin for?

Pot holder, she catches her finger in the drawer. Shit.

Try hanging on the fridge.

She spots it hanging on one of those suction hooks.

Mmmm. What smells so good? Walt drums his fingers on the table.

Mom's home made apple pie.

How Americana. And just what is it you plan to prepare to compliment this perennial favorite?

Chicken Teryaki, vegetable stir fry.

How very exotic.

Cmon, get outta here. She shakes her hair, auburn strands fall over her eyes. With one hand balled in a fist at her waist, she waves the cleaver at the door. I still have the cooking to do.

Okay, okay, he rises sluggishly. Damn. Can't even share a special moment with my long lost sister.

He raises his hands in mock surrender, appearing merely offhand and whimsical. He *had* in fact left his room moments earlier to seek communion with another, to raise his spirits, had even decided to make an effort to forget things.

Out! she rasps, gripping a wooden spoon and crouched in a mock-fencing position. He shrugs and leaves.

The famished arrive, each from their own solitude- Ellen from a restless hour in bed, Walt from the television. At last the door from the study opens at the back of the kitchen and John emerges- eyes overwrought from reading legalese, flashing a half-hearted smile at the table. After a week of hurried meals- thrown-together cold cuts, canned soups, and ordered pizzas- tonight's bounty, complemented by the good silverware glistening in the soft light of the candelabrum, is a reminder of the potential for a decent lifestyle. People of certain culture and upbringing don't eat hot dogs every night- in fact they don't eat hotdogs outside of amusement parks. John folds his arms on the table, lays his head on them a moment, then raises it and fixes a dazed look upon Walt. Have a nice rest?

    Walt shrugs. Yep.

    Good. Because I've got a nice job for you tomorrow.

    Ellen glances up sharply.

    We'll need some firewood. Any fallen trees. I'll set the axe out back. You may need some gas for the tractor- use it to haul the wagon.

    Walt remains preoccupied with his fork.

    Any questions?

    John- Ellen drops her fork- let's have a nice meal tonight. Please. Barb's gone to a lot of trouble.

    The phone rings.

    I'll get it, John bypasses the wall phone for the extension in his study, reappearing a moment later. Hand clamped over the mouthpiece, he mimes, *It's Bill*, looking dubiously at Barbara, does a sort of flip flop of the wrist.

    She pushes her chair in and John hands her the phone and obligingly closes the study door behind her. Hello?

    Did I catch you at a bad time?

    We just sat down to dinner, Barb lies.

    I can call back.

    No, it's okay. Trying not to sound too obliging, thinking to take advantage of the implied time limitation.

    He tries to pick up where they left off, launching into a breathless appeal to her better sense- she should come back, he'll agree to see a marriage counselor, running away solves nothing. She's never heard him talk so fast.

    Just want you to know, he says with finality after catching his breath. You can always come back.

I don't think that's such a good idea- she fights to contain herself and keep her voice down- My family needs me now.

There is an uncomfortable silence.

D'ya mind if I call you once in a while? his hushed voice cracks just a little.

Look, I gotta go. Dinner's getting cold.

That's not all that's going cold.

Look, I'm hanging up if I have to listen to this.

I'll call you later...

Look, just let me be for a while, okay?

For how long?

I don't know.

I can't deal with that.

You'll have to.

Look Barb, don't expect me to play this game too long.

No-one's *playing a game* she says, a knot in her stomach.

You know what I mean.

Stop crowding me. It's repulsive.

Dammit... he starts and she hangs up a screaming receiver.

The others have all finished their dinner accompanied by few words- scattered words, junk words, just throwaway lines that hold little weight or importance. Resignedly, John throws down his napkin, sighing.

Guess I'll start gathering up wood. Want something done, just have to do it yourself.

John, says Ellen, you're im*possible*.

John snatches the clump of keys from the countertop and storms out the back door.

What's worse- a heated argument with angry words and flying objects, or the uncomfortable silences that accompanied meals? John guesses the latter for Ellen- before Barbara arrived she'd taken to eating alone, heating things up in the microwave after John and perhaps Walt finished another hastily-prepared dinner. She'd take these small meals out on the front porch or up to their bedroom and carry the dishes back after everyone went to bed, or sometimes not until the next morning.

Tuesday, That Single Frayed Wire

The last time John had occasion to enter Walt's room was last spring, just before his son returned home, to paint the walls. This morning he raps an upbeat cadence on the door. It's nearly nine o'clock, he's prepared everything for a day's wood fetching, the tractor is fueled up. This sleeping-in business has gotten just a bit out of hand.

To his astonishment, Walt answers the door fully dressed. Puffy-eyed, grey-pallor, ill-postured- but awake. I'll be down in a few minutes.

Everything's ready for you.

He detects the reek of pot smoke in the dark behind Walt just before he shuts the door. He starts for the stairs, pauses at the banister then shuffles back to Walt's door, knocks again. Walt opens it to an awkward pause.

You getting high first thing in the morning now?

Walt merely grips the doorknob, eyes blinking.

I want the marijuana gone, John says, I mean every leaf, stem, seed. You hear me? Gone! That's all we need right now is a godamn Fed turnin up at my door with a warrant. Wait- he turns and approaches Walt- I'll help you myself.

No, really, Daddy, that's not necessary.

I'll decide what's necessary. We've got enough trouble on our hands to be taking any chances.

Daddy, wait, c'mon, I swear. This is it.

He fetches a single Ziploc baggie.

You giving me your word?

Yep.

You would never lie to me, would you son?

Never, Walt gulps.

Flush that godamn bag down the toilet. Right now.

John lingers, arms folded, long enough to see the task accomplished. I'll see you when I get home.

The telephone rings and Barbara rushes from her room in her underwear and retrieves the receiver in her parents' bedroom.

Hullo? she gasps, pushing a few strands of auburn hair from her face. Expecting to hear Bill's voice, she's relieved at the welcome voice of her old friend Patty.

You alright?

Yeah. How'd you know to reach me here? She stretches across her parents' queen-size bed.

I just hung up with Renee.

You in London?

No. We're in Knoxville. With the family.

Oh, uh, great.

So what are your plans?

She props herself up on one elbow, Umm...

Thought maybe we could hook up. While you're in town. Do lunch or something. Must be like what, four years now?

I, I suppose I could run out there.

Look, if it's a problem, we could run out there and see you. We've got all the time in the world, we're on holidays. Got the grandparents to watch the kids.

No no. I'll head your way. It'd be great to see you.

Okay. We're at my folks place. Say around one o'clock? You remember how to get here?

Of course.

You all right?

Of course.

She skips across the hall for the bathroom. Walt appears, fully dressed and whistling to himself. She stops with her hand on the doorknob in her own half-dressed state, blinking her eyes as if trying to discern a shadowy intruder.

My, my, she intones in mock perplexity, a finger to her lower lip and slowly shaking her head. What beckons thou from thy heavenly slumbers?

T'is the labours of the day, m'lady, Walt grins sheepishly. For godsakes Barb, put some pants on.

Doest thou trouble to be occupied by such trifles?

Worry thee not, m'lady, for I am, umm, not in haste. His majesty has, um, made all preparations for the execution of my duties by his own hand.

If thou be not in haste, to where dost thou go in thy full costume, Barbara calls from the bathroom while roughing up her hair in front of the mirror.

To the tellie, Walt calls over his shoulder while scrambling down the stairs.

Barbara looks herself over. Her auburn hair is distinctly her mother's, but the sky blue eyes are clearly her dad's. There are dimples and no sign of wrinkles yet- she looks pretty damned good, she thinks, for a woman of thirty. Younger than Janey and her other peers at the bank, she thinks. She's always thought *it must be the makeup gets them.* Perhaps it's the avoidance of facial products that's put years on her face- she never had acne, never used moisturizers, heavy makeup, or cold cream. She's had good luck with skin, good luck with looks, she could also eat a lot and not put the weight on, at least until a few years ago. Then she'd checked her diet, avoiding fried foods. Rice-based, salads. Which became just another source of tension between her and the ever-expanding Bill- Bill still stuck on fast-food joints, T-Bone steaks, double-dip cones, potato chips.

She reaches behind, pulls her tee shirt over her head and takes a step back from the mirror, with hands on her hips turns sideways, then pads fully around, glancing over her shoulder at the back of her. Not a hint of fat, her muscles toned after taking up yoga last year, twice a week on the light-weights at home.

She flops cross-legged in Levis next to Walt on the sofa in the living room, spooning the remains of a bowl of Corn Flakes in front of an *I Dream of Jeannie* rerun. At the commercial break she rises and heads with empty bowl towards the kitchen.

Don'cha wanna find out what happens to Major Healey, Walt calls after her, eyes still glued to a commercial for laundry detergent. *Tide's in, dirt's out.*

He'll be alright, she fills a plastic spill-proof mug with the last of the coffee pot. *He'll be alright*, she thinks, *they always end up alright after thirty minutes.* Walt switches off the television.

Guess I should be going myself, he sighs, pats his knees and rises as if taking a cue from her.

What about poor ole Major Healey?

Already seen it. They rescue the poor fucker.

Be nice if somebody'd throw us a line, thinks Barbara, closing the front door behind her.

On old route 35 to Rugby, this time without Mom. She thinks of her mother at that noisy school. She's decided to take a circuitous route to Knoxville, having left early enough. She feels young and invincible, nothing but winding road and the color of foliage has deepened. Time for a walk in the woods.

Having parked the car just off the gravel road by Laurel Dale Cemetery, Barbara bounces along this carpet of colors. In the woods stand tall trees whose outermost extensions of leaves and needles reveal the imminence of death, she thinks, and the tranquility and understanding of all life that comes before it. She glimpses the hint of death all around her, yet in the glorious colors of autumn, life's abundance shows. The leaves and needles drop and layer the floor of the forest with a carpet of earth tones. In the summer all was dressed in green and on many a heated afternoon she raced down this path with her brothers, Tommy and Lisa and whatever other kids happened to be around. Racing towards the Gentlemen's Swimming Hole- the rule was the last one there would be the first one in the water. The poor last-placer would be dragged by all others and heaved, squealing and protesting (one...two...three!) into the chilly depths of that ancient spot so familiar to Rugbians, and the long-time Fentress County folk. She recalls the race to that place, sprinting down the well worn path- sweating and breathing in the scent of summer pine, galloping along in her tank top and cut-offs to her usual first-place finish as Lisa came tearing up behind laughing, her braces glistening in the sun. The grown-ups would be back at Rugby-Uncle Clem and Daddy and would be outside on the porch of the General Store, relaxing in woven straw rockers and watching the customers pass as Uncle Clem tamped fresh tobacco in his pipe. Or over at the Harrow Road Cafe talking about whatever it was grown-ups talked about. Their wives doing business, plying their trade in country crafts- momma's woven baskets, plaques with words of wisdom behind lacquer, wall-mountable candle holders, dolls and dollhouses. Miriam's pottery spun with skillful hands at the urn in their basement, sugar bowls and flour jars and flower vases, all in earth tones.

*   *   *

Clem is in. His office is in its usual state of disarray, stacks of documents scattered on the floor and desk, the room is stuffy and wanting for air. He's on the telephone, fingering in turn the curly phone cord, his red paisley tie and suspenders. He motions John to one of the two chairs in front of his desk, rolling his eyes with each fruitless attempt to end the conversation. He hangs up, leans back in his swivel chair, hands folded behind his head.

Hoo boy, he says, somehow death brings out the worst in people when it comes to dividing up the bounty.

John nods, fiddles with a manila envelope.

Watcha got there? Clem plants his elbows on the desk.

This, says John, is my formal response.

Okay. Clem beckons and John hands him the folder. He opens it and fans the pages.

I'll go over this, but I can tell you one thing for sure, we're gonna cut this sucker way back.

John glances back and forth from the folder to Clem, and Clem clears his throat. You don't want to appear as if you're on the defensive, John. As if you've got too much explaining to do.

John looks deflated. But there's a lot of legal references, case precedent, that sort of thing in there.

Now you just leave the legal prep work to me John.

What about working together?

That's fine- Clem twirls his handlebar moustache, his gentle blue eyes twinkling- I just want to stay on point, stick to the basic facts. Like mainly that you had neither knowledge or consent. Save the case for the courtroom.

Isn't that what their whole case hinges on? Knowledge or consent? My land being tainted by Dawson's criminal case?

Sure, Clem sighs, but the burden of proof is still on you. To prove otherwise.

Well, I was thinking…why can't Dawson take the stand and vouch for me? Just say he didn't consult me in any way?

Well that'd have to come up in his testimony anyway. His criminal and your civil case will likely be heard conjointly anyhow.

Have they discussed it with him?

He seems reluctant to speak about it.

What?

You didn't hear this from me. He is very tight-lipped over that. There's something he's not telling.

John pounds a fist on Clem's desk. Well he better start speaking up! The nerve of him! Trespassing on my land, using it for his own, his own…illegal purposes! And now he decides to clam up? What is it? What's he tryin to beat, a trespassing charge? I'll give him a trespassing charge!

Clem pries himself from the swivel chair, behind his desk with his back turned, gazing out the picture window onto Main Street, Jamestown. When at last he speaks his voice sounds oddly detached. He says, I think we're missing something.

*   *   *

The tractor won't turn over. It gasps and moans but alas remains lifeless. Dismounting the machine, Walt lurches toward the rear of the barn- past the long-abandoned chicken coop of rusted wire mesh and rotted wood stripping, its ancient straw and feathers- where heads once rolled for Sunday dinner. He stomps past this deserted outpost to the paint-peeled side door of the barn with a vague notion of seeking tools, disregarding entirely his *ineptness in all things mechanical*, he's not prepared to give up godammit, after all he hasn't pried himself from the bed before noon for nothing. The sun's up and the son's up, the former shines through a greasy window onto the latter. Walt flicks the light switch but the room remains in murky semi-dark. What was once a thriving workshop now consigned to cluttered end-of-the-line storage. The land of lost things- battered screens unmatched to any window, scrap pieces of wood, an inflatable kiddie pool gouged with holes, a bachelor shoe, a three-wheel red wagon, all things dysfunctional. He is all the same determined to dig for that toolbox.

He unearths it from a pile of clutter underneath the workbench, opening the cover to find it chock-full of implements and suggesting that any repair may be facilitated by simply finding the right tool. He closes the cover, snaps the latches shut and picks it up with a growing sense of ineptitude. What will he do after all, dismantle the entire working parts of the Toro Yardmaster one piece at a time until he stumbles upon that single frayed wire?

He tramples back to the malfunctioning tractor. But the toolbox is set aside, foregone in favor of the good ole college try as he sits once again upon the imitation leather saddle and turns the key in the ignition. Crank, crank, the same whiny sound of failure. Attempts again with no miraculous change in fortune.

God fuckin' dammit! he cries out loud in a sudden burst of anger, pounding his fist on the plastic saddle. Again he dismounts and there's the toolbox laying in the sun, it will be utilized after all, but only as the *object of his anger and frustration- wham!* He winds up his leg and gives it a kick- *damn you toolbox, damn you elusive bag of tricks, damn you for serving to remind me of my shortcomings in all things practical!* He grabs his aching foot and hops about- anyone coming on the scene might suppose he's in the midst of some sort of ancient ritual dance of praise to the gods for bestowing the sun or the rain upon his crops. He leans up against the tractor, wipes his brow and once again turns the throttle and then the key. Nothing.

Now he launches into a *real* fury, the previous display of rage was just a warm-up, he tugs at the latches of the overturned toolbox and snares the stainless steel hammer. He curses through gritted teeth, and commences to punish the innocent tractor. It's not long before he's bashed in the ignition pretty good, as well as the instrument panel. He's about to lash out again when he catches himself, lowering the hammer and holding it limply at his side and it's a good thing he didn't get the fuel tank in his blind fury, because the tank is full and sparks and gasoline are not the perfect match.

*   *   *

Barbara

All through lunch you force a smile. Maybe it'd have been better you'd gone to lunch with Patty alone, no husband Stephen. Maybe then you'd have been able to let go, bawl unabashedly before your old confidante. Instead they bring you up to speed on their kids, their exciting life in London with budding careers, cultural stimulation in regular doses.

Now you shiver in the back seat of Patty's Dads' Lexus, and imagine your poor father tooling around in that punished pickup. Your mind races ahead to facing Renee in a few precious minutes. What is it sets you on edge so, the imminent reunion of... what? Lovers, guilty parties? Novices playing at an elaborate game, confused girls playing with fire?

Meet Renee for a drink, that's the plan, and so you and Patty and her husband Stephen hit The Library, your old favorite haunt. There's Renee, standing in the lobby and fishing doggedly through her Gucci bag for something. She looks up, shaking the blond bangs from her face. From her distracted expression springs an exuberant smile and she squeezes Patty, accepts a light hug from Stephen, then softly rubs your arm- a gesture that belies nothing more than the amity of friendship. The Library hasn't changed much, but you four who shuffle in after a long hiatus surely have. Suddenly you glimpse Renee in a new way- a tired RN getting off her shift, looking for a barstool to take the weight off of exhausted feet. Knocking back a few G&Ts a little quicker than necessary. You've downed a few vodka tonics yourself and it doesn't seem as if Renee is too pre-occupied with what transpired between the two of you a few afternoons ago- instead she's the catalyst to spark that which is shared between you three women. Stephen is suddenly relegated to observer status and Peppermint Patty's back, no longer the stuffy Lloyds of London woman exec in a tailored pants suit but rather the unbridled spew of unrelated questions and she's actually *slurring her speech* when she intones with a certain mock confidentiality,

Fuck men, they're all pigs.

No your ears haven't betrayed you, Peppermint Patty says *fuck men they're all pigs* and your eyes meet Renee's, as if on cue from Patty's drunken proclamation, neither terribly ingenious nor novel, but you have to wonder just what prompted it. Of course, she's just placating you, assuaging the hurt of your marital woes. You look over at Stephen who's playing with his nails with the vacant expression of one waiting on a subway train, nonetheless have to wonder if there might be marital issues. It's then perhaps you think you should say something to Renee about the other afternoon, but you don't, you merely return your bewildered glance to Peppermint Patty, who's polishing off another martini under the uneasy gaze of her husband. Surely he didn't overhear her drunken declaration, surely he didn't hear the conviction in her voice as she slurred it?

After they've ordered the next round of drinks, Stephen begins to check his wristwatch at successively shorter intervals. Renee's got everyone by two. You and her are breathing a little easier. On the way down you imagined a smooth night ride home listening to the radio and gathering your thoughts. But it's a long way to drive drunk and things are warming up with Renee.

So you leave Peppermint Patty in that freshly-blacktopped parking lot, gone are the potholes of yesteryear to alert many a drunken driver at the onset of the drive home. Patty embraces you with the vigor of old. You say you'll see her in the morning when you go to fetch the car, she understands Barbara and Renee have some catching up to do.

We have some talking to do, you say pensively to Renee as she fumbles the key into the ignition of the 4x4. In a wave of nostalgia and some new feeling you grasp Renee by the arm, look into her baby blue dark-ringed eyes. Smile. Renee shrugs, says, it's good to see you again, Barb.

The drive is a little awkward. Renee stops on the way to pick up a bottle of wine and a pack of cigarettes- offering one, which you accept and light. The vodka tonics have really kicked in and you feel suddenly light and airy- it's soothing to be walking up the twisting stone path under a darkening sky to her house set way back off the road, sheltered by pine trees. Renee's lost some of the exhausted RN look, taken on a strange radiance, gripping the bottle of wine and smiling for the sake of it.

I just love the place, says Renee, brightening up. No noisy neighbors, nothing but peace and quiet. You can even hang your laundry in the buff, she says.

No sooner do you place the wine bottle on the kitchen table Renee brushes past and you follow her to the back door to view her expansive yard. You stand next to her by the back steps saying how amazing is this garden Renee and expressing wonder at the cast-iron sculptures dressing up the yard. You're about to ask about them when Renee kisses you lightly on the cheek, she's just little Renee again- soft, rosy-cheeked, blond-bobbed innocent Renee as your lips meet.

Wait, Renee-
What's wrong?
I, I'm a bit confused, is all.
Let me help clear things up.

Renee directs you inside, mouths locked and sort of slow dancing through the kitchen of wood cabinets freshly painted white, back to the cozy living room decked out in the sort of crafts mama once made and, kissing passionately, you both nearly trip over the old rocker, at last to the bedroom where clothes are shed and you collapse onto the bed. Renee says *Wait, wait* and you think she's having second thoughts but instead she's just reaching across the bed to the cream-colored night table for a ziploc baggie and she's rolling a joint and *christalmighty* you think, how long has it been since you smoked one of them, and you're on your feet to retrieve the bottle of wine and fumbling around in the kitchen barefoot, naked, searching kitchen cabinets for a couple of glasses, trying not to break the moment, then you're back on Renee's bed, accepting the lit joint and pulling hard on it and passing it back.

C'mere, Renee whispers coyly and when you get closer she pulls on the joint and her lips invite you into a wet kiss as she blows smoke into your mouth. You lie down next to her, wanting to get lost in these sheets indefinitely, realizing it's been ages since you felt the compulsion to kiss someone until your lips ached.

*   *   *

John arrives home, exhausted after a long day of clearing out unsold furniture at estate sales with Frank only to discover that no wood had been gathered, the tractor sitting just where he'd left it hours ago but definitely not *as* he left it- a slew of indentations in the body and a bashed-in ignition and instrument panel- to say he was merely *appalled* would be an understatement. Walt hadn't tried to disappear, but perhaps he should have. He should have at least either told the truth or come up with a better explanation than he'd *somehow lost control of the hammer*. Or perhaps he should have gathered some wood by hand to indicate some progress. But he hasn't.

Despite all of his ruminating over his son's obliteration of the day, despite the effort in having extracted the truth from Walt concerning the victimized tractor, all John can manage to mutter in disgust is, I'll do it myself.

No, Daddy, really, Walt protests, I'll, I'll get it together tomorrow, I promise.

In the approaching darkness next to the hulk of battered machine, John rubs his chin and spits at the ground.

What– what is it son, got into you, put you in such a rage?

Walt kicks at the ground.

It's, it's… I. I think it's Cindy, Dad.

*Cin*dy?

We…we've sorta broken up. She doesn't want to see me anymore.

Oh. And why's that?

Walt shrugs with the same detachment of his matter-of-fact tone, as if it's somebody else's problems he's talking about.

Just...things, I s'pose.

Things.

It's uh, real hard to say...

While Walt digs his fists in his pockets, shifty-eyed- John kicks at the ground, pushes at the beaten hulk of tractor, shuffles about with his fists balled up and thrust into his pockets.

Look Walt. You better pull yourself together. Real soon. I need *help* right now, not broken tractors!

Walt nods his head at the ground.

For your own good, son, John continues as he spies Ellen looking on from the kitchen window. I think it best if you moved out on your own. Soon. We're all getting a little too old for this.

*   *   *

Cindy's answering machine again. He imagines her sitting on the bed listening to the dial tone following the beep, hitting star 69 to identify the caller and sighing not the sigh of love but of disappointment. He redials.

—Hi, it's you-know-who. Leave a message.

The recorded words that are all that's left of her. He badly wishes to speak to her about his dilemma, his angry father, having to leave, the mangled tractor, going to Nashville. He wants to talk to his father about Cindy and her frustrations, the way she tired of him, what a louse he's been. He picks up the phone to dial her number and hear that monotone voice and immediately hears his father's voice on the extension with the hello of the interrupted.

Oh. Sorry.

Walt hangs up the phone. He walks barefoot on the plush carpet across the hall to Barbara's room. He knocks on the door but there is no answer.

*   *   *

Barbara

Your eyes flutter awake to pain at the back of your head. The room is barely bathed in moonlight. Renee on her side facing away from you, sleeping soundly. You prop yourself up on your elbows, your head still throbbing, and glance at the glow-in-the-dark green hands of the Bambi bedside alarm clock, it's only a quarter to three, not long after you'd fallen asleep bundled in each other's arms. The pack of Marlboros is caught in the glow of the clock, in a mere few hours the idea of lighting one has gone from enticing to repulsive. Cottonmouth. Dammit you think, you didn't leave a note back in Burrville. Nobody knows where you are, you'd told Walt, but he'd been glued to the television and you can't be sure it registered. They'll worry. You should call. With no small effort you climb out from under the covers, grab Renee's robe from the back of the door and wrap it over your auburn hair and delicate shoulders. You tiptoe to the kitchen and start for the sink, tilting your head and letting the water from the tap course into your mouth.

The phone rings several times. A little odd to be checking in with your parents at your age, you think, wrapped in Renee's terry cloth bathrobe and shivering all the same.

Hullo? Daddy's groggy voice. Oh Barb? Where...where are you? Wait, here's mom.

Momma is wide awake, straight to the point. Probably she was waiting up. Where are you?

I'm at Renee's, you whisper. We met Karen and Stephen for lunch. I just woke up and realized I didn't leave a note.

My little space cadet.

Your mother's voice is soft. We were worried.

Yeah, sorry.

That's okay. See you tomorrow?

Yeah Ma. See you tomorrow.

You leave a cold kitchen for the warm haven across the living room, but the cream-colored walls of the bedroom seem to have lost all of their soft edges. Renee snores lightly. The reek of pot smoke lingers. In this new stillness you rub your eyes, return gingerly to the double bed. Laying on your back and squeezing your eyes shut you wonder, *Who am I becoming?*

Wednesday, Feel Anything?

Early morning, pre-dawn.
Cindy's voice is a gravelly whisper on the phone line. Do you realize what time it is?
I know. I'm sorry.
A very audible sigh on the other end. Walt says, I tried to get through all day. I don't know when else I can reach you.
What's wrong?
Everything.
Walt...
I need to talk is all.
It's *four o'clock* in the morning.
Got a few minutes to spare for an old friend?
Oh God, she whispers into the phone. So what's wrong now.
I've got a moral dilemma.
Moral dilemma?
I need to talk to someone. I don't know who else to call.
Look, can I call you back?
Sure, he mumbles. Talk to you later.
Cradling the phone, he reaches for the pillow and pushes his face into it. Screams.

*   *   *

Barbara

You'd woken up well after noon, Renee long gone and having left a brief note on the kitchen table, bold lettering stating simply, *Make yourself at home*.
After a few crumpled rough drafts, you left Renee a note. The upshot of the message was you had a wonderful evening and would be in touch. Nothing about your strange feelings. Nothing about the ecstasy you hadn't felt in years and thought you'd never feel again. Nothing about being confused.

*   *   *

"Probable cause in forfeiture proceeding is reasonable ground for belief of guilt, supported by less than prima facie proof but more than mere suspicion; once this initial showing has been made, burden shifts to the party opposing forfeiture to demonstrate by preponderance of the evidence that property is not subject to forfeiture or that defense to forfeiture is applicable, and if no rebuttal is made, showing of probable cause alone will support judgement of forfeiture."- Comprehensive Drug Abuse and Prevention Act of 1970 S511(a)(6,7) 21 U.S.C.A. S881(a)(6,7)

Knowledge or consent. The burden of proof rests on the shoulders of he who holds title to the property. John reclines in his chair at his desk, fingers intertwined behind his head, thumbs pushing at the tension knots at the base of his neck. It's taken the better part of the morning to finalize the response letter. He licks the envelope and seals it- somewhat doubtful about a document that began as a lengthy dissertation outlining his family's history as upstanding citizens, his abhorrence and avoidance of illegal substances, his values as such imbued upon his children- now reduced to a single page. I, John Griffith, sole Title-holder to 104 acres known in Fentress County tax and appraisal records as Lot No.109, had neither knowledge nor consent in the matter of the 126 marijuana plants discovered to be harvested in connection to the criminal case of Timothy Dawson. The rest of it just a simple letter, rife with facts and legalize, essentially saying *I didn't do it.*

When he walks outside, Walt is dragging the wheelbarrow out the barn door and toward the woods to seek out felled trees, scavenge whatever fallen limbs or logs he'd chance upon, go splitting them with the long-handled axe. John hollers to his son from the porch.

Off to the post office. See you when I get back.

Walt's throws a leg up on the wheelbarrow, rests his chin on the top of the axe handle and waves. They regard one another wordlessly for a moment, the beaten old tractor between them.

Where's Barb? John hollers.

Out looking for a job.

A job?

Yep.

Looking for a job? What sort of job could possibly interest his daughter in these parts? As he guns the pickup onto highway 27, he wonders just how deep in marital problems is she?

*   *   *

Barbara

You arrive at the Gentlemens Swimming Hole just as the sun begins to dip below the tree line. A landscape artist's dream sky, dramatic blue and violet streaks against a fading redness. A perfect backdrop for the bright red and orange leaves that seem to glow of themselves. In this path of yesteryear you walk, leaves crunching under your feet, with the same sense of wonder one walks through an art exhibit. The winding trail drops down to the river. Some of the trees down here wear summer's green. At last the sound of rippling water, a wind whistling lightly and carrying the scent of pine. Then you find yourself sprinting to the sacred spot, leaping from rock to rock, over felled trees– at last settling yourself down onto the sandy embankment, chest heaving as you remove your shoes to soak your feet in the cool water.

How was it so many significant events could occur in one spot? A traditional gathering place for generations of Rugbians and their outlying neighbors. The Gentlemens Swimming Hole. The black hole of Barbara Griffith's innocence. You roll up your pant legs, laugh to yourself and remember.

–*This ain't no ordinary cigarette Barb*, Kyle Dawson's matter-of-fact voice fell soft in the late afternoon forest. You sat cross-legged next to Lisa, bringing the Marlboro to your lips without breaking her gaze on Dawson, who sat with his legs straight out in front of him fingers teasing crumpled paper over one knee. The younger ones had just raced back up the hill minutes before.

–*Then what kind is it?* You felt thick with sleep. His eyes darted up, and he grinned mischievously.

–*Just a little something to relax the mind.*

– *That's marijuana.* Lisa's eyes widened at the sight of the dovetail joint in Kyle's hand, then she shot you a conspiratorial gaze. Kyle shrugged, bringing it to his lips with a devil-may-care expression.

—What's it gonna make me feel like? you asked.

—I dunno. Makes people feel all different kind of ways. He drew a shiny silver lighter from his shirt pocket. The flame illuminated a face with hard features, a face suggesting a knowledge beyond his eighteen years.

—Are you going to try it, you uttered to Lisa from the corner of your mouth while meeting Kyle's vigilant gaze.

—Uh-uh. Lisa spoke resolutely, kneading the sand in front of her with her feet.

Kyle was on his feet, the crude cigarette hitched between thumb and forefinger, flexing his wrist in the manner of casual invitation.

—Well, just a puff. You stubbed out your Marlboro in the sand, felt Lisa's intent gaze as she pulled tentatively on Kyle's makeshift cigarette.

—Well? Lisa stood at the water's edge, squinting and shielding her eyes from the sun. Your response amounted to a light cough, then a coarse gasp for air. Kyle retrieved the joint, blew on it, pulled hard and offered it to you again.

—Well? Lisa hovered around you. *—Feel anything?*

—Not really.

—It's getting dark, she said, eyes probing the forest, *—We should be getting back.*

—Sure. you gathered yourself, standing up and feeling the blood rush to your head.

On the way up the path you saw night as never before, everything silvery grey in the pale moonlight. Lisa was frazzled about their tardiness. You dawdled, laughed at every lamentation while steadying yourself on Dawson's elbow.

—What's so funny? Lisa queried exasperatedly.

This only caused you to laugh harder, gasping for air and grabbing your sides.

—Aw, let's go, said Lisa forcefully, *—C'mon.*

—Can't, was all you could manage to utter between gasps. All the way along the trail in darkness you and Dawson continued laughing at something entirely lost on Lisa.

Later that summer in the same spot- while the others had gone upriver hunting crawfish, you lingered with Tommy Carter in the swimming hole's cool waters- emerging dripping wet, you both flopped on the sand of the tiny beach. You were content to bask in the warmth of the sun, but Tommy couldn't lay still very long. At first you barely felt the faint pinging of minute pebbles bouncing off your belly, played dumb as larger smoothed pebbles pelted the rest of you. Shielding your eyes, with a sideways glance you caught the smirk on his face before he turned his head the other way. Propping yourself up on an elbow. His fingers probed the sand for another pebble. No sooner had he turned his head than you pounced on him and tickled his ribcage as he wormed around in the sand giggling and throwing in a few high-pitched screams for good measure.

–*No one can hear you*, you said, straddling him as he turned over onto his stomach, digging his hands into his armpits. He squirmed out of your grasp and pinned you with his knees before you could get to your feet. You tussled. In all of the fracas you pulled on his orange and yellow tropical motif trunks. He reached around to pull them back up, his pale white bottom exposed. You tugged harder amid the giggles, and the rest of them fell. It was odd, this part of a man you'd never seen in the flesh. Even water-shriveled as it was, it stood out, a stark white thing against the sunburned rest of him. He grew silent and left the trunks around his ankles.

–*Now it's your turn.*

You were still laughing, bringing a hand to your mouth. He quickly reached down and pulled his trunks back on.

–*Top or bottom?*

–*I don't know*, his voice carried the uncertain tone of one swimming in unfamiliar waters. He looked over his shoulder at the path, checking to see if his screams had drawn anyone out of the woods. The Gentlemens Swimming Hole had gone eerily quiet- no splashing, playful screams or other beach shenanigans.

You advanced the show and tell, reaching behind you and untying the skimpy rainbow bikini top, staring straight ahead as it fell at your feet in the sand. Tommy's eyes bulged, you blushed.

–*They're not much to look at*, you said as Tommy shuffled to her, –*Wanna cop a feel?*

–*Huh?*

–*Touch me.*

–*There?*

You frowned, laying a finger on your breast. –*There.*

He ran his hand along the small curve of your breast, his fingers caressed the cleft of a valley in between and then down your belly to the seam of your bikini line.

–*Hey*, you said, –*We're even.*

–*Aw, I wouldn't want to see it, anyhow.*

You dropped back onto the sand, arching your back.

–*Touch me again, Tommy.*

He glanced over his shoulder, checking the pathways.

–*There? Again?*

You didn't answer, just lay outstretched in the sand with your eyes squeezed shut. He knelt beside you, touching your pale white chest that seemed now barely bigger than his own baby fat one. Feigned an interest, then took an interest. Lightly pinched a nipple.

–Ouch. Gentle.

His hand ran gentle down to your navel, back to the seam of the bikini bottom. He gingerly passed two fingers underneath, looking over his shoulder. His hand was now submerged in your bikini– you brought your knees up and the bikini off. Told him to pull down his trunks again. He obliged, you allowed your hand to wander and work his stiffness, suddenly wet and sticky and shortlived. Later you waded in the cooling waters of the Gentlemens Swimming Hole.

On Labor Day weekend that summer you returned there hand in hand with your boyfriend of one month Bobby Lane. He gave up his high school ring. You gave up your virginity. It wasn't the playful and pleasant show and tell in the sun with Tommy Carter. Instead it was rough in the creepy darkness. You lay on your back digging fingernails into his back, looking over his shoulder for any night creatures that might smell the heat of sex. The night had the coolness of the ones at the end of summer, the sand was cold and uncomfortable. There was no foreplay, his teenage hormones anxious and compulsive. He was hardly the gentleman at the Gentlemens Swimming Hole– he'd dropped his pants and entered you so suddenly and it hurt and you couldn't wait for it to be over.

Now you sit alone on the beach and toss pebbles at the swimming hole, darkness is on the way and the moon coming up is full. An eerie silence, and suddenly it's going to be a long walk through the forest back up the hill to a solitary car parked beside a cemetery. You start along the path with a hurried gate, jumpy at every rustle of leaves that take on a new level of noise in the dead silence of night, crickets sing as your fears rush at you, you tell yourself it's silly, that every night in this forest is calm and safe without you. There are no escaped convicts, axe murderers, rapists, or insane somnambulists any other night, so what should bring them out now? Stop it, you say to yourself as your steps get wider. But you draw the line at a brisk walk, to run would be a submission to panic which should only frighten you more. Ahead of you a branch falls on the hardening ground, dead weight like a body. You run. At least five minutes more to the car. When you emerge at the trailhead, darkness has blanketed the little hill and the cemetery on it. Headstones peek from the ground at crazy angles. Squeezing the keys in your fist as if they might jump out on their own, you dash to the silhouette of the Honda, throw open the door and stab the keys at the ignition, miss, curse in whispers and plunge the key in. You hit reverse, punch the accelerator with your foot and pull away. Only when you're clear of the cemetery do you switch on the headlights.

* * *

On the drive to the post office and while he stood waiting in line, John had that irrational nagging sense that the envelope or the letter was missing something. At the counter he filled out the green certified mail form and sent the letter priority.

Then he drove over to Clem's for the sake of it, or maybe for some reassurance. Because he still has a nagging doubt about all this mess. Clem was busy and he told Janet no need to leave a message. He drives home slowly on familiar roads while his mind races. All he can think of is packing up the house to live in some bland apartment of dripping toilets, cracking paint and inefficient wall heating. He pulls in the driveway and from nearby woods he can discern the crack of woodcutting.

Gathering the long-handle axe from the barn, he joins his son in the cooling afternoon, the sun obscured by clouds. The physical exertion seems to wake him up. He swings his axe with a new buoyancy, he's cocky and soon enough his insurmountable problems are reduced to a mere legal hassle, something which has to be cleared up. All's right in the world- father and son preparing wood for a naturally-heated homestead- *why*, he thinks, *we don't do more things together is beyond me. Gonna have to change that.* He thinks of nixing his request of Walt to move out, *must've overreacted a bit from all the stress I've been under. Anyway, maybe Walt needs a little time to get over Cindy before he can get on with his own life, truth is I want him around anyhow*, thinks John as he watches his son carry a bundle of sticks towards the wheelbarrow. He calls to his son. Let's get the chainsaw on those felled trees.

Walt drops the bundle into the wheelbarrow, carves at the ground with a foot, eyes darting this way and that.

Everything okay? John asks.

No, Walt replies hoarsely, not really.

Well, what is it, what's the matter? What on earth could possibly be worse than we've already got on our plate?

Oh, I wish I could say nothing, Walt says while running a hand along the wheelbarrow.

Well go on, John says, rubbing at chafed, ungloved hands. Spit it out.

It's about Dawson. You ain't gonna like this Daddy.

Well, I guess I'd better hear it all the same.

It was that winter I came through here on the way back from Cincinnati with the band. Christmas. Couple of years ago, you remember?

John nods his head gravely.

I was down at the Colonial. That whole gang I used to hang out with in high school was there, you know, everybody was drinkin and havin a good time. Anyway there I was at the bar talkin to Gavin. Tim Dawson walks in, we, we were just talkin you know, just cuttin up and talkin about old times. There wasn't anything you could put over on Dawson, Daddy- he never went to college, but he had a knowledge of things, he knew how to get people to do things. I remember once back in high school he-

-Stick to the story.

Okay. So we're sitting there, Gavin's gone home, he's never much been one for bars-

Sometimes I wish to God you weren't one for bars, John thinks.

-Dawson stands up and beckons me over to a booth. We sit there with our beers. He starts telling me about his mother, about how she's got this debilitating illness.

Mrs. Dawson has MS, John says, she's developed cancer. So young too, it's a damn shame.

Right, well anyhow Dawson's telling me about how much the hospital bills are and how in debt they've become, how his mother, the only mother he has is sick. How they can't even get a doctor anymore, nobody wants anything to do with them, no insurance, everything you know. But Dawson's started dealing a little, just on the side-

-Dealing.

Pot. Marijuana. Just for groceries, just to keep up on the bank note. You know he can't make enough workin for Tibbs.

Yeah? John lays the axe in the wheelbarrow and folds his arms.

Walt says, he knows he can make a lot of money though. He's got connections at UT and in Nashville too. But he needs a place to grow. He needs a place that's bigger and more hidden than the little two-acre spread of grass they got on Tibbett Street. So he starts asking me about *our* place, you know, he tells me he needs good fertile ground, and he can make a ton of money in the summer and solve his momma's problems.

Solve his momma's problems, John echoes. Walt, do you know how hopeless that woman's case is? Even back then.

How was I to know the details of her medical condition at the time I made the pact.

What *pact?*

The pact. What I'm fixin to tell you about.

John cocks his head sideways. You rented out my land to that sonofabitch?

No. I- I mean not right away. But when I came home the next summer he'd already planted. I tried to put my foot down, but I caved.

Walt turns his back, kicks the ground.

It was me told him for three hundred bucks a month he could grow his stuff on our- on your land Daddy.

Walt's voice begins to quake. I'm sorry! I'm so sorry, God I wish I had the balls to run him off right then and there, I didn't know, honest I didn't know, if I had any idea... oh Daddy I'm so sorry!

John blinks his eyes in disbelief. No, he says. This can't be true. Tell me you're not serious.

They face one another in the stillness of dusk, among a choir of chirping crickets and croaking frogs.

Why Walt? Why did you?

I guess I just thought I could help a friend. And make a little money at the same time.

A little money? Do you realize what this is going to cost us? And all because you wanted to make a little extra cash! Shit! *Shit shit shit!*

John kicks at the ground, spits.

S-sorry. I just-

Damn you!

They circle each other, saying nothing. Then John grabs Walt's shoulders, shaking him.

Listen to me, *listen*. We can't tell your mother. I think I've got to talk to Clem. I've got to talk to him and level with him, he'll know how to handle this. I mean I guess he will. *Godamnit*.

Walt reaches out for his father but John turns on his heels charging towards the house and flinging the screen door open- then he senses he doesn't want to enter that house, tainted as it is with crime. Instead he turns around and runs out to the tall grass, while Walt looks on in bewilderment. In much the same manner his forebears fell to their knees and prayed for rain to deliver their sustenance, in the darkness he lies prone and begs to be delivered from the deluge of misfortune raining down on him. Walt looks on with wet eyes- unable to lend a hand, an ear, unable to speak.

Thursday, The Luxury of Time

John's eyes flutter awake and he feels his dream slip away, tries to salvage its meaning. All he can summon is a vague notion of having lost something. A piece of his dream comes back–he and Barbara rummaging around in an old abandoned house. One of Frank Lynn's jobs. Barbara is a little out of context there at his side as they frantically search one cardboard box after another. Somewhere in the dream he'd lost track of what it was they'd lost, but Barbara seemed to know it– though when he pressed her she remained doggedly at her task, and mute. Then he woke up.

In the pre-dawn stillness he lays on his back listening to Ellen's slow and even breathing. Their bedroom is a dark place, the walls painted navy blue. He ponders the expanding universe, everything moving further away from each other respectively. An image from the dream- his arms outstretched in an effort to save something, but everything out of reach.

Yesterday he'd tried to reach Steve Meigs at WHRS in the unlikely event he'd changed his mind about continuing the show after that on-air speech last week. He could only leave a message on the answering machine. Perhaps the station's been getting calls from the program's regular listeners, maybe a few of them hadn't tuned in last Thursday and might be listening for him tonight– jerking the dial back and forth and scratching their heads at the contemporary pop music blaring from tuner position 88.5. How he had enjoyed those nights at WHRS, reclining in his chair with the phone cradled on his shoulder while talking to a caller and reveling in the glory days of Tennessee musical tradition- Hank Williams, Dottie West, Jim Reeves, Bob Wills and the Texas Playboys crooning their loneliness through the station monitors and over the airwaves outside. The station all the more precious these last few lean years as a haven from a turbulent home back in Burrville. He pictures himself there in front of the console in the dark control room, alternating between the CD player and the old Philco phonograph. The collection of old vinyl 78s stacked neatly behind him, the records he'll probably have to pawn off or sell as he had the Volvo last year. The Volvo another lost object, carried off in the gravity that dictates that *all matter eventually must break down.* That car had lasted what felt to him a lifetime and ran like a charm until the transmission was deemed beyond repair and he'd finally had to have it towed after Ellen's remonstrations, her insistence that it only served to present them as *white trash*, leaving it to rust like that in the driveway.

On his back in the darkness he imagines the vacuous space above between himself and the ceiling as infinite, imagines points of light which are not fixed but moving away from each other at variable rates. There's one star fast disappearing– a faint blink of light called Imperial on the brink of becoming invisible to the naked eye. Another one- Volvo- pushing out beyond the visible gallery of stars. And yet another named Bill, a reliable and trusted annex to the star Barbara. Then a star named 88.5 WHRS blinks irregular transmissions through the ether. At last the home planet itself begins to move, but relative to what? It seems some mysterious gravitational force is pulling it from its regular orbit as it wobbles and trembles from its very inner crust, pulling itself apart at the seams.

He props himself up on his elbows and glances across at Ellen, whose eyes flutter awake.

John? Her voice is a hushed whisper.

Yeah. He rolls over onto his back, covers half flung off.

You alright?

Sure.

She toys with her gold chain and crucifix.

Maybe we should go away somewhere, her voice croaks. For a little while.

Are you kidding? We can't afford to do that at a time like this.

I just thought maybe a few days, just to... I don't know... Forget. Regroup.

The tenderness in her voice stills his objections– it's nice to be invited to her escape, he never invites her along to his– but to his mind any time away would be tantamount to jumping ship.

Sorry about the other night, he says.

Has Walt talked to you?

She turns on her side facing away from him. Not about, about anything... important. Why?

Dunno.

He sighs at the ceiling. I, ah... it's just, I, I told him, a few days ago... I thought it might be best if maybe he started to, you know, move on with things—

You mean move out? Her voice croaks as if straining to get past a whisper.

I think so.

Well, she sighs, there we're in agreement.

John stirs himself to a seated position on the bed.

But- Ellen's voice takes on a tone of authority- maybe just not right now. I know this living at home business hasn't been... healthy for him.

You're right. Maybe right now isn't the best time.

What did you say to him?

Just... I don't know, I can't recall my exact words, the gist of it was maybe it's time to move on.

Be careful John, he's really sensitive right now.

He clucks his tongue, sighs heavily, bolts up- grabbing his jeans on the chair in the corner.

What, Ellen throws her legs over the side of the bed and looks sharply at John. What's wrong now?

It'd be nice if someone worried about my feelings once in a while, he says with his back to her while fidgeting with his shirt buttons.

Oh, Mother of God...

He closes the door against exasperated lamentations, her voice fading to a faint muffle.

*   *   *

A little while later- Ellen at the chalkboard, scrawling the Bill of Rights in its entirety- slowly, methodically, pondering each word. The Fifth Amendment, *No person shall be deprived of life, liberty, or property, without due process of law; nor shall private property be taken for public use without just compensation.*

She stops writing, frozen still, pores over those words as never before. Today, she thinks, I don't want to just breeze over this, I would like to get the taste of it, digest it, try and understand what the drafters of this code of law were thinking.

Something small and hard strikes her in the back, and the classroom erupts in laughter. She replaces the chalk carefully, turns around to face a pack of kids entertained by the disruption.

Okay who did that? she demands, knowing good and well the culprit is not likely to stand or wave a hand.

That's it, she says, I want all of you to settle down. Now! And the next flying object will result in detention for every single person in this classroom until the guilty party stands up.

Most of the class has ceased laughing by now, except Billy Connolly in the first row. She picks up the little pink eraser at her feet and hurls it, hitting him on the chest.

Hey! he rasps, what'd you do that for?

If it wasn't you who threw it, you know who it was. And I don't think it's funny. I'll give the culprit until the end of class to fess up, otherwise everyone is minus five points on the next test.

She opens the teachers textbook and says to the class, Today we're going to talk about the Constitution of the United States, a document born of the revolution. The First Continental Congress drafted this document as a model for the powers of the federal government over the new independent nation. Now we're going to spend a little time on the document, yesterday we looked at the Preamble, today we look at the first five Articles of the Bill Of Rights, the debt, if you will, that the government owes to the people. Now pay attention as we see how the Constitution has been held up over time. We'll look at the Supreme Court, the body of government responsible for interpreting and upholding the Constitution. Can anybody tell me the name of one of the nine Chief Justices of the Supreme Court?

Billy Connolly's hand shoots up.

I remember the black dude with the sex videos and them little hairs on the Coke can.

Ellen closes the book and walks out of the classroom.

*   *   *

There's a knock on the door and he negotiates a path around the case law scattered on the floor and opens the door on Barbara, who stands there absent-mindedly twirling the French coffee maker's plunger in her hand.

Thought maybe you could use a break.

Ah, no thanks Barb, he says. Lot on my plate right now.

I think you mean your floor- she peers over his shoulder at the paper piles- I picked up some really good French roast in Knoxville.

Wow, you can almost drink it out of the air. I'll join you for a cup.

Leaning against the countertop, he glances at his daughter over the rim of his reading glasses. What's this I hear about your looking for a job?

Oh- she says offhandedly, twirling her spoon in her cup- nothing serious. Just something to make a few bucks, help out some while I'm home.

Uh-huh.

It's okay with you, Daddy? I mean my being here till- just until I can think things through. Properly.

Oh Barb, you know this place is always yours. You know you always got your family to turn to when you need something.

I was thinking about Grandpa this morning, says Barbara.

Yeah?

I remember like, parts of the last summer. The one before he got sick.

You couldn't have been more than what...four?

Reckon I was going on five.

Well, what d'you remember? he asks, picking distractedly at the lint on his sweater.

I remember going for walks with him, him talking about when he had the farm going. What was the name of the big black guy used to-

-Harold. Harold Earnshaw.

That's right.

Last proper worker on the old farm.

He always talked about farming.

Was his life- John shakes his head ruefully- tilling with the horses at first sign of spring. Planting, harvest time. Good years, bad years. I suppose he came to love it when he looked back on it with some distance. Sometimes you don't appreciate something much until it's taken away from you.

Did you love him, Daddy?

I guess I did. I kind of came to appreciate him more when I had to look after him. Your grandpa was a hard man in many ways. Times were tough. Lean years for farming anyway. School and an education, he thought, would be the best way to go. For the first time, we saw completely eye-to-eye on something. Then I go off and adventure around Europe one summer. He couldn't understand why I'd want to leave here, go overseas that summer. When I came back, he could see I didn't want to have any part of farming.

Bet he wasn't too crazy about that.

Yeah, he sighed, he about had a heart attack. But I came back in time to enroll late at UT. Plenty of travel stories to tell the old man.

Did he listen?

He was absolutely bug-eyed. So long as I was able to talk, he soaked it up.

What did you tell him about? You never talked to us any about Europe.

John waves his hand dismissively. Ah, all that's so many years ago. Pre-family.

Why did you come back?

Well I guess I couldn't just travel around like a vagabond forever. And besides, I love it here. I guess in a way I came back to have you all.

Barbara gushed. She said, that's the sweetest thing anyone could hear.

Well.

It's amazing how little curiosity we have about where we come from.

It's not something you spend much time dwellin on when you're young. S'pose it dawns on you when you're older. When you can look back a bit.

He strokes his chin and thinks here I was looking forward to having the luxury of time to think about such things in my golden years and now it seems more certain to be snatched away. He looks at his daughter, says, have you seen Walt?

It's only ten thirty, Barbara shrugs.

John parts the curtains at the back door of the kitchen. I don't know. Chevelle's not there.

Maybe he's out seeking gainful employment.

John places his cup in the sink, says he must get back to work. Barbara remains at the kitchen table with the application form for the bank teller position at First Tennessee Bank. Sarah Witherspoon had passed it to her with the look of a deer caught in the headlights, that was the description she'd been tagged with back when Barbara knew her from high school. She'd imagined Sarah as bewildered as any new born. She seemed so well-cast in the role of assistant bank manager- Sarah the one who played by the rules- homework on time, never had to worry about staying out late since she was never invited. Sarah Witherspoon seemed destined for second-rate, second-in-command, it was only for those two weeks annual leave for Mike Martin, the branch manager, that Sarah could assume the helm as interim manager. Mike was another former classmate low on the high school popularity pole. He'd been out to lunch and Barbara was glad because one former classmate that she and her popular clique had left sitting home Friday nights was enough to humble herself to ask for a job. When Sarah handed over an application Barbara'd spied the wedding ring on her finger. Barbara, already feeling self-conscious in her Levis glad-handing Sarah, felt an urge to convey some sort of rationalization for returning to Jamestown twelve years later to collect an application for peak-time bank teller. She stopped herself short of saying something about a *bad patch*- Sarah might be uneasy with those two words, maybe didn't have the point of reference for *bad patch* in her steady day-to-day life.

Instead Sarah had remarked, quite an interesting area, mortgage loan. In the big city, a large office. Must've been a lot to learn.

Now Barbara flips to the professional references section and begins scrawling the Union Planters Bank loan origination department information and imagines Carolyn, her well-meaning but frazzled boss getting a call from Sarah Witherspoon, hoping like hell Sarah mentioned the bank but not the position applied for. At UPB she'd felt so stuck in the Box of that PC terminal mousing through all the numeric data, spending the larger part of a working day with just her numbers. Fed up with this interaction with numbers, dreaming of a line of work that involved a steady interaction with people. Well, a peak-time teller would see plenty of people, through a shield of bullet-proof glass.

She tops off her coffee and spills some on the application, smearing the ink. A tarnished application hinting that perhaps all is not right with the applicant.

*   *   *

If only Dawson hadn't been so insistent, if only he didn't possess that damned stubbornness in his character. If only Walt hadn't been there to fall prey to it, hadn't stumbled in his *aimless cavorting* into that meadow four years ago to find Dawson pruning a few plants with his calloused hands, dirt under his fingernails. If only he hadn't succumbed to an offer he just couldn't refuse.

The light drizzle drives him to the shelter of the pines, and he lies on fallen needles and replays the scene in his mind.

At first Walt had half-jokingly accused him of trespassing as Dawson remained crouched and squinting at Walt's silhouette framed by the sun.

—Yeah well, actually Walt, maybe you could help me there, help keep me off your property. Maybe help me grow the business, so to speak.

—What are you saying, he'd asked.

—I mean I've got a lot of business lined up and I've got to work it. Maybe I could use someone else in charge of- production.

—Ah no, no way Tim.

— And I pay you for it

—I don't want to get into any of your business.

—Why not? Waddaya gonna do for the summer anyway?

—Clyde Simmons told me he could use me a few days a week cutting lawns, for one thing.

—And what's he paying you, like seven an hour?

—Seven fifty.

—Ooooh...

—Honest labor, Dawson.

—And this isn't, he swept his hand at the upturned earth, *You're still gettin' high ain't you Walt?*

—That's beside the point.

—Is it?

Last summer he'd had an uneasy feeling and considered ordering Dawson off the property, but in the end he went right back to work. It was having to save money for Nashville. It was *not wanting to work there*, it was wanting to be a songwriter. It was wanting to show up there *ahead of the game*, with a pile of money and then a pile of songs. It was a lot of things, but mostly it was a lucrative offer. He nibbled. He bit. He was reeled in- hook, line, and sinker.

*   *   *

The morning was unusually warm and he'd peeled from his summer wardrobe one of those familiar pseudo alligator polo shirts which lay alongside many he'd received from Venneman in Humboldt. Venneman was Imperial's main customer, accounting for over fifty percent of its sales. Venneman sold a knock-off of the popular IZOD Lacoste, with a kangaroo emblem stitched in place of the alligator. Imperial did the collar stitching. John had accumulated a substantial collection of these wannabees in all colors ranging from teal blue to gold. Alongside these gimmes lay two authentic originals bearing the trademark alligator stitch, the only one that would do for a business golf outing. By the time his alligator days were numbered, a few holes had been bore into the underarms of the machine-faded navy blue alligator shirt.

The worn-out shirt is on his back as he and Frank Lynn grunt at opposite ends of a red and white kitchen armoire. They ease it sideways to fit through the back door and walk it through the back door and onto the screened in porch. Negotiating the last screen door, John catches his un-tucked shirt on the latch and it is stretched like a rubber band. Stopped dead in his tracks, he has to drop his end much to Frank's chagrin.

Damn, he inspects the tear in his shirt, catches himself starting to apologize to Lynn. *Gotta get outta the habit of apologizing for faultless trivialities.*

Lura Breckenridge stands in the expansive backyard in pumps and her stockinged legs glisten in the bright summer sun. Speaking to the landscaper with a tone of authority about plans for tidying up for the exterior photos of her new listing.

They set down their heavy burden a moment there in the yard, heaving and sighing, hearing her gentle but firm orders to the young scrapper wearing a Billy Ray Cyrus t-shirt and two days beard stubble which he scratches at repeatedly while nodding and looking her over. John cannot blame the kid– Lura, after all, plies her trade with good looks. She's not just selling houses, she's selling herself– right from the glamorous color head shot which appears on business cards, real estate ads and the For Sale sign which has been staked in the overgrown grass. The smiling head shot of pearly white teeth and beauty salon flaxen-blonde hair falling on her shoulders with just the right curl. She's got a body that has obviously done time at the gym. There's a bitchiness that accompanies it– she sees those around her as if her own hired help to do her bidding, she speaks to Frank and more so to John as if they are inattentive children– explaining everything twice for reinforcement. Despite this, or perhaps because of it, he cannot deny the lure of her command as they pause to watch her go through the second pass with the landscaper– *so right, we're going to trim all those hedges back to their original sculpted design, right Jeff? And you can have all the trimmings picked up, the yard cut, the rosebushes, and I mean the Virginia roses planted by Friday, Friday at noon, right? Right. Right-* in her command of the situation is an undeniable sexiness.

They heave the monstrosity once again and empty it into Frank's Chevy van. Standing around waiting for an audience with the Fentress County real estate queen herself- she gets testy when interrupted- Lura Breckenridge. Frank's more talkative than usual today and John is keen to listen, gazing in long intervals at Lura in her silk white blouse and baby blue pleated skirt that allows enough of a display of her smooth knees and chiseled calves to sell virtually any house at any price.

The landscaper finally breaks away somewhat reluctantly and Frank approaches Lura with a single check for the entire material effects that had surrounded a little old lady's life. Clara Blaylock, deceased and leaving behind two adult children having long ago set up new lives for themselves in far away places, she having outlived her husband by twenty five years. No estate sale, just clear the place out.

Lura thanks him for the payment, asks him when he'll be back to haul off the unsightly oil furnace, makes a face when he replies he has to wait on Jenkins' flatbed and more manpower. A look of puzzlement on her face, as if these two grown men ought to be capable of extricating the three hundred fifty pound hulking mass in the basement.

They nonetheless bid goodbye and John casts a lingering glance at local real estate's top performer, a professional woman of twenty-nine years stooping down in her heels and gathering up marketing leaflets and her leather–bound agenda from the porch steps. He waves at her from the open side window of the van and she gives him a hasty professional smile.

Not gettin any at home, eh? Frank Lynn grins like a child.

Pardon?

I seen you eyein our sweet lil Loooo-ra

Well, says John, no harm in that. She's an attractive lady.

And a bitch to boot.

She has her job to do.

John finds himself again pining after the office meetings of yesteryear, far away from these undignified conversations.

Well sure, Frank rambles, but she gets her nose in the air so. Like she's sweet little Miss Jesus or something.

John lets his boss run himself dry of complaints and wets his lips with lurid thoughts of Lura. *Not gettin' any at home*, there's an accurate assessment, Frank. What's it been, three years? Ellen has run low on interest and he's stood by watching their bodies age, her battling weight incessantly. Maybe one day Lura will find herself unable to stop the spread of body fat. Lura Breckenridge, First Baptist Church member, front pew, chatting up potential clients before and after Sunday service. Maybe *during* the service in guarded whispers. He imagines her succumbing to temptation, one Sunday afternoon after a service dressed in her Sunday best after having shown a house now emptied and dark save for a few late afternoon beams of fading sunlight- him helping her out of her chaste clothing and having her right there on the dusty dingy floor in the sweat of sticky summer afternoon. The Open House sign laying face down by the backdoor and her laying next to him catching her breath and then rolling atop of him, blond hair sweeping across his face, full lips smudged with dark red lipstick pecking at his neck. *Not gettin any at home.* Trying to damn up the floodgates of fantasy- the racy thoughts flow nonetheless as Frank remains engaged in Paul Harvey's America on 650 AM. Lura Breckenridge is married to a councilman, with a two-year-old daughter. Makes it all the more spicier- her being young, married, church-going- all the more a conquest, the intimacy of the going-ons right there in that Open House where any late-comers might just wander in, perhaps even her husband or in-laws might turn up…

Everything all right John?

Sure, Frank.

But not everything is, and he can't let another day go by without mentioning it to Frank. A delicate matter.

Say Frank?

Yeah?

You got time for a beer before we go home?

The Colonial lies just off of Rt. 35 and is plain. Dimly lit, with tables for pairs or couples covered in red and white checked tablecloths of plastic, all the easier to maintain under frequent beer spillage. Frank sticks a quarter in the brightly lit jukebox and a Marlboro in his mouth. He appears to John old and worn, perhaps a surprising vulnerability is exposed in the fading light as he removes his worn baseball cap and runs dirty fingers through sandy greying hair.

So what's on your mind, he says in that rough sandpaper voice of his, lighting the cigarette once they've settled themselves in front of frosty mug beers.

Frank, it's...it's sort of a...touchy matter.

If it's about a raise John, I–

–No. It's not that, Frank. But it is about my pay.

The DEA, Clem had said, *just may be interested in how you've managed to pay the mortgage these past few years. Might just want to cross-reference with the IRS.*

It's not been an issue before you know, Frank, you and everyone else paying me in cash.

Frank looks surreptitiously over his shoulder, uh-huh.

Well, John plunges in breathlessly, it's just that I would... appreciate it if you could put me on a payroll. On your books. I mean social security, federal. I need to start paying taxes.

Frank grimaces but John continues anyway.

In fact, I...I need to get on record retro–um, going back. To the beginning.

Frank shakes his head slowly, tugging at his moustache. I can't do that.

Why not?

Frank looks again over his shoulder to an almost empty bar, just some kid slapping at a noisy pinball machine, lowers his voice to a tone of confidentiality.

I can't go back and change my books, my tax returns. It's gonna have to stay the way I've been doing it. It- he spreads his palms and shrugs his shoulders- just works out best this way.

Look Frank, I wouldn't ask if I didn't have to.

You in some sort of trouble?

Surely Frank knows, John thinks, with a deep pang of regret at his very public outburst on the radio.

No, I... Look, I just want things on the up and up is all.

The up and up. Imperial Textile and its accurate and fully disclosed payroll, corporate tax returns. Hickman the accountant, 1099s, W-2s.

Sorry John. But we've already agreed to this arrangement. Not a thing I can do here.

John has already run down his other income sources. His other odd jobs are too scattered and insignificant on their own. A miniscule 1099 from the radio station. So it's to Frank Lynn he must appeal.

Frank, actually there's a bit of a,a... misunderstanding. A legal one.

What sort of legal problem?

It's not exactly got anything to do with me, not exactly a *problem*. Just something I have to set the record straight on.

What?

I can't get into it right now, Frank. Suffice to say, it's very important to me right now that I account for all my income. *Very* important.

What will he face from the IRS upon deciding to report income three years after its being earned? A penalty, perhaps. A penalty plus all the back taxes. Beats risking having your land and house seized.

Frank's three play selection on the jukebox is rounded out by Elvis crooning *Heartbreak Hotel*. The only sounds in the room are the bells and space-age whistles from the pinball machine.

John, if you can't work for me no more like this—

No. No, no Frank. Really. Just a favor. Give you time to think about it.

I don't need any time to think about it, John. That's just how it is.

Frank downs the rest of his draft and smacks the mug down on the bar as if to punctuate the finality.

John thinks maybe it'll all come to nothing anyway, then remembers with no small panic that it was Clem who brought the matter up in the first place.

John leaves the Colonial cursing Frank under his breath. He can understand Frank's hands are tied, that if he were Frank Lynn he'd react pretty much the same way. But that does nothing to quell the gnawing sense that he was alone in a hellish battle. He recalled talking to Clem about the possibility of substantiating his income, mulling over not so much his old friend's words as his face- the calm blue eyes that customarily belied tranquility were suddenly shifty- darting about before settling on John's own steady gaze. His forehead retained the worried lines of a frown, he kept toying distractedly with his pipe, running a hand through his white hair. These are the images running through John's mind as he runs the red light, not even realizing it until he is through the intersection looking back over his shoulder at cars grinding to a halt.

* * *

With her arms full, Ellen bumps the back door open and steps in huffing and puffing with paper shopping bags pushed to their limit. Barbara starts to lend a hand but Ellen's already placed them on the countertop.

Where's the Chevelle, she asks between gasps for air.

Dunno, Barbara shrugs, slowly stirring over her makeshift tomato sauce.

Have you seen Walt any today?

She shakes her head. I just hope he's back before supper. I've made enough to feed an army.

That's very kind of you, Ellen says. Smells delicious.

Glass of wine?

Let me just get changed first.

Barbara fetches four dusty crystal wine glasses from the furthest reaches of the remodeled kitchen's teakwood cabinets, runs them under hot water and pours herself a glass.

John sticks his head out of the study and says, smells to me like something good is on the way.

They assemble for dinner, an empty chair at Walt's place. Barbara looks from one preoccupied face to another.

Must be reading up a storm in there, Ellen glances up at John and takes a delicate sip from her glass.

Yep, John nods. I think I got a knack for this legal stuff. Must've missed my calling.

Is that right? Ellen wipes at her mouth with a napkin.

Case after case, he stabs the air with his fork, these people all seem to have one thing in common.

Which is? Ellen twirls her fork playfully at the linguini.

They all seem to have been connected with the selling of the marijuana. When they're found guilty in the criminal case, it seems forfeiture is automatic. Again, the forfeiture is a civil case. The drug trafficking is a criminal case.

And, Barbara asks, what's the difference?

The difference, says John with a mouthful of pasta and pawing at his plate with fork, is that for the criminal case, it's up to the prosecution to prove guilt. But for the *civil* forfeiture case, the burden of proof shifts to the defendant. Just like Clem said. And the defendant is the damned land.

I'm really starting to worry about Walter, Ellen glances at the clock over the sink.

Maybe he's cutting lawns with Clyde, Barbara suggests.

Ellen glances up sharply at Barbara.

Did he mention that to you?

No, Barbara shrugs. Just a thought.

John, he say anything to you about working for Clyde? Ellen inquires as John wraps a heap of pasta onto his fork, head in hand, indifferent to the new turn in conversation.

It's just my wild guess, momma, Barbara says.

The dinner is delicious- the fresh herbs and garlic enrich the sauce, fresh-baked bread, the Merlot a fine complement- and yet Barbara can't wait to leave the table.

John inquires about Ellen's day and Ellen mutters *same old same old* while stabbing at her pasta and staring at her plate.

Patty's kids are just so cute, says Barbara, her enthusiasm obviously forced. Three and five now.

Ellen smiles obligingly. Have they got British accents?

Only a hair, Barbara carries her plate to the sink and says, gonna sit outside for a bit.

John and Ellen clean up the kitchen together. When Ellen has loaded the last plate in the dishwasher, she looks up at John.

Where do you s'pose he is?

I dunno Ellen, I haven't seen him all day. Tell you what though- he pauses a moment from scrubbing vigorously at a pot- I'll bet my bottom dollar he's off to Cindy's. He was telling me they're having trouble.

When?

Just, um, Tuesday I think it was.

They've broken up John, that was over a week ago.

Well, you know how these things go Ellen. Young people. Anyway, I'll bet he's trying to patch things up over there.

She drops her shoulders. Maybe you're right. Just funny he didn't tell anyone where he was going.

*Im*pulse, John says with an air of authority on the subject while toweling the saucepan. Maybe it's a good thing he's *not* back so fast. Must be patching things up.

What do you have on for tomorrow?

Got the morning with Frank, then I'm supposed to meet Clem at his place.

Ellen has a dour look as she closes the dishwasher door.

What? asks John.

I didn't say anything.

But you don't have to. Every time I so much as mention Clem, or, or the case, well... well you can kill a man at ten paces with that look.

I told you I'm fine with Clem, she says matter-of-factly.

You told us, but you sure don't show it.

Dammit, she hisses, I don't need this mind reading right now! One thing at a time, I got a son who's disappeared.

He hasn't disappeared.

I've got parents breathing down my neck on the phone all afternoon, I walked out of the classroom today it got so bad, and now you're not happy with my reactions.

Just try and show a little support once in a while, eh? I'm trying my damndest to keep a roof over our heads, prevent my land from being snatched out from under my nose.

And you think I don't care! Is that it!

I'm the one doing all the research, trying to understand as quickly as-

-I thought that was Clem's job, really-

-It is! It's why I'm meeting him tomorrow for godsakes!

Then just what are you doing? In there.

She nods her head at the study as if it might be harboring some clandestine operation.

I want to walk into Clem's with questions, not like some child waiting to be told everything. I'm trying to understand just exactly what the hell I'm up against.

We're up against.

No. *I'm* up against. Because that's *exactly* how it feels.

He turns on his heels for the study, leaving Ellen to wring her hands.

Will you please just this once not run away? You're always running away. We can't solve anything when you do this.

Maybe you should look at what it is I run away from.

The door to the study is pulled shut, leaving Ellen shaking and sobbing, steadying herself against the kitchen sink.

* * *

Barbara

Their raised voices reaching your ears, you started around the front porch, feet crunching gravel in hurried steps towards the driveway. You thought about driving away, then realized you didn't have the car keys and you sure as hell didn't want to enter the house. You don't want them to think you are running away, they're already worked up enough about Walt. So you enter the house on tiptoes and take the steps two at a time to the upstairs telephone and you dial Renee's number, because that's who you need to talk to right this minute- nobody else will do. You punch her number and hope like hell she's still on *days*, and your heart jumps when she picks up on the second ring.

* * *

Ellen taps on the door to John's study. What's going on, why is she up there packing?

She has to, he says, standing at the other side of the door.

What did we do wrong? She's not happy here?

It's got nothing to do with us. She has to do it for herself.

Hmm.

Look, she's thirty years old. Can't be easy returning home, especially when you're already looking for space from a bad situation.

Bad situation? Everything's a bad situation. You just have to tough it out.

John cracks the door open. Will you just try to be a little more understanding of your daughter.

Don't tell me-

-Will you listen-

-Sssshh! Ellen draws a finger to her lips at the sound of Barbara's footsteps.

Barbara sets the suitcase in the hallway. Her parents both appear in the hallway.

Where are you off to honey? Ellen asks.

I just thought it'd be nice to spend some time with Renee, she says with an unconvincing smile.

Let me help you with that, John hefts the suitcase.

They follow their daughter outside, looking on while she stuffs her few belongings in the hatchback. It's going on nine o'clock.

I feel like I'm abandoning you, Barbara says.

Nonsense, John replies, but it's clear to her his stoicism is only a front. Y'know, it'd do you good to spend some time with Renee. There's not much to do here but wait and see.

Who knows I won't find a job in Knoxville or something.

Will ya stop worrying about that? John pats her shoulder.

I can't just *sit around* all my life. And besides, who's gonna put gas in this old thing.

She waves at them as she backs out of the driveway.

John reaches out to put an arm around his wife, but she's already walking back to the house.

Friday, No Expected Return

Ellen wakes up alone, gathering her robe around her and stepping into the hallway. Walt's door is still open and the bed empty. She gets dressed and made up and goes downstairs to find John at the kitchen table, his head buried in the Tennessean.

Just how strongly, she asks, did you suggest it was about time for him to be moving on?

Now listen, he lowers the newspaper, I did not order him out, or anything close to it.

Ellen bites her lip, taps at the counter.

John says, don't even try to suggest what I said had anything to do with this.

No one's accusing you, she says with the detached tone reserved for clients and acquaintances, retrieving her mini cooler from the fridge. Would you please phone me at the school should he call or return?

Yes.

He tamps down the newspaper, of a mind to call off the meeting with Clem, thinking what's the point. He'll be mostly useless. And besides there's the backlog in the workshop in the basement, with the order of Queen Elizabeth chairs, the Duncan Phyfe dining room set and the custom picture frames. Folding the newspaper and throwing it down resignedly on the table, he paces the kitchen floor. The dog scratches at the backdoor. *C'mon in Sandy, there's a good girl, there's a good girl*, he hugs the dog, pats its head, empties food in the dish. Snatches the keys, locking the door behind him.

When he arrives Clem waves him past Janet and into his private domain behind her three-section desk, asking her to take messages. John has the haggard look of the unshaven.

We've got to talk to Walt, Clem declares with an urgency that pulls John away from toying abstractedly at his fingernails.

Walt?

Yes John.

What's he got to do with anything?

Maybe plenty, Clem leans on the big oak desk, both hands supporting his weight and fingers sprawled. DA opened up to me again. Let's just say Mr. Dawson's getting a little tired of a jail cell, and more comfortable to talk. It's almost certain he's gonna plead guilty. Can't afford a lawyer, can't post bail, and doesn't like the ring of public defender to his ears. DA told me Dawson's getting ready for a plea bargain. That's all strictly off the record.

And just what's he saying?

Clem looks away, drumming his fingers.

Clem, how long've we known each other. Can't you just give me the gist of it?

Well, thing to do is to bring Walt here. Or wait, maybe it's best to go to him. On his grounds. Cause I'm gonna have to ask him some pretty tough questions.

I wish you could give me a damned briefing.

So do I, says Clem, but I can't.

John shifts his weight in the chair.

He's saying Walt's involved in this, isn't he?

Look, why don't you get some rest? Christ, you look as if you haven't caught a wink in a year.

That's about how I feel.

Look, I'll come round there tonight after dinner. Talk to Walt.

Can't do that Clem.

Clem shakes his head uncomprehendingly.

He's um, gone to Knoxville. With Barbara for a few days.

Well, is it so urgent he can't come back?

I know, I *know*. I-I can't reach them right now- he wrings his hands- he's, he's with Barbara, she's got her own, her own... personal issues right now and-

-Call him. I'll ring you tomorrow morning first thing. We have got to get crackin on this. I mean it.

*   *   *

John rubs at the knot in his neck as he swings the pickup off Old Fork Road into the driveway, craning his neck, hopeful eyes probing for the Chevelle parked in its customary position at the very end of the gravel. Empty.

Stepping down from the cab, he fetches the long-handled axe from the bed of the pickup. Walking past the forlorn tractor he stops at the foot of the woods, his head heavy with sleep, and then enters the shade of the pines.

On one such afternoon many years ago a tall, lanky man passed over the edge of darkness into the pines, aluminum tanks of kerosene in each calloused hand. He'd spent the whole of two days digging up that which he had planted with the sort of tired resignation of one who must toil at a task for which there is no expected return. *Shit*, he muttered, placing the kerosene tanks on the barren ground beside his dampened army surplus boots. *Shit, oh well, the war's over, that's what counts. It was a good crop while it lasted, it fed a bank account and a new form of relaxation at the end of a long, hard day in the sun,* thought John Griffith Jr. as he showered piles of the upended hemp fiber with kerosene in preparation for a controlled fire. *Gotta play by their rules,* he thought, while watching flames lick around the dying stalks of hemp. *They needed it for a spell, they don't need it anymore. The Lord giveth and the Lord taketh away.*

*   *   *

Barbara

You yawn and stretch your legs into the colder regions of the sheets, roll over on your side and blink your eyes in disbelief. The digital clock reads 10:47. The other side of the bed is empty. Sleeping in lately, further and further in. You collapse back into the pillows and reflect on workdays, early risings. Responsibility. Stretch your arms and pry yourself from the bed, stepping around the clothing strewn about the hardwood floor. Throwing a robe over your shoulders, you spend the next fifteen minutes plodding around the house unsure of the first thing to do. Maybe that's the part of a work routine that's comforting in a way- stop the grind and you don't know quite what to do with yourself. You start the automatic coffee machine brewing and step outside into autumn scenery- in just a few days it's set in dramatically, all hues of red, orange and yellow. There on the porch is the newspaper Renee must've been in too big a hurry to fetch. You bend over to grab it and wince as a shear of pain pierces your lower back. Rubbing at it, you sit down on one of the wicker rockers and thumb through the pages of the jobs section. There on your lap in front of you is splayed offers of gainful employment- but inside of you there is no determination towards any of it. *Damnable self, I've exposed you by tripping, peeled my ego away so as for you to reveal yourself. It's three weeks and you reveal yourself as nothing.* You turn the page from banking to clerical and the paper won't fold back at the crease. Riled, you fan it, at last thrashing it and flinging it to the ground. Bringing your hand to your mouth and then your knuckles to teeth.

*   *   *

Daddy?
Hey Barb. How are you?
Oh, okay I guess.
Listen, the bank phoned you. About your application.
Oh.
John paces the room, stretching the phone cord. I took a message. They wanted to see if you could start next week.
Next week?
I don't know, seeing as you just got to Knoxville and all, but I just figured it was worth mentioning.
She flops down on the sofa, massaging her knee, sighing. I...I
You all right, honey?
I'm okay.
What's wrong? What is it, Barb?
I'm okay.
What is it Barbara, John asks. Talk to your old man.
It's- he can hear her voice breaking- I don't know.
Don't know what, Barb.
What I'm gonna do.
You mean like, today, or the next hour or-
-Today. Tomorrow. Forever.
Well.
I don't know what I'm gonna do. Things used to seem so plain and simple.
Look, you wanna come home?
No, it's not that. Unless you need me to of course.
You know by God you're always welcome. Just do what's best for yourself.
I don't have a clue what's best for myself.
I wish I knew what to tell you. I'm always here to talk to.
Thanks, Daddy.
For what?

For listening. You got enough troubles of your own.

Yeah, but I'm on the case. Of course I'd love having you around. I mean, you can always float between there and here, or whatever.

Thanks Daddy.

You'll figure something out. I'm sure.

I hope so.

How's your friend Renee?

She's fine.

Well, says John, let me know if you hear anything from your brother.

Likewise. I'm worried.

Look, we're all a little on edge lately.

I'm worried about you and Mom.

Your mother is just going through a hard time right now.

I wish things could be like before. I don't remember ever seeing so much tension.

It's gotten pretty bad I guess. We'll work it out.

I wonder.

You gotta have faith.

Yeah. Maybe.

Things just got crazy after around here after I lost my job.

She needs to get over it. Move on.

Don't I know it.

I just hate to hear all that fussin and fightin.

I know, me too.

Just when he replaces the earpiece to the antique phone, it rings and he snatches it up again. It's Clem and he doesn't waste any time with small talk.

Where's Walt?

Um, not home yet.

What's wrong over there John?

Nothing Clem. Everything right as rain. Just getting ready to hit that workshop, catch up on things.

When can we meet with Walt? He hasn't phoned you yet?

No.

John. Ring him up and get him back here. It's important, very important.

Yes Clem. I hear you. I'm on it.

Let's get crackin.

Right.

John replaces the earpiece and flops down into a chair at the kitchen table, listening to the ticking of the clock as the dog nuzzles his hand. His mind is racing, there's so much to do, but he doesn't even know where to start.

*   *   *

John

Splitting firewood's gone from an obligatory, fundamental survival chore to a more or less recreational activity for a pleasant winter luxury in just a generation. I learned how to swing an axe when I was six years old because we had a lot of wood to cut for what seemed longer and harsher winters. Not having central heat, we made do with the living room fireplace and a pair of Franklin wood-burning stoves- one of these in the kitchen and one in momma and daddy's bedroom, what is now the dining room. The heat generated from these two claw-footed devils was fierce. Peeking in through the little cast-iron door on the front seemed like gazing into the fires of hell. This contained little inferno was supposed to radiate enough heat to rise and warm my sister and I's bedroom- what came to be Barbara's bedroom and now the guest room/office. Most winter nights we ended up on momma and daddy's floor covered in blankets, sleeping soundly as the slow-burning logs daddy had strategically placed became red-glowing embers.

We'd spend whole days chopping and stacking wood. At the end of such afternoons we'd sit in the kitchen with our boots in front of the fire, daddy sniffling and wiping his nose with his shirtsleeve, the smell of ma's beef stew permeating that gathering place. The living room and its fireplace were restricted for use in valley gatherings, holidays and other special occasions. The valley gatherings were memorable in the sense that it was the rare time Daddy'd play his lap dulcimer along with Freddie Ivers on banjo, and Liza McCollister at the upright piano which now sits idle in that same spot in the corner of the living room.

The kitchen became our living room in winter. We rolled everything into it, the Zenith tombstone black dial radio, Daddy's leather-bound King James Bible and Farmers' Almanac and my stack of books, the rocker chair with its accompanying sewing implements- back then we still had our socks darned and jeans knee-patched.

From the Zenith came the programs that would serve to broaden and enrich our lives. It sat among us and eventually came to be more than just a piece of furniture. It was magical, mysterious, more than human. Its mechanical structure fascinated me, stirred a newfound scientific curiosity. I'd remove the back panel and stare mesmerized into its glowing tubes in the chassis, marveling at how its antenna pulled in signals from the very ether and sent them to this wonderful scheme of tubes and transistors, how all the complexity of power in the chassis ended up in two simple wires connected to a metal plate and caused the attached speaker cone to pulsate and produce sound waves that brought the Grand Ole Opry right into our kitchen, or we had The Shadow to bite our nails by, sitting in rapt attention anxiously awaiting the story's next twist or turn.

I gathered books as a squirrel gathers nuts for the winter. Books mostly of a biblical nature, as they were usually obtained exclusively from the parson at the Baptist church we drove to every Sunday in the Ford. Sometimes old man Cotter at the General Store had adventure series- The Rover Boys On A Hunt, or The Hardy Boys in their faraway nominal northern town of Bayport. A Websters dictionary.

Whack! I bring down the axe to the wedge and split one right down the middle.

Back then I could read for hours without saying a word, foregoing homework. I mostly hated school. I grudgingly pored over math, abhorred the schoolteacher Mrs. Sharpton's textbook diatribe on the periphery of that mysterious world of the sciences. I kept suggesting we endeavor to dismantle and rebuild a radio as a more practical and immediate means of understanding the laws of electricity. She wasn't having any of it, suspecting I had the ulterior motive of getting to spend valuable class time listening to the radio. I slept through most book readings as I'd often already read them.

One winter I read nearly fifty books cover-to-cover. My daddy'd marvel at me. Meanwhile he and momma had remained mostly wordless between each other- there was a time when I'd come to believe they weren't even on speaking terms. One day as

I burrowed my face into Huckleberry Finn adventures, my daddy startled me by breaking a particularly long stretch of silence and almost causing me to drop the book on the hardwood floor.

Martha, he'd growled, sucking on his corncob pipe. I'd forgotten my mother's name, for a moment I didn't know who he was addressing.

Momma grumbled a reply.

This here notice from Washington. Sayin we're to sess all cultivatin of hemp. What does sess mean?

It's cease, I said. Cease, and it means to terminate, to discontinue, to... Daddy looked at me quizzically through his reading specks. To stop, I said at last.

He nodded and returned his attention to the letter. Ah, of course. To *cease*, he said with added emphasis, all planting and harvesting of hemp. Destroy in place all existing plants.

Momma's ears perked up. I knew why. This was daddy's biggest crop, he had a handsome government contract to provide hemp for the military during the Second World War.

Why they askin you to do that?

Says here it's illegal. Not fittin with the law.

Let me see those papers I said, sensing the weight of its significance in causing my parents to speak to one another.

Here y'are. Y'can probably make more sense of it than I can.

Daddy's working hands had already tarnished the pristine white government paper. I translated the essentials to him. He had ten days to fully comply with the request by the government to cease all cultivation and harvesting, and to destroy in place all existing hemp plants on his farm. Hemp was now deemed an illegal substance. Otherwise he could face criminal prosecution for growing the plant.

He was pissed. Back then my sister Mary was too young to fully understand- she thought he was upset because he'd come to enjoy cutting the flowering plant off of the stalks, drying them and then smoking them in his corn cob pipe in front of the stove at night. He said it calmed him down and made him slow to argue. He'd sit there night after night in the winter with the Bible on his lap, circling words he didn't understand. Asking me about them before I went to bed, or sometimes if he remembered he'd ask while we were gathering wood.

There was and probably still is a grove of pines next to Buck's Creek. The pines my great grandfather John had planted became a full forest, with a soft blanket of needles underfoot. My sister Mary and I would camp out there a lot in the summer. A mattress of dead and fallen pine needles under the old Army tent- a gift to daddy from the U.S. government for his participation in its production during World War II. There's a good chance some of the hemp fiber in the tent sprouted from the very land it stood on. The fresh pine-scented air as I told ghost stories, frightening my little sister to the point of bolting back to the house- and then begging her to make up one of her silly poems.

In the spring and summer Daddy'd sit on the front porch cradling the pipe in his palm, gazing up at the night sky. Momma and Daddy seemed to speak to each other more often then, it was as if they too thawed and became warm with the air. Sometimes I'd hear them on the porch or later in my bedroom, the muffled sound of their voices drifting up and lulling me to sleep.

Wham! I split the last log clean through and imagine my son returning with the wheelbarrow to pick up the final load.

My son, who without my permission allowed some punk he very seldom hung around with grow some marijuana on our property. Money changed hands, he's told me. This fact will more than likely come out in Dawson's criminal trial. And the finger that points at Walt will inevitably point at me, with the burden of proof that I in fact didn't have any knowledge or consent of my son's paltry but no less significant agreement with Dawson. The property's been tainted.

My son Walt spent most of last summer sitting on his ass perfecting the fine art of doing nothing. I allowed it. And now, to put the horrible icing on a distasteful fruitcake, he's brought to my attention the fact that all these months he was involving my land, my family's land, in an illegal and covert activity for a few hundred dollars a month. And guess who's paying for it now? As if coughing up funds for an unutilized Communications degree in Chapel Hill, Partytown wasn't enough. If I'd known more about what I was sending him into before he'd been accepted, I'd never have let him enroll there. Right now I'm doing my level best to resist the urge to strangle him, choke the very life out of him. Or maybe strangle him just until the brink of death then ease off at the last second- maybe that would be just enough to wake up his better judgment, restore a sensibility, make him born again with a new awareness of self and responsibility to those around him and society at large, charge him with a new zest for life, a sort of newfound purpose. Perhaps the worst thing a parent can do is favor one child over another, but I simply cannot deny the facts. Will is up at MIT on a full academic scholarship. I picture my other son at an oak table in the library poring over a technical book, on his way to another perfect grade. Walt barely scraped by at UNC, God only knows what he was doing half the time there.

Will spent about two months this summer in Chapel Hill, Walt's old Partyville. In lieu of any all-night drinking binges, he'd worked an internship at 3M he'd been offered before he began college. Meanwhile Walt was home sleeping most of the time.

But parents are not supposed to openly esteem one child over another, that's what our child-rearing instruction books said.

That's it, I say to myself and the forest, gathering up the last bits of split wood and thinking is it not part of human nature to differentiate, draw comparisons to establish preferences, don't we need some sort of benchmark for any rational opinion? How can you possibly avoid making discriminations between your own progeny?

*   *   *

Barbara

Have you, umm... ever been with another woman before? you ask Renee, tapping your cigarette at the ashtray. I guess I never knew you to show an interest in women before. At school.

I never knew either of us to sleep with anyone other than guys, Renee says, pushing her chair back and bringing a knee up to her chin. But that doesn't answer your question, does it.

You tamp out your cigarette and cock an eyebrow. Renee draws a deep sigh.

Fact is, yes. I've been with a woman. Actually, I have a relationship.

Right now?

Yes. Her name's Margaret. Meg, for short. We've been going out on and off for almost three years.

Uh huh…

Does that bother you, Renee wants to know.

No, you say but it sounds unconvincing even to your ears. Where does she live?

She's in Houston right now.

Why so much space between you?

Her job took her there. Three months ago. On temporary assignment. She'll be moving back in November.

She live here?

Here, as in Knoxville. We've both had our own space, we like to keep it that way for now.

Listen, Renee, I don't... I don't want to get in the way.

You're not.

I mean about staying here. We never talked about that.

What we have, let's enjoy. I like being with you, you like being with me. Why not just chill out here for the next week, take your mind off of Bill, your family's problems, see if you can scare up anything for work in the meantime.

I don't know what I wanna do, Renee. It's scary.

Well, you've kind of upended your life.

Of course, but I just don't know where I want to be. And meanwhile my father phoned this morning and told me the bank offered to start me working next week.

So whadaya gonna do? Renee unburies her face from her knee and looks up sharply.

Oh I dunno. I really don't know.

        *   *   *

Ellen'd left for a church meeting, saying something about the First Grace Episcopal Church's congregation thinking she's a widow. It's turned a little chilly as John watches the sun set over the tree line on the front porch in the rocking chair, that turning point night when you begin to feel winter coming on. Lonesome in what are quiet surroundings, save for a few odd barks from the dog, who's out back on a leash. Shivering, he rubs his thin arms and is about to go inside and fetch a sweater when Clem's 4x4 crawls up the drive. Shit, he thinks, was he supposed to call Clem and forgotten to? When Clem hops out of the truck and walks up in front of him John says, I don't know where he is.

Clem's eyes blink a few times under the wire-frames as he stands stiffly. Sorry to hear that.

Get you a drink?

Sure.

Before he even got to the wood chopping, John had spent the better part of the morning helping Frank Lynn haul that huge furnace from the Blaylock estate, and he feels it in his back and knees when he crouches at the liquor cabinet to fetch a dwindling bottle of whiskey. The house feels warm, and John hopes it stays so- he can't bear the thought of Clem knowing he's too short on cash to have the furnace repaired. He returns to the porch with the whiskey and two tumblers and after he's poured they sit side by side in the rocking chairs.

Clem pulls at his moustache. How long's he been gone?

Um, about two days.

He seem upset about anything?

Lots of things. Problem is the kid doesn't talk.

He imagines Walt driving on a back road in Kentucky, or Alabama, or North Carolina- a frightened fugitive, an outlaw, just a kid with a guilty face.

I've been thinking, Clem says, swirling his glass. Not that it matters a hill of beans anyway, but there's a good possibility of an informer here.

Informer?

Yep.

I don't understand.

I mean maybe someone tipped the feds about Dawson using your property.

But why would someone do that?

Because, says Clem, there's money in it. A portion of the proceeds on the sale of your land and house.

Shit, John muses, I can't imagine who would do a thing like that.

Could've been anyone. Anyone who saw him go in or out of there.

But it's so damned remote, Clem. People just don't find themselves driving around there. Even when they're lost.

Exactly. Which means it'd almost have to be somebody who knew Tim. Or whoever it was growing those plants in that meadow.

John glances up sharply. What do you mean *whoever it was?* I thought it was dead certain Dawson was the one growing it.

Clem shakes his head. I don't think there's enough hours in the day for that boy to squeeze it in, what with two full-fledged dealing operations going between Knoxville and Nashville.

Then who the hell was helping him?

Clem draws himself another glass of bourbon. We've got to find Walt.

Saturday, For What It's Worth

Could it be that we are masters of our own destiny and as such can act as the engineer of our own undoing? Might it be that a forgotten phone call to a supplier, a missed deadline when the employees complained about the overtime required to meet it, or the sick day for a bout of sniffles, were merely the subconscious acting boldly where the conscious wasn't up to the task for a man dis-enamored of his job, his lot in life? It is with these thoughts that John plumbs through a stack of old stationary with Imperial letterhead boldly stamped. Had Ellen known something all along that he hadn't with regard to this? Could she see something inside of him trumped by the responsibility of providing for three kids-something slowly eating him alive at Imperial, then finishing him off with the arrival of the sharks from the North? Boys in suits from tidy suburban towns on the outskirts of Boston and New York in houses fully-rigged with modern conveniences, situated in exemplary school districts. Men with ties of good silk, leather-bound cases. Those men of polished shoes and department-store after-shave lotion. They whose secretaries booked flights on the spur of the moment to Knoxville and to whom John would leave the plant and drive the thirty miles to fetch, bring them back for a round of meetings concerning expansion, new plant construction, modernizing. John would gape at the sight of his beaten shoes, but somehow never got around to polishing them.

He shuffles papers around on his desk, grabs a stack and flings it at the wall. Paces about the room and then pulls the chair up in front of his desk, dropping his head to his hands.

A light knock at the study door, and Ellen peeks in. Are you okay?

Yep, he says. What's up?

I just hung up with Miriam. They've invited us for dinner later.

John glances at her over the rim of his reading glasses and smiles. Ellen smiles back.

*   *   *

You're cramming your clothes into the backpack with the awkwardness of one leaving arbitrarily.

So I guess you've made your decision.

I think it's best- you say, stuffing a pair of socks in the backpack and zipping it up- I mean for now anyway.

May I ask why? I mean, there's so many opportunities in Knoxville. I know it's not New York, or Boston, but-

-Look, Renee. It's really very kind of you and all, it's not that I don't appreciate it. It's just, well, Walt isn't back and still no word from him. Daddy's even thinking about calling the police. I'm worried about the strain on him.

I know, I understand. I just don't see exactly how it is you can help him.

Maybe just by being there.

Is that really all this is about?

Maybe.

Maybe?

Look, Renee... I-I don't know all what I'm feeling since, since you-

Since I told you about Meg?

It's a new thing for me. All of this.

I see.

We're both confused.

Renee looks out the window at the surrounding wooded hills that border her immense back yard. I'll miss you, she says at the window, there's a mournfulness in her tone that startles you, you'd imagined desire weighed heavy only on her end. You want to lay a hand on her shoulder, but only fidget with the backpack.

Oh well, Renee says, you gotta do what you gotta do. You gonna take that job at the bank?

Part time, yeah. Way to make ends meet for a while.

Sure. Just come and see me sometimes.

Of course. Look, I'll be back this weekend, how's that?

Renee turns, blonde strands of hair falling haphazardly in her mouth, speaks. Promise?

*   *   *

If he doesn't show up by tomorrow, Clem reaches for the gravy, call the police. Missing persons report.

You think that's a good idea? John toys with his salad.

Absolutely.

Why wouldn't that be a good idea, asks Ellen.

John drops his fork, shrugs. I'm just wondering if it's too early to go bothering them about it.

John, it's been two days without a word.

Miriam grabs Ellen's hand, strokes it gently. You've both been under a lot of strain, Ellen. Sometimes we just don't think clearly in times like this.

What would you know about times like this, thinks Ellen, *your simple life as a country lawyer's wife hasn't been completely upended.*

Ellen, says John, we'll get away soon. I've been thinking about what you said the other day.

Ellen looks up from her plate, a blank look on her face.

About getting away. Maybe this Christmas we'll all four of us do something completely different. Crazy.

I have this client- Clem waves his fork while downing a mouthful- keeps buggin me to make use of this fancy chalet he's got tucked away in the Smokies. Never have taken im up on it. Darn shame.

Miriam spoons mashed potatoes and gravy onto her plate. Oh yes. Old McWhirter.

Well now Miriam, he's not so much older than us- Clem wipes at his mouth- yeah, damned shame too. He brings it up every time I do his legal work. Every year. Look, waddya say we head out there this Thanksgiving?

John glances across the table at Ellen. I don't see why not.

Ellen shrugs. You mean it, Clem?

Good Lord, Ellen. You oughta know when Clem Carter says something, he darned well means it.

By the time Clem and Miriam see them off, it's almost eleven o'clock. To be conscious of the speed limit while driving these familiar county roads is strange to John Griffith who, like most locals knows every curve and bend, is only hampered by the out-of-towner, the city tourist taking in the breathtaking sight of the Cumberland Plateau. Tonight he want to avoid even a remote chance of running into the law, shifts his eyes between the slowly incoming blacktop and the speedometer on his way back from

Jamestown. Listening to Ellen talk about things which he hasn't heard her speak of for a long time, not earth-shattering things but simple ones, things that require nothing but a nod of affirmation. John resolves to languish in this leisurely pace. Hearing his wife's soft voice and easy words alongside him as he floats along at slow speed has a relaxing effect and all at once there's tears in his eyes.

What's wrong, Ellen riffles through her handbag, draws a tissue. What is it, honey?

Do you believe me?

Believe you about what?

About the pot. The plants.

Well of course. I can't imagine why I shouldn't.

It's just, that first day, when I came home and you told me about the notice.

Oh God John, I was in shock. I was in absolute shock.

And now?

She lets go a sigh. I was talking to Bob Ryan, you know the new principal? Yesterday it was. He said these cases are pretty much impossible to defend.

Clem told us that.

Oh I know, John. It's just, sometimes you have to hear it from somebody else, someone not so close to you. Sometimes easier to listen, sometimes it's easier to talk to strangers.

Wish we could talk a little easier sometimes, he replies while turning off Old Fork Road and into the driveway.

She lays a hand on his shoulder. I know I haven't exactly been the easiest person to live with. Lately.

We've both been under a lot of strain lately.

Well for what it's worth, I'm sorry John.

He can't believe it, from Ellen's tongue those two words sound like a foreign language. He kills the engine and they sit in the dark cab of the pickup in silence, neither of them reaching for the door handle. Yeah, he says at last. Me too.

Sunday, Missing Gaps

The first frost arrived last night. In the pre-dawn stillness John stood out back staring at the glistening grass beginning to thaw in the morning sun. He considered going back to bed then figured what's the point, just end up laying there eyes shut but mind open wide. Open to all the noise in his head- the phone call to the sheriff about a son gone missing for three days, mortgage payments yet to go on the remodeling and addition to the house, homelessness and dire need, having to tell his sister Mary and son Will up in Boston that his life has taken an unexpected turn into a dead end- a fifty-something without a job or prospects and no home as he nears the end of his useful working life.

Barbara spent another night at Renee's. She'd started for the car with her backpack, and felt a sudden compulsion to get a bottle of wine, it being a cool and crisp Saturday night and Renee off Sunday. Well, she thought with her hand on the door handle, why the hell not? Renee's face brightened as she started walking up the stone path to the front porch. They finished the bottle of wine and then another. They watched a clear night sky with a full moon in it while Renee strummed drunkenly, lazily on her guitar. They collapsed exhausted in each other's arms under a patchwork quilt drawn from of a chest of such winter accouterments.

In the morning she drives home. It's past noon when she walks into the kitchen and is greeted by a nod from her father, who has the phone cradled in his ear.

I just wanna know where my boy is Sam, now do your godamned duty.

John glances over at her, shrugging his shoulders.

Y'know, the more I get into this Sam, the more I smell a rat. Maybe you can tell me who it was snitched to the DEA about Dawson using my land. Meanwhile, he says getting to his feet, I'll phone the authorities in Knoxville about my missing son. Maybe they'll be quicker to get off their asses.

John slams the phone back in the cradle, his back to her.

Hello Barb. Welcome back, he says, his voice tinged with irony.

It's really getting to you, isn't it?

Doesn't look good.

But we've got Uncle Clem-
-Yeah, yeah, we've got Clem, but Clem isn't God.
What's this about a snitch?
John shakes his head slowly.
Nothing certain. Clem has a hunch someone tipped off the feds. Reward money in it.
Reward money?
Yeah. Informants get a pretty good part of the proceeds.
I don't get it. Proceeds from what?
Sale of the forfeited assets. The house. The land.
Who would do a thing like that?
John clasps his hands together under his chin and closes his eyes. He says, usually the local authorities.

After Ellen and Barbara prepare an early Sunday dinner of roast, potatoes, green beans, and buttered rolls, John shuffles off to the living room and the recliner. Ellen pulls the ottoman up under his feet and throws a blanket over him.
Sorry, he mutters, let me know if there's a call...
Don't be sorry, John.
I- I've got to do something.
Sssh. There's nothing to do but wait.
She kisses him lightly on the forehead.
Get some rest.

John is soon fast asleep in the recliner as the sinking sun in the living room's picture window gives way to an autumn chill and another frosted night. On the television the football game at low volume. Barbara throws an old shawl over her shoulders and looses her auburn hair from under the collar. She determines to build a fire as her mother lies curled up on the sofa under a quilt. Off to the barn, beside which lies a dwindling stack of firewood. She bundles a stack of split pieces against her chest, sets them on the steps and forages the woods for kindling. In the living room, amid the light snoring of her parents, she builds a fire. The phone rings.

She scurries off to the kitchen, catching it just before it can ring a third time. It's Will and he's surprised to hear her voice at the other end.

She tells Will that Bill's on a business trip and she thought she'd take the opportunity to drop down for a visit. When John takes the phone he tells Will that his brother is at Gavin Sharpe's and that there's nothing new and everything's just fine. When Ellen takes the phone she says the same.

After she's hung the phone up, as John lays a fresh log on the fire, Ellen says, why don't we just tell him?

I don't want to disrupt his studies.

But doesn't it kill you to keep this locked up? From him? From Mary? She's all the family you got.

I got family enough right here in this room.

She shakes her head and flops on the couch, as if a joke's been told and she doesn't get it.

John feels another nap coming on, would that it were just another Sunday night to wake up to, a cozy fire and a few shots of bourbon before an early turn-in and a Monday morning in the basement finishing cast-off pieces, remnants from the houses of the dead. How many fires graced that hearth, how many Sunday nights before another week at the mill did he sit reading thrillers, mysteries while Ellen went the *I'm OK You're OK* route on the couch just opposite? How they loved to read when the kids had all left the nest, and it was only when Walt was back those last three summers that the television would impede such tranquility. However much it might irritate John, he bore it in silence. Put up with it, as with so much of Walt's behavior these last three years. Lumped in with the heavy sleep schedule, the television left little time for the lawn cutting, house painting and the other odd summer jobs his son occasionally mustered up the energy for. But there were still missing gaps.

Monday, Let's Get Up and Run Away

This, says Sarah Witherspoon, is the break room. There's the coffee maker and you'll find condiments and everything here in the cabinets.

The room is windowless and bleak. Barbara can envision lonely sandwich meals, the peak-time teller with a break opposite everyone else. Just as well- she'd prefer not to be subjected to idle conversation over children, shopping, weather and problematic mother-in-laws.

Cars pull in at the drive up, deposits and withdrawals, ingoing outgoing, the exchange of commerce, the flow of money through Barbara's hands. Computers facilitate transactions, and there are procedures for which there is a neatly printed manual. So there's on-site teller training for Barbara, whose previous banking experience has allowed the bank to condense the usual three-day teller training to a half-day at the Knoxville branch this morning, and now there's an afternoon with Sarah Witherspoon, Barbara looking over her shoulder observing, then her looking over Barbara's correcting. At first she's not too crazy about this peak-time teller position, but after a few goes at the simulated computer she reminds herself it's only three afternoons a week, only for money. And Sarah's cheerful enough, if over-polite. That professional distance which precludes asking straight-out *what are you doing here anyway Barbara*. But of course there will be plenty of break room postulating between Sarah and the other employees. In one day, she has learned her job. Well, maybe not mastered the data input routines on the massive hulk of a computer in front of her, but she'd drawn up cheat sheets along the way.

Thanks, she says to Sarah outside when she's locking and double-checking the doors after they've closed the bank.

My pleasure. You're a fast learner. Nice to have you on board.

Barbara dashes to her car just at the onset of a downpour. Soaked to the skin moments later, she fires up the engine, thinks about going home, wonders where that is.

*   *   *

Frank Lynn sold him a punished Duncan Phyfe dining room set for next to nothing this morning. Just fifty bucks, and when he handed it to Frank, Frank studied it and then crushed it into John's palm and said with a wink- ah hell, you're doing me a favor taking this old thing off my hands.

So he's in the basement wearing plastic protective glasses as the electric sander buzzes away along chairs and tables and the ventilator fan pulls dust out the window. Restoring the sculpted wood, infusing beauty back into where it once was. Focused on nothing but wood and curves as the radio plays Vivaldi, Schubert, Shostakovich, Stravinsky. He'll be mindful of the pressure applied to the electric sander, he'll plod along as always with hand sanding the little curves, the little nooks and crannies along the legs of the table. He'll run his hand along its baby-smooth surface checking for knots or little missed spots, humming to himself as he mixes the coat of varnish, leaving the exhaust fan running to empty the fumes.

On the workbench is a slab of wax for candle-making and that is in the cards for this week. They may be dropped round the Rugby General Store as all of the handcrafted candles he dropped off at mid-summer have sold. All of this hustle-and-bustle on-the-fly entrepreneurship hasn't exactly made him a staple in the community, placed him on board the Chamber of Commerce or elected him to office in the Jaycees, but it has given him a sense of holding his fate in his own hands. And with one piece of paper posted to his front door that feeling has been stripped away like one strips away at old varnish leaving just a dull bare wood.

Barbara hollers down from the top of the basement stairs, *I'm home, I'm home Daddy*, and he wonders if she really is- *home*. He wonders if any of them can consider themselves home anymore. She perches on the topmost cellar steps and asks, watcha doin?

Gettin back to my own work. Kinda takes my mind off things, he says. How'd things go at the bank?

Well, you know, it's money.

John purses his lips and nods, well-acquainted with such resigned sentiment- *it's money*, that's exactly what he said to Ellen when he started clearing out the houses of the dead with Frank Lynn four years ago. Barbara says it's already after seven o'clock and she'll put the dinner on, leaving him stirring a can of varnish. The phone rings and he jumps up from his workbench, takes the stairs two at a time, waits with a hopeful stare as Barbara cups her hand over the mouthpiece and nods.

But it isn't Walt nor is it about Walt. It's merely a message concerning the cancellation of Ellen's womens group meeting at the Grace Episcopal Church. Barbara replaces the receiver, draws a chair and sits drumming her fingers on the kitchen table.

We've got to find him, she says.

How?

I'm going to pay a visit to Walter's room for a start. Call it invasion of privacy, but I'll shoulder the blame. I just want to see if I can find any clues- she heaves a sigh- then I'm going to pay a visit to Cindy.

What do you think you're going to find there in his room? I mean besides empty cigarette packs and rolling papers? Might as well make sure he got rid of all the pot.

She shakes her head. Oh our Walt. Whatever are we going to do with him?

Later, opening the door on her brother's dark tomb, she gets right down to business. Underneath the bed lie crumb-ridden plates and glasses with milk residue. Clothes are strewn about the floor, piles of books as well, pages marked by pieces of Marlboro packs. She pushes on the window to allow some fresh air in and decides to start in the big oak desk, the top of which is heavily laden with old magazines, crumpled papers. More dirty plates and glasses. Underneath the desktop, a top drawer and a side cabinet. She flings open the top drawer and finds a ruler, a few Bic pens and a mechanical pencil. She runs her hand along the back of the drawer. Finding nothing there, she pulls open the side cabinet. At the front of a pile of mess- an address book and sheets of paper filled with what appear to be song lyrics. She fans the pages with a grim idea about plumbing through the melancholy-laden prose of suicide victims for clues. Were things that bad with ole Walter, and nobody saw it? Was all that sleeping and television viewing not just a phase but indication of a long and haunting depression? The thought that her brother might just turn up dead is hardly a comfort as she stops fanning the paper at a random page-

Don't let them into your bed, don't let them fuck with your head,
Let's just be ourselves today, let's get up and run away.

Jesus, she thinks, a little dilettante, ole Walt. She scans the rest of it, page by page. Just a lot of angst and anti-society ranting, nothing new there. Nothing very dark, even a few stabs at humor. Nothing's dated. Nothing to suggest in any way that the writer might be toying with the idea of doing himself in. Not to her eyes anyway. She places the sheets on the desktop, plunges her hand to the back of the cabinet, yanks out the remaining contents and they spill onto the floor. She flops indian style on the dusty carpet in front of them. Something in the pile of mess catches her eye, that familiar six-leafed plant, and she draws a tiny pamphlet that stops her breath-

Grow Your Own, A Guide to Cultivating Cannabis

Under the pamphlet lay more guides in the same vein, she leafs through them. There among the pile lays a notebook and on its pages scrawled notes in Walt's hand, showing dates, prunings, waterings.

Shit, she mutters. Shit, shit, shit.

*   *   *

There was a time not long after after his wife died in his tired farmer arms that Seamus Griffin considered selling his lot in Tennessee and going back up to the industrial North with his only son to join his aging father, brothers and assorted cousins in Boston. But it only took a few letters written in his brother's aching, calloused laborer hands to dispel such notions.

Padraic Griffin's letters were now wrinkled and yellowed but survived four generations in the Griffin attic trunk, and John would read those letters to his father on winter nights around the hearth. Letters in neat cursive hand which unfailingly began with an apology for the lapse in time between them and then went on to say Padraic hadn't but glanced at his fiddle, his calloused hands were too tired and beat up to rosin the bow, much less press the strings to the neck. Sixteen-hour workdays and still barely enough money pooled between the lot of them sleeping on floors in run-down flats with leaky toilets and mice traffic. Seamus must have read these letters with great dejection, because though his letters in response are quite possibly buried away in someone else's attic in Boston, Padraic's reference to them indicated more than one invitation extended to them to make the journey south through Appalachia and back to their farming roots. Perhaps Padraic and his family believed that their new start required an unequivocal denouncement of their former agricultural life, or supposed that although they were now the ones paving the streets, working the factory lathes, and emptying the multifarious garbage waste of the new industrial dynamo; their sons would be the ones supervising such menial monotony, and their sons' sons would ascend to ownership of enterprise. Whatever their reasons, none of them joined the young widower and his only son. In the first years, he probably struggled. Knoxville was a burgeoning city within range for horse and buggy. Whatever gaps exist with the absence of any personal written record from John Jr., it can be deduced that Seamus' only son John Griffin Sr. worked extremely hard. The surviving farm records reveal that he raised chickens, cattle, pigs, corn, tomato, peppers, beans, kept a team of horses for tilling and riding into the small settlement of Jamestown and longer excursions to market in Knoxville. He hired farmhands and paid them decent wages. Around 1920 John Jr.'s scrawled handwriting replaced that of his father's in the farm ledgers. The figures in the ledger columns swelled and then diminished somewhat under the reign of John Griffin Jr., John's grandfather, who died at fifty-one years of age, when John was six. John would only remember him as bedridden with rheumatoid arthritis and a liver ravaged by alcohol. The grandfather slept in the same room as his parents, what's now the dining room, while John and Mary hid themselves away from death underneath blankets in the drafty room upstairs. Now, having extracted the mess from Walt's room, Barbara sits on her bed in this very room without the benefit of furnace heat, and the chill is no longer negligible. Winter is fast approaching and the twelve-thousand dollar check her father mailed off seems to have only bolstered an inclination towards frugality. She holds Walt's scrawled farming ledgers in her hand and notices the dates are all for 1988 through 1990, from May through August. Damn you Walt, damn you silly fool of a brother, damn you for playing with matches and setting everything to blaze, damn you for your want of the quick buck, easy money. *Damn, damn, damn*, she whispers as footsteps sound on the stairs.

  Daddy?

  Where are you?

  In the guest room.

  John appears at the doorframe rubbing his hands together against the chill. What is it, he asks.

  You better sit down.

He draws the desk chair and straddles it with his forearms perched over the backrest.

She says, there's more to this than Dawson.

What?

My um, my search... has turned up something I think you ought to know about.

She hands him the notebooks and the pamphlet, wringing her hands as if to rub off the taint of malefaction. He studies the pamphlet and books, dropping them to the floor in turn until he pores over the cultivation ledger. He clears his throat and drums a fist on his knee.

We've got to burn this.

Which?

All of it.

Daddy, think it over.

I don't need to think it over.

But what if he's gone to the police?

John shakes the ledger, and drops his head to his arm. Oh dear God, he says.

Why would he even need to keep such records? Barbara looks incredulous. I mean after the first summer, you'd think he'd have gotten a knack for things.

Walt can't remember what he did yesterday, John gathers the other books off the floor and starts for the hallway. Barb, let's ransack that room. Make sure it's clear of any more of this crap. I already have a fire going to throw these into.

She follows her father out into the hallway. He pauses at Walt's door, says, not a word about this to your mother.

*   *   *

I'm freezing, Ellen announces.

John resurfaces from a dead sleep in the recliner to find Ellen silhouetted against the harsh hall light, the dying embers in the hearth behind her.

C'mere, he mumbles. I'll get wood. Build new one, fire...

This is no way to live.

What time is it? he asks, yawning and rubbing his eyes.

Two thirty in the morning.

Right. I'll call the service in the morning.

You coming to bed?
Why not sleep here? I mean just for tonight.
Sleep on what?
I'll rekindle this fire. We can pull the mattress down and-
-John, we're not teenagers.
Just for tonight, he says.

      *   *   *

Barbara

You lay in the dark dead of night like a mummy- wrapped in blankets, body warm and face cold. You cannot sleep. It's not the cold that keeps you awake, but your racing mind. You curse that fireside cup of coffee you had before bed because it's making your stomach churn and your mind race with a negative taint on everything. But where, after all, is the silver lining in this cloud? Turn over on your side and think of calling Renee. Decide against it. Wonder about just where it is your brother might be sleeping tonight. Surely Cindy knows something. There's a rustle of wind and a branch from the sycamore tree scrapes at the window. The quiet of an autumn night in Tennessee was meant to be savored, out of Bill's bed and in your own peaceful rest. Instead you finger your wedding band and wonder just when you'll have the guts to remove it. In the morning you'll make a trip to the ATM and withdraw three hundred dollars from the joint checking account to cover the cost of the furnace repair. Your father will protest, but you'll lie to him that you've got plenty of money. You worry about your father, worry about your mother, worry about what happens next with Bill. The alarm clock reads two-twenty. Giving up on sleep for the moment, you reach for the bedside table and switch the light on. Beside it lays that hodgepodge of papers- your brother's bits of sophomoric prose. You reach for them and thumb through the stack again, not knowing where to begin, at last settling on the beginning. A few pages in, your eyes begin to get heavy. And there wedged between the pages- a piece of loose-leaf paper folded in half. How was it you missed this one, a letter written in almost illegible cursive-

Cindy,

I have been trying to call you for days now, and I guess it's just time to put it all down on paper. Why it is that you choose to abandon me at such a time of crisis I'll never know. But I would like to know, and on these dreadful nights I lay awake and wonder why it is you stayed with me so long. I wonder about this more and more and I hope it's not the devious reason stuck in my mind tonight as I sit to write a letter to someone who doesn't even answer my phone calls. Sorry about the lateness of my call last night, but I don't know when else to catch you. I hope

And there it ends, there's just a few more words that have been scratched out with such force as to penetrate the loose-leaf paper. You sigh and place the unsent letter in your lap. Picking it up again with eyes that can barely stay open, you reread it. *Devious reason.* You wonder what the reason stuck in his head is all about. Just before giving in to sleep, you resolve to pay a visit to Cindy's place after work tomorrow. You have no doubt that it's the first stop on Walt's flight.

Tuesday, A Fork In The Road

The morning dew glistens while yielding to the rising sun on the Cumberland Plateau, as all around this remote region in East Tennessee the few remaining birds chirp their song to the chilly morning air and those who awaken to encounter whatever it is the day may bring. Just off of Old Fork Road, the windows of the Griffith household begin to glow with light. From the mantle above the fieldstone hearth in the kitchen hang ancient cast iron implements- tongs, sturdy-handled pots and crockery, and a huge stirring spoon. Collectively they appear more like museum pieces. This primordial fieldstone hearth sits in the wall opposite that of a wall of modern appliances- electric stove, dishwasher, double sink, blender, toaster, can opener, automatic coffee maker which now chokes and gasps at the end of its brewing cycle. John squats before a bundle of sticks and twigs while layering larger pieces of split wood amid the snap and crackle of the fire in the old hearth. Hovering behind him, Barbara has a clear view of the crown of a balding head with hair thinning to gray.

Daddy, let me pay for the furnace.

It's not your responsibility.

Neither was my college education.

I chose to see it as my responsibility.

And I choose to see this as my responsibility.

John fidgets, rubs his chin. Look, he says, when I really need it, I'll come to you for it.

I don't need to wait for it to come to that. So take it now.

Look honey, I just don't want to be the cause of any more friction between Bill and you.

I'll deal with that. You know he'd give it to you anyway, he'd do anything...

As her words trail off she's left with a sense of contrition at the realization that for all of his shortcomings as a husband, Bill made a decent enough son-in-law.

Look, she says at last, I'm training at the bank until three and then I'm going to pay Cindy a little visit. I might just stay at Renee's and come up for work in the morning.

She fetches her handbag from the small marble stand just beside the front door in the hallway. Tell you what, I'll just leave a blank check.

Barb, it's really not necessary.

She scrawls her signature at the bottom of the check, tears it from the checkbook and leaves it on the kitchen table.

Look, John says, if you ever want to talk about it.

About what?

You know, you and Bill.

I'm not sure you'd want to hear it.

Is it another woman?

Barbara shakes her head lightly, a wry smile. No.

John lays a skinny pine log in the fire, and its sap makes it pop like a firecracker.

I guess, Barb says, we just don't see eye to eye on much.

Money?

Barbara shakes her head. We have enough of that.

Kids?

I couldn't bring a kid into the mess that is our lives. Oh Daddy, Bill hates his job, he feels stuck, and all he ever did was take it out on me.

He ever hit you?

She fingers her bead necklace. Yeah. Just once.

*   *   *

"The Government is permitted to use hearsay to prove probable cause for instituting forfeiture suit."- 21 U.S.C.A. S881(a)(7)

She had to chase down Cindy's address from information. Neither of her parents had ever chanced to drop by her place for even a brief visit. From what she could tell, Cindy hadn't dropped in on them much either. And those few occasions when she did were mainly spent cooped up with Walt in his twelve square foot domain. When Barbara asked her father about Cindy's mother he merely shrugged, and she was startled at the fact that he could be so in the dark. A four-year involvement, and nobody really knew anybody. And from what she could glean from Walt's unfinished letter, that was pretty much the case between he and Cindy.

She lights a cigarette and rolls down the window to allow the heat of the sun to be stirred by cool crisp autumn air, wishes she were on an open highway out west driving among new vistas with fresh eyes instead of here on the old familiar pot-holed road to Knoxville. At the Gas n Go she spreads the map on the trunk while filling her tank and uses the street index and then the grid to locate Cindy's street in Maynard, an outlying suburb just south of Knoxville. She realizes she's embarked to a destination with no idea what she will say when she arrives, or if Cindy will even be there to say anything to. Repeated phone calls last night and this morning yielded nothing but a voice on an answering machine. And now Walt's older sister springing herself at Cindy's doorstep with a load of questions. But what questions? Well, where the hell is Walt for starters.

It's almost four o'clock so she's just in time for Knoxville rush hour traffic, cars crawling around the bypass and then she's dropped into the stop-and-go traffic of route 135 heading south, wrestling with the map between tiny advances. After the highway and a series of winding back roads, she comes upon a strip mall shopping center and at last the final turn, down another winding road and then into the parking lot of a non-descript apartment complex. Why, she wonders, do these places always seem to be painted the same drab shade of beige? The Whispering Oaks sign is chipped and birdshit-stained, like the picnic tables and terraces of the ground level apartments. She imagines her brother coming and going here. Did he feel out of place here in Whispering Oaks, himself a country boy raised among the tall whistling pines and momma's cozy country trinkets dressing up a home, a real home that didn't need assigned nomenclature such as Whispering Oaks to provide a sense of haven from the demanding world beyond its doorstep? What if her parents will have to move into a place like this in just a few months, her mother huffing and puffing-struggling along with taped cardboard boxes filled with her pop psychology books? Her father lugging wood-crafting tools and wondering where the hell to put them? She shakes her head and walks up two flights of cast-iron stairs in Building F to apartment 3D. She takes a deep breath and raps her knuckles boldly against a steel door. Nothing. Pressing an ear to it- the television and low hum of the heat and air system. Steps back, unsure of what to do next. Then she drums on the door with a flurry of fists. There's evidence of stirring within and a girl's voice calls harshly as if from the abyss, who is it?

Barbara Griffith, she replies. I'm looking for Cindy.

She aint here.

Well where is she then?

Don't know. Now go away.

Perhaps it's the long drive in rush-hour traffic, or maybe the cumulative fatigue from the whole of last week. Whatever the catalyst, she rears her foot and kicks at the door with the steel toe of her hiking boot. The metal on metal makes a deafening blast.

Hey, *what the fuck!* The voice on the other side has lost any indifference.

That's better, calls Barbara. Maybe the police will help jar your memory.

What's this all about?

A police matter.

You aint no police.

Well maybe that's just your bad luck, says Barbara. I may not be so nice. There's a missing person involved.

Cindy aint gone missing.

Yeah well, my brother has.

Well I don't know nuthin bout it. So fuck off.

Barbara steps back, arms folded, regarding the unopened door. Then she rears back and kicks with the bottom of her boot full force.

Look, cries the agitated voice, *I'll* call the cops!

Open the goddamned door.

After the sound of the deadbolt unlatched the door opens as far as the chain lock will allow and the owner of the menacing voice appears- an overweight teenaged girl in tee shirt and sweatpants. Over her shoulder, a familiar baby blue-eyed face appears, a towel wrapped around her head, bearing a soft angelic voice.

Barb.

Cindy. So you *are* here after all.

It's been a while since they crossed paths at the Griffiths, and greeted each other with customary familial hugs. Not today.

Why have you not answered our calls, Barbara demands.

I've been away at my mother's house all week.

We've been trying to contact you. About Walt.

I'm sorry about that. C'mon. Get in out of the cold.

Cindy steps aside. The carpeted room she admits Barbara into is bare- only a sofa, a chair and a coffee table. Stacked on the linoleum floor of the adjoining kitchen area are cardboard boxes, taped and sealed.

Moving out?

Mm-hmm. Lucky you caught me here. I've only been by a few times over the week to pack.

The automatic drip coffeemaker is still hooked up, Cindy retreats to the kitchen and calls over her shoulder would Barbara like a cup?

If you have enough left.

I was just going to make a fresh pot anyway.

She brings a sugar bowl and a little carton of half and half on a tray to the coffee table. The pudgy sentry remains mute, but stares daggers at Cindy's show of hospitality, as if the service tray holds treasures far beyond the merits of this strange intruder.

So how's Walt doing? Cindy wants to know.

I have no idea, Barbara sighs as the sentry continues to shoot her dirty looks from her seat in the well-worn sofa in front of a silenced television. I was going to ask you the same thing.

Me? I spoke to him briefly like, I think, three or four days ago or something. But to be honest I think it's best right now for he and I to um, chill the communication a bit.

Cindy removes the head wrap, retreating to the bathroom and shaking her wet hair in front of the vanity. Barbara meets the unrelenting glare of the mute stranger across from her. Well, she says, he's certainly chilled it to a freeze with us. Did he happen to call you at your mother's house?

I don't remember when it was exactly. He called me in the middle of the night.

Middle of the night.

Cindy returns to the kitchen, groping in the cabinets with her back to Barbara, returning with coffee mugs and setting them on the counter. I just stopped by to pack some things.

The heavyset girl saunters over, hair matted, unwashed. What's this all about anyway, she assumes a challenging posture, fists on hips.

Who the *fuck* are you? Barbara whirls around to face the strange creature. The pudgy girl doesn't flinch.

That aint none of your business.

Take it easy Cookie, Cindy says in the sing-song tone of one admonishing a restless pet.

Cookie? Barbara squints at the girl. She live here with you?

She's staying for a few days.

Not very good at taking messages are ya? Don't you pick up the phone when it rings?

Fuck off, the girl's face reddens.

Well what a cute little sweetheart you got on your hands Cindy, Barbara shakes her head at the girl.

Cindy shrugs, perches on her kitchen chair Indian-style. What exactly's the matter Barb? What's happened?

Walt's gone missing. Five days now.

Cindy's on her feet to the coffeemaker.

I thought this is the first place he'd hit, says Barbara.

Ready for another one? Cindy asks.

No thank you. Did you hear me?

Cindy refills her sentry's cup then her own. She sits cross-legged on the sofa next to Barbara, the affable hostess. Yeah, she says while twirling her hair. Who knows, he may've been by. Like I said, I've been gone most of the week.

Ain't nobody been here but me, states Cookie with an air of authority.

Anyway I wouldn't worry too much, Cindy says.

Whaddya mean?

Cindy absently twirls a teaspoon in her coffee mug.

He's alright.

How do you know that?

I just... feel it. I sense him.

Barbara drops her cup down on the table with a thud and a bit of the coffee spills. Oh great, that's just fucking great. So we can all stop worrying now, because Cindy's got a good vibe on that Walt is roaming around somewhere, happy as a lark.

Cindy licks her lips and shrugs.

Do you do happen to do thought transference? Barb says. Maybe you could ask him if it's cold out there sleeping in the car.

Cindy stiffens and draws back as Barbara leans in at her.

Do you have any idea what the hell is going on back in Burrville? Do you know the mess my family's in right now?

God Barb, I'm sorry. I wish I could do something.

Barbara studies a pale face with high cheekbones framed by blonde strands of hair, as if considering which way to go at a fork in the road. Well, she says. There is something.

Yes?

Help me find Walt. And I don't mean by fucking ESP.

Cindy sighs with an air of resignation.

I'm afraid I can't do that.

And why not?

Look, I- I'm trying to get over Walt. Or he's trying to get over me. The last thing I wanna do is go chasing him, she shrugs. Might give him the wrong idea.

The paucity of concern at this last exchange jars Barbara into debating whether Cindy is cold and callous or just cute and simple. Or maybe clever enough to pull off the latter by means of the former. In any case, though she's drained her coffee, she's not ready to leave.

Write me a list.

A list? Cindy meets a significant glance from Cookie who stands across from them at the side of the table.

A list, says Barbara, of all of Walt's friends and contacts.

Have you phoned the police about this yet?

Yes.

And haven't they been-

-They've done jack shit.

Barbara slumps in her chair, glancing over at Cookie. You got any ideas there little sourpuss? Do you know my brother?

Cookie makes a face.

You young people, Barbara clucks her tongue. Haven't all those hours of television taught you how to speak just a little?

I aint gotta watch no television.

Wow, says Barbara, you can string a few words together. I'm impressed. Now that we got your mouth flapping, maybe you can tell me when the last time was you saw my brother Walter.

Cookie looks confused.

Walt, she presses, you knew Walt, *know* Walt, don't you?

Yes, she does, Cindy says.

So when did you see him last? Cookie? Can you speak for yourself?

Oh, sighs Cookie, I don't know.

Think. Barbara taps her forehead.

Cookie fidgets. Over a week ago.

Where?

Here I guess. He was here with some dude named Tim.

Now we're getting somewhere, Barbara shoots a glance at Cindy, regarding Cookie warily while pulling on her cigarette.

What brought them out here? If ya don't mind me asking.

Cookie shifts her gaze from her feet to Cindy.

Just, I don't know, nuthin. Just to hang out.

Well, my brother's pretty much a pro at that.

Look, Cindy says, I'll write you out a list. I'll jot down everyone I can possibly think of.

Good, says Barbara, then why don't you get started?

You mean... like *now*? Cindy looks genuinely perplexed.

Well I sure as hell am not coming back for it. And I'm not going to wait for a letter in the mail. You can just jot it all down while I have a nice chat with Cookie here. Why don't we sit in the living room where it's more comfortable Cookie?

Really Barb, Cindy starts.

Uncomfortable, Cindy?

Cindy shrugs. Not in the least. It's just... she's already told you she hasn't seen Walt in ages.

Now you didn't say that, did you Cookie?

Cindy fetches an address book from the countertop and begins to thumb through it for names, scratching at the pad in a hurried manner. After five minutes of grilling Cookie, Barbara is able only to glean that Walt and Tim paid a visit approximately a few weeks ago, and judging by the way she imagines Cookie must spend her days, she can see how easy it is for the girl to lose track of time.

Cookie says, I hope your brother's not really gone missin. My old man left one day and we ain't seen im since.

Really.

Yep, Daddy aint nuthin but a ghost now. He had trouble with the law too.

Who said anything about trouble with the law? Barbara replies to Cookie while glancing over at Cindy.

Well, Cookie says, it's jes that usually when a dude just up and skiddadles, there's usually some kinda messin with the law.

Any idea what Walt might've been doing, put him at odds with the law?

No, Cindy replies immediately, then qualifies, outside of smoking the occasional reefer.

Occasional, Barbara says.

Cindy scrawls hurriedly at the paper. I'm sure you know we got pulled over last week. They almost took the Chevelle.

Wish that was all we had to worry about, says Barbara, a bitterness in her voice. I don't think that would be enough to make Walter take a powder though. Don't suppose you know anything else would've put my brother on the run do ya Cindy? I mean, besides a broken heart?

Cindy drops a sheaf of loose leaf with hastily scribbled addresses under Barbara's nose. These are all the people we knew real well at UNC.

Great, says Barbara, so you'll help me on this, yeah?

Help you?

Yeah, help me, Barbara meets Cindy's startled gaze with a disarming smile, get to the bottom of this. Find Walt.

Look, Cindy says while dipping a shoulder and placing her hands in the pockets of her corduroys, I told you Walt and I split. It's really important for me to have this space right now.

No *you* look, Barbara bolts up from the sofa, my brother's been missing four days. No phone call, no nothing. How can you just shut off your feelings for someone, just like that?

How can *you*?

Barbara throws her head back, swipes the auburn strands that fall in front of her face. How did you know about that? I thought you said you hadn't spoken to him in a week. I only just arrived Thursday.

Okay, okay, so I talked to him Thursday. I'm not exactly counting days.

Well we are. Four fucking days.

Well I'm sorry about that, alright?

Yeah, Barbara starts for the door. I'll bet you are.

C'mon Barb, be reasonable, Cindy appeals to Barbara's back. You of all people must understand the position I'm in. Barb, c'mon, how long have we known each other?

Barbara turns around, her hand on the doorknob.

I don't think I know you Cindy Blum. Not one bit.

*   *   *

The pickup won't start. John steps on the clutch and tries to push start it, rolling, letting out the clutch and giving it gas. Nothing. He rubs his hands together and glances in the rear view mirror. Frank's Chevy is long gone around the bend into autumn foliage. Lura's Lexus is still in the driveway of old lady Eldridge. One more attempt and he is in the same muddy rut as rain begins to sprinkle the windshield.

Damn, he lifts the door handle, climbs out of the cab and starts for the huge mansion with lurid thoughts about the woman within. Why can't he stop himself thinking those thoughts, they aren't something he'll ever act on for godsakes, he was already a father when she was in diapers. Now it's a grown woman who greets him at the door dressed in a sleek grey pinstripe pants suit, white blouse and a wedding band.

Sorry Lura. Truck won't start. Can I use the telephone?

Of course, she says, it's in the kitchen. Oh wait, it's been disconnected.

Oh.

You can use my mobile she says, extracting what looks like a walkie-talkie from her large Gucci handbag.

John wonders who the hell he's going to call. It's too early for Ellen, she's got a faculty meeting after school today. Barbara's in Knoxville. Clem? He's asked enough of him already. There's an emptiness he feels, standing there in that empty hallway with an astonishingly beautiful woman who is between appointments, then perhaps going to grandma Breckenridge's to fetch her two-year old daughter and home to put on dinner, just a normal day in a very normal life. He stares at the keypad of the mobile phone which he doesn't know how to operate, and he's ashamed to tell her, the same way he was ashamed to tell her that his ten-year old pickup won't start.

She stands waiting, arms folded, as John pushes buttons in vain. I guess I don't know how to work one of these, he says. Don't own one myself.

Lura smiles obligingly. I'm still trying to get a grip on it.

He hands the clunky phone back to her and she asks him what number to dial. He blurts out his home phone, though he knows nobody is there. But when she hands him the phone and he hears the ring tone, there's suddenly the pang of hope that Walt will pick up the line.

No answer, darn. Thanks anyway, Lura.

Look, I can give you a lift if you need.

Well, I don't want to put you to any trouble.

How are you going to get anywhere, out here without a phone? C'mon, where can I take you?

I-I guess home would be as good a place as any, he laughs affectedly.

Sure, give me just a few minutes to lock up, and I'd be happy to take you home.

He idles on the front porch. The drizzle has turned to a steady driving rain. He has calmed his fantasies in this meeting of a practical matter with Lura Breckenridge. She's a young mother in a pants suit, with regular cotton underwear underneath, not the frilly, lacy things of his imagination. He is grounded, grateful of her having stayed on here a little longer, because what else would he do? It's at least five miles to the nearest main road, a long enough walk even on a sunny day.

Ready? Lura swaggers towards her shiny new Lexus.

A hard rain beats at the windshield, wind blows newly-fallen leaves across State Highway 52, and the heat in the Lexus is non-intrusive, comfortable.

How's Barbara doing?

Oh, great, Lura. Funny you should ask. She's just come home for a little visit. She's off to see friends in Knoxville today.

How's um, her husband, what's his name again?

Bill. He's, he's...great. Just busy and all with work, like all you young up and comers.

Oh right, she says, What is it he's doing now?

Selling cookware.

Lura seems unimpressed.

To major distributors, John qualifies.

And how's Walt?

He's okay. Will's up at MIT, you know.

Really.

Yep. Full academic scholarship. Studying applied physics.

John can convey pride through his son, anyway. A son at MIT the great equalizer, bridging the gap, connecting John in some sense to the reputation, modest yes, but substantial enough class and community standing that is the Breckenridges. All this catching up, here in the intimate proximity of the Lexus. John is suddenly anxious for the sight of his driveway.

I'll bet you're proud of him.

Yep, we sure are.

John glances across a polished faux wood interior at Lura. Her chiseled features, high cheekbones, perfect nose. Her rouge applied just enough to pick up what is undeniably raw and natural beauty maintained by a privileged background. He craves her all at once, wants to invite her to warm and cozy sheets, imagining the pretense and restraint of the ride home decimated as she pulls into the driveway. But he knows that wouldn't do much for her business acumen. Given the problems already on his plate, having word spread around that he'd hit on Lura Breckenridge might not exactly be the best thing. He wouldn't try it anyway. He shuts the door, thanks her, waves goodbye.

*   *   *

Barbara

You curl up beneath the warm sheets, Renee's light kisses skimming along your back, teasing you into turning over on your back to meet her mouth with a full kiss.

Renee wants to know does it bother you. The thing about Meg. Oh, I don't know, you tell her, you really don't know what you can do with this right now, you've been thinking a lot these last few days. You just need time to find yourself again, you say. Time alone. She says, guess that's just how it is. You don't sound very happy about it, you say. No, she says, actually it's good for me to know. Really. It'll help me to make some decisions about other things. You sit up, throw your legs over the side of the bed and say you're sorry, it's just all you have to give right now. Renee pulls you back into bed. You collapse onto her and she presses her lips hard against yours. You look wiped out, she says while rubbing your arms and searching your eyes. Do I, you say. Yes. Wiped out and gorgeous, she says. You'd give a hundred bucks to hear that.

*   *   *

In Burrville John Griffith picks up the extension phone in his study. It's Clem. Well, he drawls, thought I'd let you know the news. Dawson pleaded guilty and his trial is set for next Monday.

Oh my God.

Yeah, guess he got tired of jail and decided to cut a deal.

That was sure as hell fast, says John. Sure was says Clem.

Later in the kitchen, John says to Ellen, Barb will be back tonight anyway. Meantime, he says while removing the keys from the station wagon from the key rack, I'll just head into town for a few errands.

Ellen busies herself wiping down the sink with a dishrag. When are the police ever going to find our son?

I don't know.

Did you call today?

Yes, he replies although he didn't. When he'd phoned the Knoxville main precinct yesterday and insisted he wanted to file a missing persons report through them, the desk sergeant told him without reservation he must file in the precinct of jurisdiction, namely Jamestown. So it was to Jamestown he'd gone to fill out the paperwork under Sam William's watchful eye.

Know any reason he might have run away, John?

John gave Williams an even stare.

I have to ask you, John.

John pushed the form back at Williams.

Now I'm sure you're gonna work real hard for me like I do for you. It's my taxes pay your salary Sam. Don't forget that.

Those having been his last words, and leaving behind an air of mutual mistrust, John's not exactly of a mind to phone Jamestown Precinct regularly. He's pissed as hell at Walt. He also worries incessantly about him.

* * *

When Seamus Griffin laid down to his final rest, he begged his only son to work harder. It was his only dying wish. Stay out of the Tabard Inn, set your hands not on the glass of beer but on the plow. Plow these fields and make a life for yourself. It's a good life, a life without war, only killin you have to do is the fatted pig or the clucking chicken, and that hurts all the same but it's a far cry from watchin your best friend die with cannon fodder in his chest and a frozen look of terror on his face. It's a far cry from watchin children die in the hold of a sailing coffin. May you never know war, may you never know famine. Stay out of the Tabard. Read the Good Book. Live a good life.

John Griffith Sr. led a good life alright, most of it sitting at the bar of the Colonial Inn while fortunes dwindled. The Tabard Inn had burned to the ground twenty years before his father had spoken his last words and the dying man hadn't taken a drink since. John Sr. had the benefit of well-tilled earth and sharecropper families who paid him to gain their sustenance from the earth.

He also had a hard-working wife who bore him three children. They broke new ground, literally and figuratively. His son Jim went to the big city and worked for John Deere, used an engineering-oriented mind to help design the tractors that would largely diminish the human struggle of raising crops. His son Tom went on to know war first-hand, he died on the front lines in World War I. His third son, whom subsequent generations would render John Jr., went on to dwindle fortunes just a little further, inheriting an uncanny determination for the same public house as his father, and ultimately the same muted interest in the property he inherited. In between treks to town in the horse and buggy that he refused to lay down for the motor variety, he kept farm records of frugal spending for meager yields and collected rent from a few more sharecroppers. He managed to make a living and his liver held on long enough for him to see the onset of World War II and the sixth birthday of his grandson John Griffith, who now draws a barstool at the Colonial-haggard-looking, cheerlessly raising a finger, begging a double Scotch.

Wednesday, A Different Tune

Barbara pours herself a cup of coffee, cradling the phone on her shoulder, Cindy's list in front of her on the kitchen table.

Gavin?

Speakin to im, says the voice at the other end of the line.

Hiya, Barbara Griffith here, 'member me?

Barbara! Well long time no hear. Although word gets back occasionally through Walt.

Yeah, would be great if that information channel were still open.

Huh?

Seems we've lost our intermediary.

Walt?

Yeah. I got your number from Cindy. I've been on the phone all morning trying to reach people and mostly just leaving messages on answering machines.

Yeah, well, ole Gavin doesn't currently have himself an employment obligation to report to.

What is it with you guys, allergic to a little honest work?

Allergic to workin for somebody else I reckon. Naw, I'm gettin my own thing together here.

So was Walt, thinks Barbara.

What kind of thing you gettin together Gavin? Nothing illegal I hope.

Oh totally not. Buildin a recording studio. Bought loads of gear, soundproofing the basement, y'know, gettin it together.

Yeah, so how's business? Got many clients yet?

Nah, but y'know, Rome wasn't built in a day. Hey, what's up with Walt anyway?

Gavin, can we meet soon as possible? Like today?

Sure. You know I don't live at home anymore. Janet and I bought a place just near Pickett. Let me tell you how to get here.

Well great, except daddy had to borrow my car today and it wouldn't be until tonight-

-You at the old house?

Yep.

No problem, I'll be right over.

* * *

Ellen's hands are folded on her lap as she faces the stage of the auditorium, picking at pieces of lint from her green wool skirt and glancing up at the principal at the podium. She's glad of there being no classes today, glad of the half-day. Because today teaching would be almost impossible, she'd have called in sick for sure, something she's never done in her four years at Jamestown Elementary. Today it's just hall monitoring at the breaks between acts for Patriot Day, a full day event featuring dramatizations of significant events in the history of the United States of America. The nation's flag graces one side of the stage, the Tennessee state flag on the other. The home stretch for what's been an agonizing four hours in the doldrums, shifting in her seat while a circle of kids join hands tentatively, all garbed-out in hippie gear, it's the social revolution of the sixties and they're singing the theme from Hair with marked indifference. *Amen,* Ellen thinks, *let's get this over with, let's pack up our lockers and go home for the day* as Tracy Williams, this twenty-something fresh out of university, whispers over her shoulder from behind, *Were you a hippie in the sixties Ellen?* Ellen fears this might be the opener in a long line of questioning so she turns slightly, shaking her head and smiling dismissively. She does not wish to be spotted talking during an assembly- the teacher charged with the duty of setting an example- chastising the young ones for talking during her lectures, she simply looks straight in front of her and wonders *was she a hippie during the sixties?* No, she reckons, she wouldn't have qualified. No marijuana smoked, no acid dropped, no rain-drenched music festivals, no public nudity. Just raising a little daughter, the boys, going to crafts fairs, a little substitute teaching on the side. Perhaps the aspect of the Ellen Griffith of the sixties closest to hippiedom would be the beaded necklaces she sold to the long-haired peaceniks that occasionally rolled through the Cumberland Plateau in their Volkswagon vans, or motorcycles.

When Patriot Day rolls up and Ellen leaves the school she hits ClearCuts, a hair salon franchise in a strip-mall in Jamestown. There's one customer in front of her. She sits in the waiting area up front and takes a battered magazine. Commercial R&B blares from a boom box planted on the wall-length shelf of implements. A handsome man with clean-shaven chiseled features sits in one of the swivel chairs watching the mirror and the frizzy-haired girl who chews and intermittently snaps bubble gum as she flicks up his grey streaked hair and pokes scissors at it. When the girl has swung the chair around, holding the mirror with an affected smile at the back of his head he nods agreeably. Ellen is certain she's seen him somewhere, but can't place the face. It's only when he's paid and on his way past her sitting on the ugly orange waiting couch that their eyes meet and his smile bears the dimples.

Ellen? he squints at her, your John's wife, aren't you?

Why yes she says, shaking a warm and clammy hand. Tell me your name again.

Steve Meigs. I'm the program manager at WHRS.

Oh right. We met at the fundraiser.

When they've steeped outside, he glances around furtively and lowers his voice. Sorry about what happened.

I-I'm sorry, I don't understand.

Oh, he didn't tell you?

Tell me what?

We had to let him go. I felt awful about the whole thing, feel awful still. John did our best show far as I'm concerned. He knows the high regard I held for him.

What happened?

Well, Meigs says, maybe it's best to ask him, Mrs Griffith. Basically, he got on the air and spilled his guts. I agree with every word of what he said. It just wasn't exactly the right forum.

I see, she says and they shake hands and walk away from an awkward moment.

* * *

Gavin Sharpe, elbows planted on the kitchen table, chin placed in his palms, tries to talk above the steady clatter of the furnace repairman from the basement.

So how long's he been gone? he shouts.

Almost a week, Barbara shouts back. Last Thursday we woke up and didn't see the Chevelle.

My God, Gavin leans back, shifting his coffee cup to and fro on the table as the noise below subsides.

What, Barbara shrugs.

That's a long time.

Yeah.

Why didn't anyone call me? Has my approval rating taken a nosedive in the Griffith family?

Well just look at ole Gavin with his feelings all squashed.

I'm worried is all, he sighs.

I know, so's everyone. But we've had a lot of shit going on around here, lotta fires to put out. And they're still burning awful hot.

Gavin sniffs, screws up his face. Barbara draws a deep breath, deliberating, standing up and entering the study to fetch the cursed document from top of the rabble of papers, dropping it under Gavin's nose on the kitchen table.

He studies it, furrowing his brow. Who else knows about this?

I wish it were nobody except myself, momma, daddy and the Carters. But you know how word can spread like wildfire in these parts, she sighs. Oh well, I suppose it doesn't matter much anymore. I'm surprised you haven't heard already.

I'm really out of circulation Barb. That studio, workin on the house. And there's good news. We've got a baby on the way.

You gonna be a daddy?

Yep.

Well I'll be damned. Congratulations, Barbara says as she pats Gavin's hand and gives it a squeeze.

Well thanks, he says. I've been out of circulation. Maybe too much for Walter's own good.

How long've you and Walt been friends, anyway?

Fifteen years, I reckon. I remember the first time momma dropped me off here.

All them sleepovers, Barbara sighs. You little pests were always up to your mischievous little pranks. Scribbling eyeliner all over my Peter Frampton records. Remember the damn beard and moustaches?

Gavin's eyes brighten.

Y'all hiding in my closet, Barbara says. Nosing around in my diary, gum between the pages of my schoolbooks, remember that one? Stealing my lipstick and writing all over my mirror?

Yeah well, you stole my pubescent heart anyway, Barbara Griffith.

That's sweet- Barbara is blushing, shifty-eyed, shaking her head slowly from side to side- That's really, that's like... well, finding out something you never knew, may've never guessed... but I guess it makes sense, I-I mean, well I was always a bit aloof.

Gavin shrugs.

Barbara draws a breath, her face still reddened. I'm really happy for you.

You ever thought about kids, Barb?

Not yet, she shakes her head. Not with Bill anyway.

What?

We're, um, separated.

Gavin wiggles his thick neck as if to clear his ears, Wait, woa, hold on now. Bill? You're leaving him?

I've left him.

Sorry to hear that.

It's okay, really. I feel good about my decision.

Well that's good I guess he says, leaning back, drumming his fingers on the table, squeezing his eyes shut in deep thought, then blinking them open. Now about this mess with Walt?

Yeah, just how much do you know about all this?

He draws a breath, kneading his bottom lip, fidgeting with the document in front of him.

C'mon Gavin, spill it. Remember, I'm *still* Walt's older sister, she says. Payback time for all the shitty pranks you punks used to pull on me?

I told you, you won my heart in exchange, he shrugs, but the lopsided grin quickly gives way to a grave look over his wide face, he rubs at the developing pouch under his chin.

I told him several times he was a fuckin idiot for doing it. Damn, the first summers, we were on the road with Astroglide, Dawson was just *leasing*, few hundred dollars a month. But then... then the band ruptured, that month-long tour last Christmas break, no money, freezing cold, we argued. He had his ideas, I had my own. In the end, Walt and I figured we had a friendship before the band. Then last summer, he came home. Back here. I told him not to.

Why?

I didn't think it was a good idea. From the very start.

Why not?

Because there was nothing for him to do here. He just ended up hanging around with that... girlfriend of his.

Do I detect a trace of fraternal jealousy here?

No, absolutely not. Perhaps a little mistrust. Lot of anger. But jealousy, no. She's nothing to be jealous of.

Really.

Barb, maybe y'all met her, I don't know, on *your* terms. She's a very flexible girl, I'll give her that, she can fit herself right into anybody's terms. *Any*bodys. But you have yet to meet her on her terms. That's something completely different.

Barbara meets his sharp gaze.

I told Walt from day one, four fuckin years ago, to leave it alone. Let Dawson solve his own problems, few hundred dollars a month was hardly worth it. But he wouldn't listen. He can be a stubborn bastard sometimes, that brother of yours.

Really, I thought Walt was as gullible and impressionable as they come.

Yeah, a regular pushover. With Cindy anyway.

Why?

He was nuts about her. But I wouldn't say the feeling was mutual.

I don't get the sense she's too stirred up about anybody but herself.

*Bin*go, he stabs a finger at the air. You know, she can put on an act, that soft twinkle in them baby blue eyes, make you feel mushy all over. But I see right through it.

So do I, Barbara says.

Really? *All of it?* he gapes, running his fingers along the table. Well anyway, I also had more than a sneaking suspicion ole Walt would get into more no-good with Dawson. Never cared much for them Dawsons, not a one of em. Had a bad experience involving Kyle's fist and my face.

They've been through a lot, I mean their daddy leavin, their momma's sickness...

Everyone's got their problems, some more than others, Gavin drums his fingers on the table. Doesn't give anybody the right to run around doing whatever the hell suits their own damn interests. Like planting pot on other people's property.

Fair enough.

Anyway, he said, Dawson was dealing more and losing a lot of ground being tied up on the farm. Cindy really pushed your brother to get into it.

So she knew all along, Barbara gasps.

'Course she did. Think she hung around here all that time and didn't have a clue what he was up to?

My parents live here and they didn't.

Let me tell you, she wasn't blind to it. I godamn guarantee she got her own delicate little hands dirty from it.

So how do you know for sure Cindy knew the score? Had the *dope* on him, so to speak?

Because I was there when he told her.

Barbara leans in, planting her elbows on the table.

It was during spring break. Walt and I had thawed the ice between us. You remember we all went down to Florida?

Vaguely. Go ahead.

Well anyway, we went to Lauderdale. Last spring break. We're in some bar getting drunk, talking about what we're gonna do after UNC. Walt starts rambling on at me about re-connecting to make some music, he's all keen on going to Nashville to write, record, play in a band, all that shit-

-Right-

-So I tell him, straight out, I'm not lookin to be the next Hank Williams, he says neither is he, that's not what Nashville's about, it's changing, blah blah blah…- Gavin waves a dismissive hand and sips at his coffee- I tell him look, I just want to take my business degree, move back to the pristine forests of the old Cumberland Plateau, and bang out a living. With Janet. Period.

So what'd he say to that?

He didn't buy it, said I was growing old before my time, wouldn't last, I'd get bored, that kind of shit. He was very drunk and very annoying.

Did you have an argument about it?

Hell no. Remember, we were down there patching things up. I had a few beers in me anyway, and I just laughed it off. But I got the sense Walter really believed I'd continue that elusive and illusory pipe dream of going to Nashville and becoming famous.

I found some of his lyrics. Not exactly country.

Yeah, he grins, but a little bit rock and roll. My attitude was like, if you wanna do that, fine, go for it. Just not where I'm goin. I'd seen enough of the road and paying your dues to know that it wasn't anything I'd wanted to keep on pursuin.

Gavin shakes his head vigorously, as if to shake himself back on the track of his story. Anyway, Walt says in the meantime he met Dawson when he went back home to get some things for Lauderdale, spring break and all. Dawson put it straight to him. Would he be interested in taking over the production side of the little enterprise and free him up to work the sales. Walt said he'd think about it, over the week like. Dawson says *don't take your time.* So there's Walt telling me this at this joint in Lauderdale right in front of Cindy. Saying he'll make a wad of cash in the summer, head for Nashville with me in the fall. He asks me what I think, I tell him I think what I always thought. You can get in a heap of trouble growing the stuff. Should've kicked Dawson's ass off the property in the first place. Well, *no no*, he says, Dawson's very careful, discreet, all that shit. Says he can manage growing and it's easy money, all that. Well I guess right about that time Cindy starts nodding her head, elbowing her agreement into Walt's ribs. Even though she mostly couldn't be bothered about Burrville and environs. Man, how she hated this place.

Really?

Oh man, she *hated* East Tennessee. She's a city girl, inside and out.

So she was for Nashville, I presume.

No.

No?

Not at all.

Then why stay with Walt? This summer?

That's a damn good question.

Barbara and Gavin remain silent, only the sound of the grandfather clock ticking from the living room.

I paid her a visit yesterday, Barbara says at last. At first, she disarmed me with all that charm. But I left there pretty much in a huff. And that's how I'll return, pick up where we left off.

Why do you want to go back?

Because I need to find my brother. Figured it was a pretty good place to start. Not a bad place to continue either.

Makes sense. Well, almost. Would have been better to call me before you went out there in the first place. I'd have gone with you.

Id've had to talk to her to get your new number anyway.

My parents have it.

Whatever. I'm going back to our little charmer. I want to find my brother. Are you in?

Am I ever.

So when can you go? She's in the process of moving out. She's a hard one to contact, I doubt she'll answer the phone.

I can't go today. Janet gets off work at four, and then we got an appointment with the obstetrician.

I have off tomorrow, Barbara says.

Where you working?

First Tennessee. Peak-time bank teller.

What are you doing working *there*?

Just making money.

Local job. Wow, you really *have* gotten out of dodge.

I wasn't making up stories.

I'll pick you up in the morning. Let's say eight o'clock.

What if she's not there?

Then we try her Mom's place.

But I don't know where that is.

I do.

He rises from the table and walks his cup over to the sink.

Gavin, I sure do appreciate this.

Hell, he says, we gotta find that bugger after all.

*   *   *

John knocked off early with Frank Lynn. In the kitchen he wriggles out of his jacket and says to Barbara, I need to finish that Duncan Phyfe table. Dot Everly has been waiting forever on it. Swears she can sell it in five minutes, what with Thanksgiving coming up.

Well, says Barb, it'll sure be warm enough for you down there with that furnace up and running.

Hallelujah, it's sure nice to have a cozy home again.

Listen to this.

She beckons him into his study to the answering machine, pushes play and a man's voice crackles. *Yes, ahem, my name's Early Chase. Callin fer Barbara Griffith. I got your message this morning, I was out walkin the dog. I believe I might be of help, uh, here, about your brother. Ring me up when y'can. Right, bye.*

Well, I'll be damned, John says. You sure are on the case, Barb. What do you make of it?

Won't know til I get there.

Where?

Black Creek.

Who's in Black Creek?

Early Chase, Barbara says. I was out walking the dog when he rang back. But I rang him back alright. Told him I'd be out as soon as I got the wheels back.

Why not just talk to him on the phone?

I don't like doing important stuff over the phone when I can help it. And Black Creek's just a half hour's drive.

Well not exactly just around the corner.

This could be a hot lead.

You sound like a private eye.

I guess I feel like one too.

So who is this guy and how do you know he's gonna be there when you get there? Do we send a search party if you're not back by five?

Dad, really. He's an old codger. Retired, home all day just waiting for me to get there. He's a safer bet than Cindy.

I don't mind to tag along for the ride.

What about the Duncan Phyfe?

It can wait.

Stay here and do it. I think it'd do you a world of good. I'll tell you everything I find out.

Pulling out of the driveway, she glances in the rearview at her father, standing on the front porch steps and scanning the sky as if expecting something to fall from it.

*   *   *

It's warm enough for John leave the double doors open in his basement workshop. In dirty old coveralls, over the strains of the Bach concerto, John hears someone enter the house. The basement door opens and Ellen peers at him from the top of the stairs.

We got a letter from the IRS she says, handing him a large white envelope. He wastes no time tearing it open. It turns out to be only informational materials for EZ filing.

Well, he says, picking up his brush and pointing it at the table. What do you think of this beauty?

Looks like it's shaping up alright. Nice looking table.

That table, he says while picking lint from his coveralls, is the finest piece of furniture I've ever laid eyes on.

Is it?

Yeah, absolutely.

You don't say as much about your wife. You didn't even notice I got my hair done. Y'know paying a compliment once in a while wouldn't kill you.

Well lately here you don't give me much cause to.

He regrets the words as they leave his lips.

Ellen's face turns red. Oh dear God I can't deal with this anymore, this marriage is just, just-

-I'm sorry. I am so sorry.

Ellen buries her face in her hands. John drops the brush and rushes over to her.

-I'm sorry, I didn't mean that.

You did, or you wouldn't have said it.

John places his arms around her and she shudders against him, her voice muffled in his chest. I just can't take this anymore. You always have something to lash out at me with. The constant bickering.

He kisses her neck and gently runs a hand along her back.

The house is all ours, he whispers.

What? she thinks he's referring to the forfeiture case- it's all over, it's all been a big misunderstanding. *Sorry bout that Mr. and Mrs. Griffith. Y'all can go home now.*

We've got this warm house all to ourselves.

Yeah? she lifts her head, stands up straight.

Yeah. Let's go upstairs and roll around in the linens.

John Griffith, are you coming on to me?

Playful accusation. She follows him up to the kitchen and to the staircase. Watching him climb the stairs, she whispers protestations to herself. More than one of her books states that it's absolutely foolish to try to settle marital issues with sex, but it's unconvincing at that moment. At the top of the stairs, John faces his hesitant wife standing at the foot of the stairs. Okay he says, continuing to the bedroom. Have it your way.

Wait, Ellen says.

The lovemaking is rushed. They meet in front of the bed with the awkwardness of teenagers, John kissing the nape of her neck and noticing up close the advance of grey hair, thinking how long has it been since we last made love? Ellen thinking how long has it been since I began the habit of dressing and undressing in the bathroom? They give short shrift to kissing, there's precious little of the soft caresses of yesteryear and foreplay is disregarded almost entirely. They collapse onto the king-size bed, he squeezes his eyes shut- to her, to the world. Afterwards he lies on his back and neither of them seem to have anything to say.

This is silly, Ellen says while they dress. I know this is not the way to solve our problems.

John fetches a balled-up sock and says it's as good a start as any.

*   *   *

After long stretches of gravel and dirt back roads riddled with potholes, she spots the turnoff just before the river bridge. She slows down and the car bumps along the steep gravel road in first gear, past trailer homes. At the fork where the road levels off she bears left and follows the tree-lined dirt road to the end.

About fifty feet from the road is a shanty. Smoke billows from a chimney on an uneven weatherworn roof. She parks the car next to the guardrail at the dead end. Beyond it the landscape plunges into great depths of forest. She starts toward the makeshift house. A weathered door opens and a man in a turtleneck shirt under denim coveralls appears. He's hunched over a cane, a full head of cottony white hair, whisker stubble on a craggy face. She enters a modest living room with a large fireplace and a good fire crackling in the hearth. A little terrier sleeping beside it comes to life and starts towards her.

Don't pay any mind to her, he says. She don't bite.

She gives the dog a pat on the head and drops herself into the deep cushions of a beat-up sofa.

Early Chase limps to the kitchen at the back of the house, drawing a battered metal teapot from an old wood-burning stove.

Your brother, says Early after he's set the teapot down on the table in front of her and settled himself gently into the rocker on the other side of it. Well, he used to come by every now and again with Tim. Kindly good-hearted, your brother. A little heavy with words. God amighty, if you aint the spittin image of him. I can see you's kin alright, just settin here lookin atcha.

Well I'm glad I came out here in person, she says.

Reckon I am too. Cause I sure don't get much company these days. You hungry?

No that's okay she says, sipping timidly at the scalding tea and gazing into the fire. Early gropes around the floor beside his rocking chair for a box of cinnamon crackers. The terrier jumps into its master's lap.

Here, have ye some to warsh up that tea.

So what was it had my brother and Tim coming out here to visit?

Early raises a finger, sipping at his tea. My wife. God rest her soul.

Your wife?

Yep. Lost her last July. To cancer.

I'm sorry.

Much obliged.

He wipes his mouth with a flannel sleeve. Yep, cancer it was took Loretta- I won't bore you with the details.

Anyhow, he says, scratching at his knee. Might as well tell ya, doesn't matter a lick now. My wife endured a couple months of awful pain. Wa'nt much we could do, no health insurance and all. I've spent a good bit of my life underground. Coal mines. West Virginia. We moved down here five years ago when I got too old to work em. Always thought fer sure I'd be six feet under long before Loretta. These lungs must be made of steel.

I guess so.

Anyhow, wasn't much we could do for the pain, y'see? I-I wa'nt too keen on marijuana for a painkiller, unnerstan? Really, I wa'nt. Now you look the type wouldn't be too, now don't get me wrong here, bothered by it. I mean most of you younger folks try it or do it, whatever, but I aint much of a mind for it. Still aint. But it sure eased Loretta's dyin, that's fer sure- he scratches at his whiskers and sighs- I can't tell you who it was told me about Tim, seein as he's pretty much a public name, but he told us about him cause that's where he got it from, see?

She nods while patting the head of a dog badly in need of a bath.

Tim would bring the stuff right here. Walt'd tag along sometimes. Ever' so often Walt'd carry it over by his lonesome.

He ever come with anyone else? A girl named Cindy?

Coupla times, sure. Pretty little thing, her. They come up here once, spent the night on this floor. Woulda been, lemme see, last August. Shortly after the wife passed on.

Well, have you heard about Tim? What happened to him with the law?

Yep, Early wags his head. Damned shame too. Nice fella, he was.

Some people don't think so.

Well, that's the way of it with every body, I s'pose. Caint have every soul likin ya. But that Tim. First he starts sellin us at a price we and our, our friend knows, is just way below what price he coulda really fetched for it. Then, an I beg ya not to tell a soul, he starts leavin it here, towards the end y'know, last two times he jes leaves me a bag- Early frames a sizable packet with his hands- I said Tim, how much I owe ya, he says Early only debt you owes to God an yer payin him takin care yer wife. Well Im payin you anyways I say. He says I aint havin any of it Early.

Barbara thinks about Eliza Dawson, raising four children on her own, barely making ends meet while facing death daily.

How did you hear about Tim's arrest, Early?

Why, from Walt, course.

Walt? When?

Just a coupla days ago. He was here. Stayed two nights. That's why I was answerin your call.

*   *   *

John crouches beside the Duncan Phyfe under the bright fluorescent light, dabbing around delicate ornamentation with a foam brush. Scans the tabletop as the second coat of finish dries. Draws an oval-backed chair from under the stairs, an upholstery and refinish job that's been waiting on him and pulls a book from a line of books above the workbench, flipping the pages to the chapter on Re-upholstering.

Upstairs Ellen is sprawled out on the sofa, leafing through the pages of *You Can Heal Your Life*. She flips to chapter fifteen. The List. A vertical table- *I am healthy, whole and complete*, she roams this alphabetized list of physical ailments.

Problem- Frigidity. Probable Cause- Fear. Denial of Pleasure. A belief that sex is bad. Insensitive partners. Fear of father. New thought pattern- *It is safe for me to enjoy my own body. I rejoice in being a woman.*

Problem- Bronchitis. Probable Cause- Inflamed family environment. Arguments and yelling. Sometimes silent. New Thought Pattern- *I declare peace and harmony within me and around me. All is well.*

All is well, she gazes once again at the framed portraits of her husband's ancestry on the wall next to the fireplace. *All is well*, she repeats to herself, looking into the eyes of the Confederate-uniformed Seamus Griffin, in the yellowing photo under frame and glass that isn't the airtight container of museums. *All is well* she repeats, but Seamus's eyes don't give the slightest hint he's convinced.

* * *

Barbara freezes, the teacup just shy of her lips.

Walt was here a couple of days ago?

I wasnt lookin at no ghost.

Early Chase sets the dog on the floor and pushes himself out of the rocking chair with his walking stick.

What was he doing here?

Just hangin out, Early says, fetching a piece of wood from a stack beside the fireplace and feeding the fire- Least that's what he *said* anyway. But I seen there was more to it than that- Early taps his temple just below the shock of white hair- More like *hidin* out. Real uneasy like. Restless.

Uh huh says Barbara, watching the man fetch a cigar box from a shelf over the hearth. My wife left few earthly possessions, some of it green stuff I aint got no use for. Walt smoked most of it, there's a little left here, he reaches for a cigar box laying on the table next to him. Maybe you could use it, I don't know.

That's okay, I'm good Early.

The man returns to the rocking chair and the dog settles in his lap.

Barbara places her teacup on the table between them. So, she says, when did he leave?

Day before last.

Where to?

Said he was a goin *home.* S' why your phone call struck me kinda odd.

Oh my God. He didn't mention any other place?

Nuh-uh. Just stood on my porch, smilin like, nighttime comin on, said he was goin home.

Did he say anything about what's happened. At home?

About the law findin plants growin there on the land, you mean.

Yes?

Yep. Didn't seem real concerned like. Jes said it'd all be cleared up.

Cleared up, she thinks, *cleared up, well then come home and clear it the hell up Walt.*

Did he say whether he was coming back anytime soon?

Didn't say for sure.

Thank you Early. Thanks for telling me all this.

Well now, I don't reckon I coulda not tried to help, you look mighty worked up settin there an I caint say I blame ya one bit. Silence'd git nobody nowheres. I reckon I caint never tell any bold face lie.

I appreciate that.

I wish the same could be said of Walt, she thinks, brushing the crumbs from her knees into a cupped hand. Goes to the fireplace and throws the crumbs at the fire. Despite a pang of guilt at what to him must seem an abrupt close to her visit, she grasps Early's hand, gushing gratefulness and telling him to call her day or night in case of any news from Walt, saying she'll do the same and oh yeah she says, about that little bit of…

No bother Early says, drawing the plastic baggie from the cigar box. You're doing me a favor.

They regard one another silently a good while, the old man thumbing his whiskers.

I dunno but I guess I oughtta tell ya this.

What, Early. What is it?

He pitches his elbows to his knees and draws a long sigh, gazing into the hearth. That fella I told you about.

Which fella?

The one who, let's just say is pretty durn connected to the law in this state-

A judge?

I caint say either way.

She holds his gaze a moment, nods.

He got word, it seems, there was somebody done told the law. Bout your brother. Back a while ago.

How long ago.

Dunno. But long enough for them to stake it out.

Who to stake out?

Local cops.

Any idea who this person was that tipped em off?

Early shakes his head slowly, drops his gaze to the floor. That girl, he says at last, that pretty little thing your brother runs around with.

She bows her head and heaves a deep sigh.

I didn't have the heart to tell im.

I'm not sure *I* do, Barbara says.

Early pats her on the shoulder. You take care of yourself. Troubles come, troubles go. I hope your brother turns up soon.

Early sees her to the door and she leaves the cozy shanty for the cold crisp air and darkness- shivering as she skirts around the puddles.

*   *   *

A home cooked meal is keeping warm in the oven and its aroma wafts through the house.

I'm going to build a fire, John announces to the air- Ellen having nodded off to sleep on the couch, *You Can Heal Your Life* laying face down on the floor beside the sofa. He dusts the ashes out the hearth, sets the kindling like a teepee and strikes a match to the crumpled newspaper at the base. He adds a few pieces of the split wood and the fire begins to catch.

Ellen's eyes flutter awake. Ummm, that's nice, she utters in a husky voice just above a whisper, propping herself up on an elbow, mesmerized at the lively dance of fire and outburst of snaps after he's placed the tiny pine log on the glowing sticks.

The shrill ring of the antique phone in the kitchen breaks the peace and quiet. John hurries to answer it. It's his sister Mary.

How's things? Her cheery voice over the line.

Oh, can't complain, just putting the fire on. It's freezing outside, I reckon it's turning cold up there.

Well, I wouldn't notice, I'm cooped up in the office most of the time listening to a steady stream of former soul mates trade insults and doing my best to referee.

Right, he chortles, but at least they pay you for it.

Most of the time anyway. Hey listen, I've got Willy here at my place tonight, he's getting ready to play bartender for one of my crazy dinner parties. We were discussing Thanksgiving and I just thought when was the last time you gang came up north, eh?

Oh, replied John.

Yeah, *oh*, she mimics, I'm calling to invite you and Ellen up here. Tell Walt to tag along too, if he can. And if Barbara and Bill don't have plans, tell em to join the party.

Okay well, look, Mary, she's... she's having... well I guess she's having the kind of stuff with Bill they might could stand a visit to you about.

Oh dear. Well, tell her to come along as well then.

Sure.

So do I take it that's a yes?

John pauses, glancing over at his wife finishing the dinner preparations at the stove. Umm... yeah, sure, why the hell not?

Great. See you then.

Just after he hangs up, headlight beams play on the ceiling of the living room and soon Barbara strides into the kitchen- out of breath, not even having bothered to shed her jacket.

Walter's alive, she says.

What? Ellen turns from the stove. *Where?*

Don't go all hysterical Mom. I don't know.

What?

I said I don't know.

How can you know he's alive and not know where he is?

I don't know, Barbara shrugs.

My little space cadet, Ellen grimaces. What do you mean you don't know?

Well, I mean, like we know the President's alive right, but like, we don't know where he is at this very moment.

He's in Kennebunkport playing golf, John suggests.

Stop it, the both of you! Ellen bangs a wooden spoon on the stove range.

John takes Barbara by the elbow and steers her into the living room. Obviously he says, this has to do with... who was it you went to see?

Early Chase.

Ellen, let's sit down and talk about this.

Ellen shuffles into the living room and Barbara relates the afternoon's events, talking over Ellen's frequent interjections.

So that damned Cindy Blum snitched on us, growls John.

Well it's hearsay, honey. We don't know that for sure. It's just this man's word.

Well momma, I don't know that he has any reason to lie. Barbara shimmies her arms from out of the jacket, pulls the clear plastic bag of pot from its breast pocket. Ellen says, oh Jesus.

And now if you'll excuse me, it's been kind of a long day, Barbara rifles through her pocketbook, fetches a packet of rolling papers and begins the machinations of producing a joint.

What on *earth* do you think you're doing? Ellen glares.

Well, I thought I'd just have a little spliff by the fire.

What?

Look, ma, I'm just a tad bit wrecked, all this drama with Walt, she says, pinching leaves from the bag and dropping them into the paper. You may as well know that your daughter enjoys the occasional joint. Early Chase said he wouldn't be needing this anymore. So...

She goes about her business, licking the gum-lined edge of the rolling paper.

Lord Jesus, Ellen looks appealingly to John but he's lost in thought before the fire.

You're just going to sit by and let her light that thing?

He shrugs.

Barbara gingerly pokes the joint at the blaze in the hearth, places it to her lips and draws an orange glow. Ellen storms off to the kitchen, honest to God she says, I thought I'd seen it all but doesn't this beat the band.

Barbara blows a stream of smoke at the fireplace, and a pungent odor lingers. She sits indian-style on the woven rug in front of the hearth, glancing at her father. After another puff she proffers the joint to him and he shakes his head slowly. She's flicking the ashes to the blaze when tentatively he reaches out a hand. Taking it, dancing it through his fingers as one would a fine cigar. He pulls lightly on it, lets out a stream of smoke, coughs a little. Takes another light puff, then returns it to Barbara. She smokes what's left, tosses the last bit into the embers.

All the while Ellen fusses in the kitchen. She reappears in the doorway with a potato encrusted wood spoon bobbing in her hand, sniffing at a mingling of marijuana and cozy home-cooked odors.

Well I hope you've had your little bit of fun, she says to Barbara, anything to get a rise out of your momma.

Barbara looks up, shrugs indifferently.

Huh, isn't that it? Well this is our house and *I* sure won't just stand by and keep quiet. No marijuana smoking here! Never before and certainly not now!

Never before, says Barbara. Guess ya never noticed what was going on in Walt's little corner of the world up there, she jerks her head at the ceiling.

You have nothing to say to this, John Griffith?

He clears his throat. I-I ah, don't know what to say Ellen. Don't feel like I want to say anything. No harm done.

No harm done! Look at you, sitting there like a blank book.

Aw c'mon momma, you mean to tell me you haven't tried it? Barbara screws up her face.

Ellen recalls the night long ago with the house to herself, rummaging through her daughters personal effects upstairs. She's not about to confess it now. I don't need it. I don't need anything to get me high but the love of the Lord.

Sure, Barbara says airily, don't drink wine, the occasional spirits, eh momma?

That's different.

Barbara sighs.

Ellen says, look devil's advocate I'm not going down that road of conjecture, stand here and debate over what constitutes a drug and all that. I just don't need any drugs in my house. Period.

John starts after her, then sits back down on the sofa, feeling the weight of the situation and the change of atmosphere in the room. His thoughts become painfully self-conscious, years since he smoked the stuff. *You smoke when you're twenty, that's one thing.* He looks around the room, seeing the details- quiet and pensive before he inhaled, he is now positively a tomb. Inside the tomb are restless random thoughts, one leads just as quickly to another, he considers the weed, and then one solid horrifying thought sticks. He begins to grope at articulation, but he wouldn't want Ellen to hear it. It's simply this. *That pot we just smoked sprung from this tainted property out there beyond the window and this tomb that is me. Now I've tasted of it and it has tainted me.*

They assemble in the kitchen. Ellen considers returning the red silk napkins, china and silverware that she'd pulled from the antique server in the dining room in a more festive mood. But she hasn't and they remain, brightly adorning the table, a mockery to the mournful countenances on those gathered around a spread that could be a holiday meal. Crisp southern fried chicken, sweet potatoes, baked potato, green beans, hot biscuits and apple cider are spread about the table.

The doorbell chimes the eight notes of Shandon Bells *dum dee doo dah, dah doo dum dee* fracturing an uneasy silence. Ellen bolts from the table to the hallway, reappearing in the doorframe with stifled hysteria whispering *it's the law*. John jumps out of his chair to the sink, grabbing a can of pine-scented air freshener from the cabinet underneath. He bolts into the living room, dancing about and spraying pine in every direction to cover any lingering traces. Barbara flits about batting a newspaper at the air.

Evening Sheriff.

Ellen holds the oak door open wide and blocks the door frame, letting as much cold fresh air as possible waft past her and into the house. What brings you out our way?

Evening Mrs. Griffith, replies Sheriff Williams. May I come in a minute? Won't take up much of your time.

Ellen steps aside to let him pass over the threshold as the sound of aerosol spraying from the living room subsides. An insurance blast, *tss tss*. Ellen blinks her eyes, smiles at the sheriff.

Just then the two-way radio clipped to his waist squawks and he brings it to his mouth and barks, go ahead. The voice on the other end is garbled underneath white noise. No no, he says, that's alright Pete. G'wan home. I'm packin it in too, on my way home now. Bag it. He cuts the two-way, tips his hat and says, I hope I didn't interrupt your dinner.

John has Barbara by the arm, wrestling the newspaper from her while Ellen takes the sheriff by the elbow, whisking him past the living room door and propelling him to the kitchen. She asks him if he's had any dinner yet, hoping his police nose will give over to the scent of good ole home-made cooking.

No, thanks all the same he says. I'm headin back to the ranch myself. Mighty nice spread you got here.

The sheriff gets comfortable, plunking himself down in an empty chair, stretching his legs and crossing his ankles. He nods over at John, who returns from the living room sans the can of aerosol. John returns the nod and reclaims his spot at the head of the table- pulling the chair out to sit and lean forward, elbows on knees, propping his chin on his interlocked fingers.

I'm not here on official business. Just thought I'd drop by on my way home.

He removes his hat and places it on his lap, pushing back his thinning grey hair over the balding crown of his head.

So how you folks gettin on? Williams glances from one face to another. Barbara is serene, shrugs. Ellen smiles, taking the lead, the sober spokesperson. We're, you know, doing our best, Sheriff Williams.

John stares blankly at the table. Williams might take this for his previous displays of resentment and mistrust, but in fact the few pulls at Barbara's joint hit him stronger than he expected. The sheriff's sudden arrival wrenched him from a path of mental abstraction and introspection, and he's still not fully back on the main path. He's a little jittery, gathering his thoughts and wary of what may come out of his mouth.

Folks, I'm not here to apologize, I've got a job to do. I don't always like it, don't always, l-let's say... *agree* with all the laws which the courts and politicians task us police folk to enforce- he runs a finger along the brim of the tan Stetson hat in his lap- but I just want you to know John, I've known you a damned long time, neither you nor your kids have caused a lick of trouble for this community. You're... this place here is part of our history, Burrville's ancestry. I don't want to get all mushy here, just want you to know plain and clear I didn't initiate any of this. When

TBI and then the Federal Marshals come knockin at your door, you can only resist so much. I know what you're up against, I know you've been hard at it tryin to make an honest living. But you just got to understand John, my hands are tied. There ain't a thing I could have done then and there ain't a thing I can do now.

Ellen smiles and says in a voice just above a whisper, Thank you Sam. We sure can understand that.

And I want you to know me and my force have been on the lookout for Walter. Just hope we can locate him soon. We've alerted all other precincts in the state. Soon's we find him we'll bring him right to your doorstep.

Barbara sits with her arms folded, glancing now and then over at her father, who remains seated away from the table.

Thanks Sam, says Ellen.

Williams sighs and replaces his hat to his head. I wouldn't want to keep you folks a minute more from this divine meal. I'll show myself out. Let you know soon's we find out anything.

After the front door is pulled shut, the three sit silent a good while.

Well, Ellen glances at John. What do you make of that?

I'd say that's a man with something on his conscience, John muses.

That's exactly what I was thinking, Barbara says.

Thursday, In the Here and Now

From the bed Ellen hears them shuffling about between downstairs and upstairs. John and Barbara, readying themselves for another day. When John looked in on her a little while ago, she muttered *sick day*, and he asked if he could do anything for her. She said no and thought to herself *there's nothing anyone can do for me*.

The house has gone quiet, the room every bit as dark as the thoughts that bombard her. She feels incapable of facing the kids at Jamestown Elementary, facing her family, facing the fact that things are spinning out of control very fast.

Every time she thinks of getting up to brush her teeth and get going, she rolls onto her side to resume tossing and turning.

*   *   *

At Cindy's they encounter a not-so-amiable Cookie, who fumes at having her solitude interrupted once again. She doesn't crack the door any further than the chain lock will allow and she doesn't invite them in for a cup of coffee or anything else for that matter.

She aint here.

Let's beat it, Gavin says. Barbara suppresses an impulse to attempt a forced entry just as the door shuts and the deadbolt is engaged. They return to the truck and get back on the road.

Gavin says it's not far to Cindy's mom's place. Barbara glances over at him as he cuts the wheel of his pickup for a sharp exit ramp off of Route 40 just outside of Knoxville. Just what are we going to say, anyway?

Just leave that to me, he nods self-assuredly.

So you've actually got something in mind?

Not really, he furrows his brow.

Not really?

Well I mean, not exactly.

What do you mean not exactly?

I mean I wasn't up all night preparing my lines. Will you stop worrying.

I'm not worrying, just wonder what you might say.

What about you? It was your idea to come back here.
Yes it was.
So what are you gonna say?
I don't know yet.
You haven't a clue what you want to know?
I want to know where my brother is.
And you think she knows?
She may have some idea, Barbara says, working lip balm across her mouth.
So just ask her where your brother is.
Sounds too easy.
So what are you going to say then?
I don't know.
They drive past filling station convenience marts and strip malls that line the road to Cindy's mother's place in Sharpsville.
You sure she's gonna be here? Gavin asks.
Barbara pulls a makeup case from her bag, touches up her rouge in the tiny visor mirror. I don't know. I didn't want to tip her off that we were coming.
So what are you gonna say to her, Gavin says.
Shut up Gavin. Barbara snaps her makeup case shut and repositions the sun visor.
Not far off the highway they park in front of a townhouse in a neighborhood of houses wrinkled by peeling paint, their toy-littered front lawns speckled with mud patches. There's a porch full of rotting appliances across the street. On the sandlot of the house next door lay the rusting sculpture of a pair of bicycles.
Cindy's mother answers the door clutching her dressing gown at the collar, hair in curlers. She says Cindy isn't here and the puzzled glance she gives them through the partially opened door indicates she wasn't expecting any visitors. Nonetheless she cracks the door open and motions them into a tiny vestibule with a coat rack on the wall. Leaving their coats on, they follow her into a makeshift living room decorated in seventies-style faux-wood furniture, the kind that can be assembled in minutes with a screwdriver. Ashtrays and dirty plates are strewn about an orange shag carpet. A cat sleeps on its back on a brown leather sofa with its upholstery sheared here and there. More than a few cigarettes have been smoked here, with brief interruptions of fresh air in the comings and goings through the front door.

They are invited to sit down in black metal folding chairs in front of a soap opera on a television set on a card table. She glances at Gavin. I know you. Tell me your name again honey.

Gavin. When do you expect her back, Mrs. Blum?

I don't know what time she said she was droppin by. You sure she said today? Mrs. Blum furrows her brow and takes a drag off her cigarette, then commences a coughing fit.

Yep, says Gavin when the coughing subsides. Oh well, we can always hang out with Cookie over at her old place, he says with a wink to Barbara.

Barbara glances across the living room to the kitchen area and a beat-up refrigerator sat next to a sink abundant with dirty dishes. She returns her attention to Mrs. Blum. What caused Cindy to move out of there anyway?

Mrs. Blum bats a hand at the smoke in front of her and says, she's just staying on with me a little while. She's gotta take care of some business before she heads for California.

California? Barbara shakes her head in disbelief.

Mrs. Blum looks bewilderedly to Gavin. She didn't tell ya?

No. How long's she been thinking about this move?

Not very long.

Mrs. Blum throws one skinny leg over the other, folding her battered dressing gown. So what is it brings you two around here anyway?

The sound of a key in the lock at the door before either of them can respond. The door opens and Cindy Blum appears, framed by the sunlight, shoulder length blond bob around a soft-featured face. The angelic bearer of all light and goodness. She closes the door and removes her RayBans, eyes darting from her mother to the guests.

Didn't know you all were coming today, she glances from Barbara to Gavin.

Well here we are, Gavin says.

She nods at them and drapes her leather pocketbook over the back of the rocking chair next to the television. She smooths the pleats of a low-cut skirt, and remains standing. Barbara would prefer to have the soap opera on the blaring television turned down, but thinks it better not to push the issue. Cindy shoots her mother a meaningful glance and Mrs. Blum quits the couch and shuffles off somewhere upstairs.

So what brings you both here to my mother's?

My best friend disappeared, Gavin drawls. Been about a week now. Thought you might just be a little concerned.

Of course, Gavin, she grabs the remote from the floor and silences the television. It's just that... well, cold as it sounds coming from me, life goes on. Walt and I split up a while ago.

A while ago? Barbara says. Seems to me you were going over to the house regularly until a few weeks ago.

Look, what's the point of all this? You really think I know where he is? Well, I wonder. Nashville? Back to Chapel Hill? It's anybody's guess.

Not any more, says Barbara.

What?

Up until a few days ago, he was staying at Early Chase's.

Who?

You don't know Early?

No.

Well, you gave me his number, but let me stroke your memory. *Black Creek* Early? The old man whose wife had cancer?

Oh right, okay. So there you have it- she raises her palms to the air- Walt's still at large.

Yes he is and I'd like to know why he's running. What happened between you two.

That's our business.

Right you are, Barbara says as she draws Walt's unfinished letter from her purse. I found this. Going through his things.

What were you doing going through his things?

Just making *his* business mine, Barbara waves the letter and proffers it to Cindy. I wanted you to see this.

Cindy snares the letter, her lips moving as she reads it.

Barb clears her throat. I'm just curious about what might be the *devious* reason, as he puts it, for you *abandoning him in a time of crisis*?

Look, cool the Perry Mason routine. I- he was emotional, obviously. Anything could have crossed his mind.

Of course. But what's the *devious* reason?

That's easy. His lack of ambition, dwindling funds, any number of things.

But those aren't what I'd call *devious*, Cindy, Barbara says, shaking her head.

Look, just what are you getting at?

How much did you know about what Walt was doing on our property?

What? He... I don't know. He, well sure he was growing a little, Gavin could tell you that.

I don't suppose you mentioned anything to anyone else about his little crops, says Gavin.

Never! Why would I?

Well why wouldn't you? All kinds of things come up in casual conversation. You swear you never said a single word in passing to anyone about it?

No! Why?

Because, says Barbara, someone snitched. The feds didn't turn up without a tip.

How do *you* know? They do all that aerial surveillance, any flyover would have detected it easily.

I thought you said he was only growing a little.

Look, I've had about enough of this cat and mouse shit. I have nothing else to talk about, now if you'll excuse me...

Cindy makes a move towards the door to empty the room of visitors. But Gavin isn't having any of it.

Look Cindy, he bolts up from his chair, I'm sick and tired of-

-Look. Gavin. I would like it if both of you left. Now. Do I make myself clear? And take this damn letter with you!

What's this I hear about you shoving off to California so suddenly? he rasps like a reporter trying to get one last question at a press conference.

Yeah, Barbara says. What's up with that?

I don't have to answer that. C'mon, let's go. Both of you.

She makes a sweeping gesture, as if whisking petulant children from a room.

Not very communicative are we? You act as if you've got something to hide.

Look, Cindy says, planting fists to her hips. I'm calling the cops if you're not out the driveway in five minutes.

Oooh, aren't we getting ugly now, Barbara says, following Gavin to the door.

I'm well within my rights. I owe you guys nothing, you have no legal basis to question me.

Barbara pauses at the threshold, turning around to face Cindy. You're right, we don't. But having seen your true colors, I have to say I'm glad my brother dumped you.

I dumped *him*, she hastily replies.

Well that distinction seems *mighty* important to you. I'll remember that important point as I dig further into this.

Into what?

Whatever *devious* reason it is Walt mentioned in this letter.

Just why in the hell are you so bothered about somebody terminating a relationship?

It's the timing of it- Barbara looks Cindy dead in the eyes- the *timing*.

Cindy rolls her eyes, clutching the door.

Somebody snitched, says Barbara, and whenever my fool of a brother turn up I'll find out what the hell that devious reason is, and who all knew about this mess.

Your family's trouble is all Walt's fault. And what would anyone stand to gain for going to the authorities about it, beyond a sense of, I don't know, civic duty.

Money, says Barbara, lots of it. Money from the proceeds of the sale of our home.

I don't believe that for a second.

That's just what I'm starting to think Cindy, Barbara says, every time you open your mouth.

* * *

Upstairs in the bedroom, Ellen lies flat on her back. Her raw voice rings out to every corner of the house. She doesn't merely cry, she howls. She begs *Lord have mercy, Lord take this away*. She pleads amid tears for nothing but *help, help, help*. She tries to stir, thinks about putting dinner on, how much longer can this go on, how much longer until John or Barbara appear at the door and tell her to pull herself together? Then the pain hits her like a lightening bolt again in her chest. She rolls over on her side. The sun seeping through the curtains mocks her. She glances at the telephone on the bedside table but can't think of anyone to call who won't just say pull yourself together Ellen. Miriam? No, she'd think Ellen's having a nervous breakdown. *Am I having a nervous breakdown?* The thought causes her to shudder. She calms her breathing, settles on her side brings a tissue to her nose. Then it comes back to her mind in waves- she thought she knew what the pain was all about, but the more it manifests itself the more uncertain she is about what lies at its core.

She hugs herself, wraps her hands to her elbows, then her sides and moans with great despair *help, help, help*. Her words echo around an empty house.

*   *   *

John

Back from spending the morning with Frank Lynn, I sit at my workbench and fiddle abstractedly with the fine woodworking tools, cans of varnish, bottles of screws and nails, shuffle things around on the shelves. At last I get up from the stool to fetch a shredded tea chair and begin undressing it, rubber-tipped pliers prying rusted upholstery tacks that will be replaced. I'll use foam rubber to cushion the seat. I wonder which pattern of material might best dress this simple chair. I wonder how I ever came to worry about such trivial matters.

Would that I could drop myself back to just a month ago. I'd be strolling around my one hundred and four acres, perhaps imagining myself a wealthy lord in feudal times, mounted on his steed among the peasantry occupying the empire my grandfather had doubled with one stroke of the pen at the courthouse and a negligible sum after the neighboring land lay long abandoned. I imagine myself trotting about the estate on my horse, executing some annual assessment of the state of the empire. I'd be stunned out of my revelry at the sight of neat rows of marijuana plants in that secluded meadow. I'd cease daydreaming, run to the barn to fetch a shovel and that ancient sickle from the land of lost things and return to that meadow for the plant slaughter. I'd have erased the scourge on my land, knowing damn well that there would be repercussions with the law had they beaten me to it. The penalty, had I guessed back there on that imagined afternoon, would be nothing more than a minor fine. I'd have finished the inspection of the remainder of the kingdom very much in the here and now, leaving the playful dalliance in make-believe for a very real chore of the utmost importance and then I'd set myself to the task of finding out from whose hands the weeds, too neatly arranged to have been wild growth uncorked from my father's subsidized hemp days, sprung from. But this imagined afternoon remains a mere fiction. I know the weeds sprouted at my son's hands, as yet the government does not. But it hardly cares in building its case against 104-acres of land that cannot speak for itself, indeed its case didn't need to be built, it came incidentally with the arrest of Timothy Dawson. Throw it into the pot, boys, just a civil hearing and the land is ours. My son's direct involvement in the business has only served to muddy the waters. I can't tell my wife, she'd only exacerbate the problem by lecturing Walt. I could always do that better than she could.

Oh yeah, my wife. She's tucked herself away upstairs in a dark room, but more than that she's tucked herself away inside a shell that I can't seem to break. I arrived home this afternoon to a murky house with not a single light on. I called the name I have called for thirty years with increasing vexation, a gnawing sense that something had irrevocably changed. At last I climbed the stairs and saw our bedroom door shut, where it would usually be open. Inside I gazed upon what looked like a corpse. I was dead certain, because the body that lay on its back in the calm repose of the dead didn't answer, not when I called out from downstairs nor whispered to it there in our bedroom. At last my wife spoke- tiny tiny utterances about being very very sad.

* * *

Gavin pulls off Old Fork Road and into a dark driveway. They remain inside the pickup a good while in silence.

Well, Barbara yawns. I feel like I'm just banging my head against the wall.

I'm so sorry your family has to go through this, he says. I'm sure everything will be alright.

Thanks Gavin she says, pushing on the door handle and hopping out of the truck. Thanks for everything.

When she's walking towards the house he calls out to her. Good luck.

She turns around. Bows her head and waves.

The porch light comes on and a silhouette appears at the front door. Her father opens the door, steps aside and then takes her elbows in his shaking hands.

Your mother, he whispers with a nod to the ceiling. She's been upstairs all day.

What's the matter?

I don't know.

She talking?

A little.

Well what'd she say.

Just that she's very sad.

Barbara brushes past him and climbs the stairs two at a time. She knocks on the door, and can barely distinguish a small voice from within. She pushes the door open and gropes in the darkness for the light switch.

Please don't turn on the light, the tiny voice comes from under the blankets.

Can I light a candle?

No answer. Barbara retrieves one of her votive candles, cupping a protective hand over the tiny flame and scuttling back across the hall to her parents room. In the dim light she can see the form of her mother lying on her side, half of her face crushed into the pillow.

What is it? What's wrong momma?

Ellen blinks her eyes open but says nothing.

What is it? Barbara traces a finger on Ellen's shoulder.

Ellen barely moves her lips, Barbara has to lean over her mother's shoulder and strain to hear the thin voice, lightly grazing her mother's back. I'm just sad. Terribly sad.

Any physical pain?

A little. In my chest. My heart.

Do you want to go to the hospital?

Heavens no.

You sure?

They couldn't do anything for me.

Barbara pauses a moment, considers.

I love you momma, she says, placing the back of her hand to her mother's forehead. Ellen's head is as cold and clammy as the hand that Barbara squeezes.

I'm very sad.

I know. What can I do?

What can anybody do? I'm terribly sad.

You need to eat, Barbara says.

No.

Look, I'll bring you some soup. Toast. You need to eat.

Nooo, Ellen whispers.

I'll be right back.

I'm terribly sad, she hears her mother mutter before she's out the door.

I know I know, she whispers and shuffles off downstairs.

Well, says John, what happened?

Not much, Barbara says, emptying a can of soup into a saucepan. She just keeps saying that she's terribly sad.

That's exactly what she said to me, says John.

I'd say it's just all catching up with her. How are you?

Fine, he shrugs, just...fine.

Will you take this up to her when it's finished?

Okay, he says, sure. What happened at Cindy's?

Barbara sighs, Well, she didn't come right out and confess it, but-

-Confess what?

You know. What Early Chase said. About snitching to the authorities.

Right.

It only makes sense, she says. She wasn't in anything close to love with Walt, she hated East Tennessee, she had no interest in Nashville, so what was she doing here? What was she doing riding around and getting stoned the night before? Great timing, that's gonna look real good before a judge. And now she's just quit her job and is shoving off immediately for California. And probably to plunk a nice little down payment on a beach condo with her snitch money, if I had to guess.

Well doesn't that just beat all, he says, tapping a letter on the table. Oh, this is for you. From Bill.

Leave it there. I'll look at it later.

Cindy, he curls his lip, ruminating. Doesn't change a thing for our case. And she'll never admit it anyway. Doesn't have to.

Yeah, says Barbara, that's the hell of it.

*   *   *

Dear Barbara,

I really don't blame you for leaving the way you did. It doesn't make it any easier, days here have been dark and lonely, I live without heat because I feel I don't deserve warmth of any kind. I leave the house in complete darkness in the morning and I keep it in darkness when I return at night, because I feel I don't deserve any light either. It is my wish to be together, to work our problems out, to rebuild what I feel is after all, as good as life gets, holding down a regular job and coming home to you and kids at night. Don't fool yourself imagining there's much more in life. We are not children, we have to lose our longings for things we cannot have. But the love remains. You can never have the old Bill back, just as I'll never have the old Barbara. I'll always be here, Bill Fortney, waiting on you to come back to this life we shared, simple yes, but no less beautiful in the eyes of God.

Your ever-loving, Bill

Friday, The Crying Ghost

Ellen has called in sick for school again. Last night John fetched a blanket and curled up on the sofa. Through narrowed eyes he watched Barbara reading Bill's letter on the floor in front of the hearth. Crumpling it in her hands and tossing the paper ball into the fire.

He wakes up fully clothed and drooling against the crush velvet upholstery as the aroma of coffee, bacon and eggs waft in from the kitchen.

Barbara hands him a tray to take upstairs. The bedroom is a dark tomb. Setting the tray down on the bed, clearing his throat and announcing breakfast in bed.

Ellen's voice is muffled in the pillow. I have no appetite.

Aw c'mon. You've got to eat something.

I'm just so damned sad.

Ellen sit up for godsakes, John says from the foot of the bed. We're all in the same boat. Doesn't mean anyone's giving up.

I give up.

So where's your mighty God now he asks, toying with the breakfast tray.

I don't know John, she sighs. I really don't know.

*   *   *

Miriam Carter sits on the sofa and sips her tea, steeling herself for the daunting task ahead of her. She nods at the ceiling.

How long's she been like this?

Since yesterday morning, John shrugs. We've tried everything. Begging, pleading, full breakfast.

Well. Miriam dusts off her skirt, sets the cup and saucer down on the coffee table and rises with a determination. Entering the hall she draws a breath and bellows at the top of her lungs.

Fire! Fire! Everyone out of the house! Fire!

John and Barbara bound into the hallway, eyes darting in all directions. But there are no flames, just Miriam staring up at the top of the stairs. Ellen stands there in her nightgown- pale, luminous, an apparition seeming to float just a bit above the crush carpet.

Well, says Miriam. So our Lazarus has emerged from the tomb at last.

That was a nasty trick, says Ellen and storms back to the bedroom, slamming the door shut behind her.

Miriam hikes her skirt and starts up the stairs.

Ellen is seated on the edge of the bed when Miriam enters and draws the curtains to let in light.

Oh don't do that. Please, please don't do that Ellen says.

What's gotten into you? Miriam whispers.

I'm just very sad really.

You've got to pull yourself together.

How Miriam? How?

I don't know. Pray or something.

Oh, as if that will solve anything.

No. Just help you deal with it.

I can't deal with it.

You can't deal with it because you're not praying.

What's the good in that.

Look Ellen, you can't just lay around and give up. John needs you. Get up and help him deal with this.

Ellen props herself up on an elbow.

Deal with it? Look at you, Miriam Carter. So easy to stand there and lecture me, as if you'd do any better given the same circumstances.

What's that supposed to mean?

What could you possibly know about any of this hell? Just go back to your cozy life and leave us to our hell.

Cozy life?

Y'don't know pain like this, you've been given everything you're whole damned life-

-Well I never-

-That's right you never! *Never* had to deal with anything like what it is we're going through. So don't tell me to pull myself together. Close the damn curtains!

Miriam strides briskly out of the room. Alright Ellen, she says, if that's the way you want it.

Wait wait, Ellen says. I'm sorry Miriam. Please don't go.

Miriam stands in the hall clutching her pocketbook. Well are you coming downstairs for a cup of coffee then?

Could you bring it up here?

Fair enough.

Miriam shuffles down the stairs with a wink to John and Barbara.

That was brilliant, John beams.

Not quite the way she saw it, Miriam says.

I'm sorry Miriam. You know she doesn't mean any of it. We appreciate all you've done for us.

It's nothing John, she says.

But both John and Barbara can see in the way her hands shake with the serving tray, the deliberateness in each step as she marches it to the steps, the way her shoulders have sunken a little, that the harsh words Ellen fired had found a target.

*   *   *

There's this flannel shirt with a simple plaid pattern, two breast pockets, one bearing a stitch of the foxhunter. A lining which renders it a light jacket, the better to wear on a cold winter morning. The shirt carries the odor of the lavender soap Ellen drops in their dresser drawers. This simple shirt he's fished out of the bottom drawer was a Christmas present from Walt four years ago. John packs it for their getaway with the Carters.

Well, he says to Ellen, how do you feel?

Ellen merely shrugs and asks what time they have to be at Clem and Miriam's.

Five o'clock. That'll put us in Sevierville by seven.

Barb staying home?

Barb will be right here watching the phone and the door. I'm gonna do some shopping, make sure she won't even have to run an errand.

Ellen crushes a cashmere sweater into a suitcase crammed with what is more clothing than necessary, riffling through the contents to insure that those socks are among them, those wool socks that Walt had given her for that same Christmas four years ago, the one with a week-long ski holiday near at hand for the Carters and the Griffiths, one that would see them usher in 1988 with a welcome overdose of champagne. Clem was in good form, teeming with an abundance of his whimsical jokes and dry wit, pollinating the Griffiths with good humor. It was the culmination of a particularly joyous year for the Carters, the silver lining in a bad patch for the Griffiths. Ellen can remember that week, puttering around the glass-walled chalet in her warm wool socks and sweat pants. It was a crystal palace where they could sit in front of the blazing hearth, insulated from the frozen snow-laden pine world just outside the wall-length windows. The two women sipping at cappuccinos, while the tenderloin marinated and pies baked, their ski enthusiasm having waned long before that of the men. John and Clem would return with rosy cheeks and whiskey breath and kisses for their wives. It would mark the turning point in the intimacy between she and her husband. How would it look, after all, with Clem nibbling on Miriam's neck, wrapping his arms around her and cajoling her to their private domain off of the loft in the log heaven. How would it look for John and Ellen to do nothing but exchange indifferent stares, shrug their shoulders and set about engaging themselves in their respective distractions. But that is exactly what happened after the obligatory greeting peck on the cheek. Both sat before the fire, each to their own book as stifled noises of frolic and ravishment drifted down from the loft above them. Ellen felt like an old lady, busied at her stitching, prudish, clearing her throat but stopping short of glancing over to John to roll her eyes at the friskiness over their heads.

Maybe that's why she wishes that she were the one to stay home and monitor the phone and the door for the return of the prodigal son whose woolen gift she presses her fingers to. That other of his gifts of practicality, John's shirt, cushions warmth up against her from behind and she meets it with a cold stiffening.

Are you alright? You sure you're up for this?

Sure, she says, squirming out from under his arms. Then pinching his flannel shirt.

That's a nice shirt. I always liked it.

*   *   *

The pizza guy arrives just as they are about to give him up for lost. Barbara crushes a ten dollar bill into his palm and shoos Renee back into the living room, insisting she leave her purse in her pocketbook.

This is cozy, Renee uncorks the bottle of burgundy and pours two glasses, squatting down on the woven rug before the hearth. A seemingly interminable wait for delivery has left them both ravenous, and they make short shrift of the pizza. The film Renee brought goes largely ignored on the television screen.

Look, I'm gonna break the rules a little, okay? Barbara says while closing the empty box and setting it onto the blaze in the hearth. Then she fetches the sparse remainders of the plastic bag Early Chase'd given her.

Oh you're an angel. I left mine back at the ranch. Didn't feel right to bring it. I mean under the circumstances.

Barbara shrugs indifferently, rolls the remaining contents into a very large joint. We'll just take it outside if you don't mind.

They clink glasses and lock lips, a lingering kiss.

Oh what the hell, let's fire it up in here, says Barbara when their lips have parted. Just exhale towards the chimney.

She lights the blunt, meeting Renee's mouth to shotgun the smoke, hands the joint over to Renee to reverse the exchange. On the television screen behind is a close shot of lovers, their tongues lolling and darting at each other- a strange backdrop to the real life scene on the floor in front of it.

What a striking spectacle for the pair of eyes outside the window to take in.

* * *

Here's to old friends, Clem lifts a glass of zinfandel. Ellen downs hers and tips it back at Clem while Miriam nods to each in turn. Across the fine white linen tablecloth, John's studying gaze lingers on Clem, who's eyes are just a little shy of that gleam that would suggest all was right in the world. On the ride up when John'd asked him about the morning telephone conversation with district court Judge Sanders concerning the forfeiture proceeding, Clem'd waved his hand with his eyes fixed on the highway and said *let's pick it up on Monday John, no business this weekend, just put our worries aside and have a big time*. But it's clear to John behind the steady stream of light-hearted banter that Clem can't quite heed his own advice. And that makes John a little restless as his glance shifts between Clem and his somewhat affected merry making, Miriam as usual prompting the comedian, and Ellen getting tipsy sipping from her crystal glass. An uneasiness creeps over him, all the more disturbing is the fact that he can't place the root of it in the usual way. It's not all the things he can run through his mind-the case, his son's disappearance, or his wife's breakdown and remoteness on the ride up. The wine's making his head heavy and sleepy- he'd prefer a whiskey, a shot of beer and a cigarette. He sips at his wine- maintaining a pretense of affability, scanning the entirety of a gourmet restaurant. Candlelit dinners are underway, enough space between tables to insure that conversations won't collide. Anyway, the clientele aren't prone to loudly broadcast any personal angst, air their dirty laundry in front of complete and total strangers, clap each other on the back with full belly laughs, or otherwise *create a scene* in such an impeccably polished room beset by glowing candles and a blazing hearth that sets crystal, fine silver and china sparkling. In between checking in with those in his own corner, John's wandering gaze takes in the main floor on which his own party is seated. After a brief interlude to meet Miriam's hand-covered laugh with a smile, he looks past her at what is an open-air porch in summer, now dark and enclosed. And then he starts at the sight of this woman, her elegant blonde hair bouncing along with glimmering diamond earrings for some animated story that is out of earshot. She leans forward to her dinner companion, whose hand is placed on her black-stockinged thigh- prominent against the short crush velvet dress with a low pearl-bedecked neckline. He brings his hand from her thigh to the table where their fingers lock, then he leans in and brushes his lips lightly against hers. The woman is indisputably the real estate queen herself, Lura Breckenridge. Her dinner companion is not her husband. There is no infant set in a high chair at either side of a table for two. And John's glance has been too long, Lura turns her head to meet his gaze and he averts his eyes too late. His own dinner companions look at him imploringly. He knows there's only one way off the hook- leaning in, saying, Hey, isn't that the Breckenridge girl? Don't let's all look at once.

    Clem recognizes the stranger sat across from Lura whose fingers are now withdrawn from hers.

    I'll be damned. He's a recent client of mine.

    They return to their meal, and Lura Breckenridge is left unobserved and uninterrupted. Just after they've ordered dessert, the party of two on the outdoor porch pass their table on the way out. John has watched from the corner of his eye, the paying of the bill, their making ready to go, and as Lura walks in front of her beau onto the main floor, there's a brief meeting of the eyes between them before she scans the table, her attention resting on Clem.

This is David Harris, my right hand man for hunting real estate in these parts, she says in the starch manner of introducing a business associate to a group of esteemed colleagues. *That and whatever else he wants to hunt*, John thinks, wondering if Clem or Miriam might be on to them. If they are, they have the utmost discretion and social graces, because their faces don't betray even the slightest hint of bewilderment. David Harris's unremarkable looks are punctuated by the onset of a paunch John's sure Lura's spent a good part of their meal disparaging. He shakes hands all around the table and sidles up to Clem to talk shop.

Thanks for all the help with the deposition, Clem.

Clem waves a dismissive hand. It was nothing. Well look here, he says as the dessert tray is presented by the waitress. I must've spoken the magic words, he says, beaming at the carrot cake plunked down in front of him. S'posed to be keeping this figure buff for retirement.

You and somebody else, Lura replies, poking playfully at David Harris's burgeoning waistline. An awkward moment at Lura having betrayed some level of intimacy, having in so familiar a manner chided he whom is supposed to be a business associate on his weight. Clem and Lura conduct a banter that ingeniously interweaves business and frolic. John merely observes, in his lined flannel shirt that is too warm for this room, a white cotton shirt would have better suited both the setting and his comfort level. He catches Ellen observing him, excuses himself to the restroom, all smiles and waving precipitately at Lura.

Once inside the black and white tiled washroom, chrome-polished and scrubbed tile sparkling where he stands in front of the mirror, he unfastens a couple of buttons to let some cool air carry under the shirt that is always too hot for indoors. After he's splashed cold water on his face he starts through the bar for the restaurant Lura and her David Harris are heading towards him on their way to the door. Lura extends one of her black-gloved hands to catch him by the elbow and he expects some accusation, some passionate denunciation of his rather racy inner thoughts, a claim that she can see right through him, because from the onset her detached professional demeanor seems to have been hijacked for a more convivial and familiar one.

Mr. Griffith, I-I just wanted to express my regret... I'm sorry to hear about your problem with the law.

Aw well, that's mighty kind of you, Lura. Clem's gonna help us fight it to our last breath if we have to.

Well I was saying to Lura, says Harris, sidling up beside her as he sticks his arms in his overcoat, feds are generally pretty narrow-minded in these cases.

Lura shoots Harris a reproving glance for having betrayed their discussions of John Griffith's personal matter.

Well says Harris, jiggling his keys, we've just had two of them right here recently. Just outside Sevierville. Government put the property up for auction sooner'n you could say spit. Owners claiming they were innocent, didn't make one bit of difference- he shakes his head, clucks his tongue- Wicked law.

Lura shoots Harris an admonishing glare. Harris quits the key-jiggling and says he'll fetch the car. Lura returns her attention to John. I'm sure Clem'll straighten it all out.

Up here for the weekend, are you?

Yes, she replies evenly, Daddy's wanting to get into a little condo development.

Nice parts for it.

Yes, we think so. Anyway, we'll miss hearing your radio show as well. That was some fine music they'll just never be able to replace.

John bows modestly, it's beginning to dawn on him that Lura's had a few cocktails today, because she normally doesn't carry compliments let alone drop them.

Well, he says, I sure do appreciate that. Just hope you weren't tuned in to the final shebang.

To this Lura has only a blank face in reply. Then this top selling professional breaks out into what may actually constitute a *giggle*. John's a little unsettled, debating whether he should laugh along. She pokes his arm playfully, grips and squeezes a shoulder, saying actually my best friend was listening. She said it was a little heavy-handed- she locks her hands on his elbows- but true Mr. Griffith. You know, you really spoke from the heart, not many people do that these days.

John has by now placed his hands on her elbows, mimes *thank you* just as Ellen appears at his side in the dimly-lit bar. John and Lura Breckenridge unlock arms with a swiftness that makes an innocent enough situation seem like a delicate one.

*   *   *

On second thought, Barbara thinks, the pot lingers in the air, and it's not so far-fetched Williams might return. What would they say to the benevolent officer of the law then? Toss the joint into the fire, only to have police digging the hearth for incendiary evidence. On this wave of paranoia, she bolts up from the floor to the front door to allow cold fresh air in. She pushes the storm door open and rushes out into the chill night air, turning her head at heavy footfalls across the porch to her left just in time to catch a glimpse of a fleeing figure in a red down jacket.

Walt!

Barbara clings to the storm door while staring with a fixed intensity towards the crashing sound at the left of the house, eyes fixed on the ominous intruder bolting away from the porch and into the woods.

Come back here! she screams, sprinting across the porch, leaping onto the frost-hardened ground and tearing through the yard after her brother, whose silhouette disappears into the edge of the woods.

The sky is star-riddled, a diminished moon spills no light. She continues hollering out his name as she sinks into the foliage. The forest is a dark tomb. She calls out her brother's name and stops to listen for the crunch of his footfalls on brushwood and sapling, and to allow her eyes to become adjusted to the darkness. It's an inky black that serves to attenuate her sense of hearing to the sounds of her brother clumsily groping around in the dark. She can hear Walt's heavy breathing plainly just up ahead and to her right, struggling blindly to negotiate the standing pines, moss-backed logs, fallen branches, thickets. She thrashes around in the darkness, branches sweep across her face as she tries to narrow the margin between them.

Pricking up her ears and running blindly as a fresh fear infiltrates her heightened senses. Just how long was Walt spying on them from the window? Does he carry her dark secret with him into these woods? She runs smack up against a pine, wincing at the sharp stab of pain to her shoulder- clutching it and rubbing at it through her sweater, shivering.

Walt! a fresh urgency injected in her voice. You little shit! Get back here! Her voice rings out, leaving only an eerie silence, for a moment she thinks she's lost him, then the footfalls ahead resume and with them her frustration mounts. God only knows where he's running to, it's like chasing a frightened kitten devoid of any logic. Her fingers are numb as she gropes her way through a thicket. Just when she thinks she's cleared it she tumbles over underbrush and falls on her chest into a puddle, the muddy water soaking her shirtfront, splattering her face.

Walt you son of a bitch!

She pushes herself back up on her feet to chase footfalls that are getting further away.

* * *

The waitress returns the card and receipt to Clem, who insists on picking up the tab, along with all other bills for this excursion in the Smokies. John makes his usual protestations and Clem waves them away. They return to the highway, yet another billboard for Dollywood, its namesake cute-winking an invitation. Clem makes a glib joke, referring to a part of Dolly's anatomy and likening it, or them as it were, to the immensity of these very mountains. John barely manages a light grunt. Ellen sits far across from him in the expansive back seat of the Lincoln- the buoyancy she'd previously displayed over a few glasses of wine having given way to melancholia.

At Mullen's Farmhouse B&B they are ushered in by a middle-aged woman with the carriage and disposition of old age. After the matronly proprietor matches names to faces, Clem and Miriam shuffle off with their few bags to a converted barn just behind the farmhouse and their suite above. John and Ellen haul their bags up a wide staircase just off the dining area at the front of the farmhouse. John unlocks the room and Ellen carries her travel cosmetic bag to the bathroom to commence her ablutions, closing the door tight.

John changes into his flannel pajamas and lies down on the bedspread of a massive double bed, imagining a long night of tossing and turning. He fetches his paperback from his bag. It's a collection of short stories of contemporary Southern writers, something he picked up at the beginning of summer and hasn't got very far into. He's been looking forward to devouring it, his hunger for stories hasn't subsided a bit, but tonight he can't *taste* it, his eyes pick up the words across the page but he is unable to digest it. Placing it down, he sets the alarm clock on the night table and stares at the bathroom door. When at last he hears the door handle turn, he swipes the paperback and replaces it under his nose, lying on his side there on the edge of a generous bed. Ellen pulls the covers back on her side of the bed and climbs in without a word. When it's clear her silent treatment won't elicit response from John she sighs and says with her back to him.

Just what was it had you so piqued back there with that Breckenridge girl? I mean all that… poking and, well, wrapped in her arms and laughing.

We're not a little jealous now are we?

C'mon John, she's half your age. Last time I saw her she wore pigtails, she sighs. You want to grope a girl, at least have the good sense to do it in private.

I wasn't *groping* anybody, he flings the paperback across the room at the mirror.

Let's not go breaking things now, we're guests.

John leaps off the bed, pulling his corduroys over his flannel pajama bottoms.

Where are you going? she says to the wall.

For a godamn walk, he rasps with such acrimonious bite it startles even his own ears. Though I'd say it ought to be you leaving this room.

He picks up his socks and shoes. Calling up restraint so as not to slam the door and possibly disturb the other B&Bers, he tiptoes down the hall, sitting on the top step to finish dressing. In the dining room Mrs. Mullen is arranging the tables of white linen for tomorrow's breakfast.

Just out for a little fresh country air he says, his smile an effort to put on.

Cold air. Gotta dress warmer than that in these parts, she says, shuttling napkins around a table.

Just a short walk. I'll be alright.

Whereabouts are you from, she queries, I mean, if you don't mind me askin.

Just outside of Jamestown, he says, trying to determine the path of least resistance across the table-scattered room to the front door.

Wait. I'll have to open it for you, the woman interrupts her table-setting, reaching into the breast pocket of her denim dress to extract a ring of keys. Now he's all the more ill-at-ease at having put her out with this anomaly in the routine. At the same time, an idea hits him right then and there, and he knows as awkward a request it is he must put to this somewhat reserved woman, it will greatly serve to calm his nerves over the next few hours.

Pardon me, but I wondered if I could beg a favor, he says and the woman's brow begins to furrow.

Need a wake-up call?

Actually, um... I-I don't suppose there's an extra bed, um, somewhere about the premises. You see, my wife, she- he lowers his voice confidingly- she has this terrible snoring problem and I just haven't slept a wink these past few nights. She's already fast asleep up there, and I'd just leave a note inside the door so's not to alarm her in the morning.

I'm sorry but we've got a full house tonight.

Oh, I see, he considers asking about anywhere, a barn, something. Don't suppose there's a cot or something? I could set up in our friends' room?

Well, sure Mister um-

Griffith.

Mister Griffith, that's no problem at all. As long as you don't mind to help me drag the old thing out. It's in the laundry room.

He follows her under the stairs and through a door to a basement. Amid whitewashed concrete walls, a washer and dryer, paint cans, Clorox bottles and massive laundry detergent boxes is a very narrow cot, a metal folded frame with a thin mattress.

Sorry, it's not much.

It'll do just fine.

Now will we ring Mr. Carter's room?

Actually, this is going to sound a bit ridiculous, um, but I'd rather not disturb Clem and Miriam. If it's alright with you, he yawns at his fist, nodding his head, I've no problem just pitching it right here. That way we don't have to go lugging it up the stairs at any rate. Really, he shrugs at her blank look, I really don't mind. I'm just tired and need a good night's rest. I can fold it up in the morning.

Look, Mister Griffith, I don't know what the situation is, and I reckon I don't want to know. But for all the trouble you're going to in order to sleep on your own, I do have a single room at my house in the back that I'd be happy to let you have.

He takes it. They walk up to the lobby and John goes up the wide staircase with the pretense of gathering up his hygienic necessities and leaving a note with his sleeping wife. He listens in at the door. Nothing. After what he feels is sufficient time, he shuffles off, back down the stairs where Mrs. Mullen hands him a set of towels and leads him down a hallway to the last door. He nods gratefully and prepares for a good night's sleep. But when he lies down on the heavenly featherbed mattress, his mind races.

*   *   *

Barbara is doubled over in the blackness of deep forest, coughing and cursing at the footfalls ahead of her that she's been doggedly pursuing, the gap between them closing.

Walt you fucker, listen to me. I know you can hear me. I'm lost. I don't know, maybe you are to. But Renee's back there at the house, and so help me God if I'm not back there soon she's gonna have the cops out, I godamn guarantee it.

There's only silence. Then she hears it, from the darkness just off to her left. The sound of sharp and staggered breathing. Tentatively, she steps toward the sound. Leaves crunching lightly under her feet are as unwanted as a coughing fit at the symphony. She plods on towards sobs that reach her ears clearer with each measured step.

Walt? The trepidation in her voice carries a fresh spell of fear- what if it wasn't Walt back there on the porch? Wishing the crying ghost would identify itself. *Walt*, she whispers urgently.

A grunt in response. Then a soft muffled voice, words indistinguishable. She plunges ahead haphazardly in the darkness, twisting and turning in every direction. A splash and water creeps into the sole of her sneaker and her sock is soaked. Cursing under her breath, she reaches down to feel the current of a creek bed.

Stay put, she calls, *Where are you?*

Here.

A soft reply so close to her she nearly screams. And then she spots it, underneath her, the red jacket, leaned up against a pine. She goes to it and drums her fists at the hood.

What the fuck are you doing out here? Dragging me out, I'm soaking godamned wet freezing and what for! Momma and daddy have both gone to pieces!

She slaps at the jacket and he offers no resistance. What the hell's wrong with you?

The sobbing starts again and her rage begins to dissipate, a strange ache welling up in her throat. She drops onto the cold ground next to the jacket and folds it into her shivering arms while the body in it shakes uncontrollably.

I'm sorry, the muffled voice repeats between gasps for air.

Shsh, there there, she repeats, because that is all she can think to say. She pulls the hood back and what was once a long mane of brown hair is now reduced to a peach fuzz- but the eyes that stare back at her, the wet ruddy cheeks are none other than those of her estranged brother.

Why did you run Walt? Didn't you think to at least call to let us know you're alive? We were worried out of our minds, God only knew you weren't lying dead in a ditch somewhere.

God knows I tried.

Tried? Tried what Walt.

I would have done myself in. I just didn't have the guts.

Oh please don't talk like that.

For a while there's just the sound of the soft ripple of the creek bed and the wind whistling through the pines.

Where are we? Barbara stares into the inky black.

I'm not for sure.

Well let's get going back.

I'm not going back.

The hell you aint. What're you gonna do, stay here and live on nuts and berries? she asks. Just how long have you been out here anyway.

I don't know. A few days I guess.

A few days.

Yeah.

Oh that's great. And so, like what exactly is it you intend to do out here?

I don't know yet.

You don't know yet. Well you better make a plan, because the government is gonna be at your heels pretty damn soon. Although that's not exactly the assessment you gave Early Chase.

How do you know Early Chase?

I didn't just start looking for you tonight asshole.

She grabs the jacket with both hands and pulls him up to a standing position.

Let's start making our way back. Before Renee has Sam Williams' men crawling all over this godamn property.

But it's pitch dark and I'm as lost as you are, Walt replies.

Barbara releases her grip on the hood and presses a warm hand to his cold whisker-stubbled cheek.

Yeah, right you are brother. You're just as lost as I am.

Saturday, A Mutual Air of Futility

A knock on the door stirs John out of a deep sleep. He rubs at his eyes, squinting at an unfamiliar room.

More knocking.

Mister Griffith?

Yes.

There's a telephone call for you.

Light creeps in from behind a curtain on the room's lone window. He gropes along the carpet for his watch- it reads seven o'clock. He gathers yesterday's clothes from the floor and dresses hurriedly. Outside the door, Mrs. Mullen wrings her hands, then leads him back to the reception desk and the telephone.

He knows who's calling and hopes for good news.

The prodigal son, says Barbara, has returned.

Walter?

None other. Wanna talk to him?

Put him on.

He drums his fingers on reception desk, glancing around him, waiting for the voice at the other end of the line. The voice arrives, dull, sluggish. Hey.

Where the hell've you been?

Here and there. Listen I'm sorry. I just came back to pick up a few things.

Well, why'n the hell didn't you call or something?

I guess I was ashamed. *Am ashamed.*

Well y'damned well ought to be, John eyes the breakfast room where Mrs. Mullen serves the early risers. Dammit, you had us all worried sick. Dammit.

A pause. John traces a line along the desk with his finger.

I love you son.

Love you too.

Hate you too, at the moment.

Can't say I blame you.

Sit tight. Don't go anywhere.

John replaces the phone and riffles the brochures on the desk. Sunlight spills into the dining room, setting all the glass and silver on white table linen sparkling. Mrs. Mullen whisks through the dining room door holding an empty milk pitcher and a vacant stare. She shuffles to the kitchen with a polite smile.

John steadies himself against the desk and massages a stiff neck. Cotton-mouthed, stomach grumbling, glancing at the stairs.

When he opens the door to the room, Ellen is wrapped in blankets at the far side of the generous bed. He shuts the door behind him and the room is dark but for a line of glowing white under bathroom door. Silent, not even the muffled breathing of sleep from the body under the blankets. He gropes along the wall for the light switch. The bedside table lamp throws a soft light as he crosses the room and kneels beside the bed. His wife is curled up in the fetal position, the bedspread pulled up under her chin, her face a pale mask.

He whispers her name, but the statuesque face moves not a muscle.

Ellen?

He gives the bed a good shake.

Ellen.

Shaking her by the shoulder. Digging a hand beneath the covers and grasping her cold clammy hand.

Ellen!

He gets to his feet and vacillates between staying in the room or running for help. Glances over at the line of light from under the bathroom door.

In the bathroom towels are strewn all over the floor. On the basin is a brown prescription bottle beside a ravaged makeup case.

Secanol.

Oh shit, oh Jesus Lord, oh my God!

Bounding back into the room, flinging the covers off the bed, grabbing her wrist for a pulse, putting a finger to her delicate nostrils to feel the slightest trace of breath. Rolling her onto her back and cupping his hand around her neck. Pinching her nostrils shut, he places his lips to hers and blows with all the air he can muster from his lungs, each breath shorter and more forceful as panic mounts. At last he disengages his lips, panting, searching her face for signs of life. He drops his mouth upon hers and once again begins attempting to revive his wife with waning hope. Just as he goes to inhale, he tastes her exhale. Places a hand over her ribcage and there's a light pulsing.

Ellen!

She gasps for air. A cough, then staggered breathing. But breathing no less.

*   *   *

It's a damn good thing Renee doesn't scare easy. It would have been longer getting back to the house last night in the inky black if she hadn't thought of bringing the flashlight to lead them back. After she and Walt had stumbled over all manner of nature scattered about the forest floor with a mutual air of futility, they'd heard the faintest sound of hollering, and hollered back in unison. Presently a ray of light swept from the wall of trees in front of them. They could make it out dancing about the branches until at last Renee shined the beam at their faces. *You didn't call the cops did you*, Barbara wanted to know. Renee shook her head vigorously and then they trudged behind as she trained the flashlight on the branches she'd stuck in the ground with their tops duck-taped on her way in, reflective flags that the flashlight could pick up. It was pretty much a straight line to the house and when they got back it was nearly two o'clock. There wasn't much chance to talk in the forest and when they removed their jackets, Barbara said we'll talk in the morning. Walt flopped onto the couch and Barbara covered him with blankets. She and Renee'd collapsed in her bed. She woke a few times and went downstairs to check on Walt.

This morning she finds him in the Griffith living room on the sofa in a dead sleep and prods him in the ribs. When the three of them are assembled in the kitchen for breakfast Barbara turns from the frying pan, waving a spatula at him.

Just what the hell did you intend to do anyway?

I dunno.

You don't know.

It's like a told ya, I was just waiting on a chance to gather some clothes for winter, I don't know, head for Nashville. I'm not thinking straight.

You got that right she says, dropping the spatula to steady herself on the kitchen table- squeezing her eyes shut and shaking her bowed head. What're we going to do with you Walter.

Walt glances between his sister and Renee, leaning against the counter, arms folded. So like, maybe it's not my business, but are you two an item now?

Barbara brushes the hair from her face. Renee clears her throat. Walt leans back in his chair.

Where's the car anyway? Barbara asks.

Over at a friend's.

Who? Please don't tell me Tim Dawson's.

He shifts in his chair.

Oh my god.

Nah, he toys with his coffee mug, that'd be the first place they'd look.

What the hell were you aimin to do?

I told you, I don't know.

Walt lays his head on his folded arms. God, I don't know anymore. I just don't know anymore.

What did you come back to the house for, Renee asks.

Just some winter clothes and stuff, he says, head buried in his hands. He glances up to find dubious looks on both of their faces. What?

Barbara shrugs.

Okay, okay, he throws up his hands, *Je*sus.

They follow him into the hall and upstairs. In the hallway, he snares the pull string for the ceiling door and the crawl space. The sound of uncoiled springs and Walt unfolds the ladder to the floor. There's just skinny denims and soiled Converse high-tops as the rest of him disappears into the dark confines. He gropes around for the drawstring for a bare light bulb. Light spills from the attic while he pulls himself in the rest of the way. They hear his footsteps above their heads and it's not long before his face appears at the ceiling. He passes them a sizeable Tupperware tub and between them they manage to wrestle it down the ladder.

Kinda heavy, I know. Walt says from his perch.

Can I open it, Barb wants to know.

Go ahead.

She pries open the lid and her eyes bulge at the sight of what lies within. Neatly wrapped clear cellophane packages tinted with the green of their contents.

Damn Walter, you're lucky the cops didn't come crawling all over this house. Why didn't you remove this a long time ago?

Hadn't dawned on me immediately.

Hadn't dawned on you?

He sighs. Too much on my mind.

Well, says Renee, what other illegal boobie traps do we need disable?

That's it, says Walt.

*   *   *

John and Clem hoist Ellen down the stairs and past Mrs. Mullen and her bewildered breakfasters, Miriam scuttling in front of them holding doors open. Mrs. Mullen's directions are written in bold cursive, clear and concise, directing them along a series of back roads to an emergency medical clinic. Ellen's head is in John's lap and he strokes her hair, squeezes her hand.

Clem is very much in command of the situation, prodding John to rummage Ellen's purse for her insurance card, badgering Miriam to repeat directions as she cries unabashedly. When at last they've rolled up to a brick building bearing the sign Sevierville Medical Center, Clem bolts to the reception desk and convinces the nurse his friend needs immediate attention. There are few scattered about the ER waiting room and none appear to be likely patients. As John produces the insurance card, Clem says save the paperwork for later, we can't wake this woman up.

The staff gets right down to business. Later, after assuring them Ellen's stable after a stomach pumping, the doctor wants to know was she prescribed the Seconal.

Why no, John gapes, I don't know where she got them.

When they assemble in the waiting room, Miriam wipes at tears. I told her the dosage, she says, blowing her nose into a Kleenex. I never thought in a million years.

How many did you give her? asks Clem, placing a hand on her shoulder.

Seven, eight, something like that.

Miriam shudders, looking up at them imploringly.

It's not your fault Miriam, says John.

Bet that's the last time you'll dispense medicine without a prescription, Clem says.

Oh shut up! Miriam bawls.

I'm so sorry dear, Clem squeezes her hand, guiding her to the sofa. That was a stupid thing to say.

*   *   *

Barbara replaces the phone and turns around to meet the expectant gazes of Renee and Walt.

That was Daddy. Said they won't be back until sometime tomorrow. They're having a great time, you know, taking their mind off everything. Said stay put Walt, and he means it. Sounds way more glad than mad.

She meets his incredulous glance and wonders if he isn't somewhat vexed by their lack of urgency.

Look, she says, they've been really cooped up here Walt.

I know.

You know, it's not as if you didn't worry momma nearly to death. We had to resort to drastic measures in order to pry her from bed yesterday.

I know.

A flurry of fists on the front door. It has the urgency and brazenness of official business, but when Barbara peers into the tiny window it's Gavin cupping his gloved hands and breathing the vapor of a frosty morning. When she lets him pass through, closing the door on the chill, he removes a pair of wool gloves and rubs his bare hands together.

Any news on the dumbass?

Barbara jerks a thumb at the kitchen.

Well, well, the sumbitch's come home at last.

Gavin strides up behind Walt and claps him one on the shoulder. Don't get up, he says and then glances over at Renee.

Cops bring him or did he just show up by his lonesome?

Shee-it, Walter drawls, I needed the law to get back here Id've called them for a lift.

Well, Gavin helps himself to a chair. He spins it around, folding his arms over the rail and perching his feet on the rungs. What've you been up to?

Nothing much, Walt says.

Nothing much, Gavin mimics, kneading the stubble on his wide chin. Well aint that something.

He spent last night right here under our noses, Barbara's voice sounds from the living room.

That right? Gavin says while reaching to accept a cup of coffee from Renee, stirring in sugar calculatedly. Haven't bumped into that girlfriend of yours lately, have ya?

Ex, Walt qualifies. And no. Why?

Did you know she's movin out west?

What?

That's right, chuckin it all in- he sips tentatively at the coffee- gonna hitch her wagon and shove off to Californy.

How'd you know this?

Right from the horse's mouth, ace- he points his spoon at Walt- from the mysterious lady herself.

Just wish I'd have wised up sooner, Walt says.

Just out of curiosity- Barbara spreads her palms at those present- seeing as we're amongst friends, what's your theory on why she dumped you?

Walt cocks his head indignantly.

Oh hey listen Walter, we've all been dumped before. No reason to be bashful.

Bashful? I'm not bashful.

Well go on then. What's up with this up and leavin?

He appears to them a scientist rummaging an overworked mind to articulate a theory. I thought it was odd. The whole thing with the DEA. Just how they...I don't know...turned up at our door. I mean, far as I know Tim took the fifth from the get go. I can't see him cavin. I'll be damned if he'd have spilled anything.

Walt glances over at Gavin. I know you don't think the world of the guy, but could you see him draggin other people down with the ship? I mean, what does he stand to gain by that anyway?

Well I don't know. I think it's more than coincidence that the forfeiture notice turned up on the heels of his arrest for crying out loud.

She was going two for one, Barbara ruminates. She blew the whistle on the whole operation. She stood to collect a little cash for turning in a drug dealer. Plus it makes Timothy look like the snitch. At first glance anyways.

Cindy, Gavin says, played Dawson for a fool. She was getting tired of him. Yeah, in all likelihood she snitched the whole operation for her own gain.

Walt shakes his head in disbelief at his friend's words and the light they shed upon the sum total of the relationship.

What a bitch, Renee says.

Just when exactly did all this begin to dawn on you Walt? Barbara asks.

Guess it was something Dad said, just after he got all that material together in Nashville. About snitches, informers. Taking a share of the proceeds. Of the land.

Now our wires are starting to connect, says Gavin.

So you don't think I'm talking out my ass with any of this, this um, theory I'm coming round to.

Quite the contrary, says Barbara, I'd really hate to hear you defending her.

What do you know?

Just what I gleaned from um, oh dammit Walter, I gotta confess. I'm sorta guilty of some invasion of privacy. Yours.

He wags his chin at her to continue.

The letter. The one you started to write. It was on the back of one of your um, song lyrics I guess. In your desk drawer.

What else did you find there?

Enough. At least enough to know it wasn't all Dawson slaving away in that meadow back there.

He shakes his head, shuffles over to the fridge.

C'mon Walter, Barbara prods. It's a little late in the game to be playing coy. If you're gonna come back, at least bring the truth with you.

Walt absently rummages around the fridge. Does Daddy know about all this?

Yeah.

He must be real pissed.

Wouldn't you be?

Of course, he says, closing the door and returning to the table empty-handed. Flopping back down in the chair with a great big sigh. I wanted to believe so much she wasn't tied into it. With the cops I mean.

Ah well, says Gavin, sliding his cup across to Renee for a refill, don't guess we can pin anything on her. Not that it would matter a hill of beans anyhow.

Walt hunches his shoulders, shivering. It's just hard to imagine all this. To be sitting here right now... Jesus, a few weeks ago you couldn't have told me-

-Damn right, says Barbara. Not what you expect from our sweet Cindy.

Sweet and cunning, Gavin says.

Yeah, Walt says, but you've never seen her sweetness go sour.

Oh yes we have, Barbara nods.

Did you talk to her?

I told you I wasn't exactly sitting on my ass waiting for yours to turn up, she says, Where the hell you think's the logical place to start?

How was she? I-I mean what was her vibe?

Well Walt, the *vibe* started out nice enough, but chilled a bit with our line of questioning.

Well how did she seem, what did she say?

Hmmn, Barbara purses her lips, mindful not to expound on Cindy's reluctance to join the search party.

It's more what she didn't say, says Gavin with a glance to Barbara. I mean, like, you had to remind her about Early Chase, didn't ya?

I suppose it was her guardedness about this sudden move to California, says Barbara. She pretended to know nothing about your sordid activities at first. Before Gavin and I teamed up.

I just know she snitched, says Gavin, just wish I could glimpse her bank balance in the next few months. I-I mean, if this forfeiture thing should, God forbid, go through. Just wish we could prove beyond a doubt that Cindy-

-It wouldn't change a thing now, Walt glares and they fall silent a moment. He slides his chair out, heads towards the living room. It's too late to change one damned thing now.

No one in the room has anything to say to this.

Sunday, The Test of All These Things

No church services for Ellen today. Everyone sleeps in at the motel they booked, foregoing a second night at the B&B to the relief of a sympathetic but wary Mrs. Mullen. They've just finished breakfast and John glances at his watch, anxious to get home. Everyone seems to have come into his stewardship now—it's solely in his hands to prevent Walt running away from home, to prevent Will learning of a mess back home, to prevent Barbara going back to Pennsylvania, to prevent Ellen getting her hands on anything that might constitute a fatal overdose.

They check out ten minutes late and after breakfast at the Waffle House next door they pile into Clem's gigantic Lincoln. Miriam sits beside Ellen in the backseat trying to placate her with small talk and, that having no effect, pats her hand and tries to convince her things are sure to take a turn for the better. John's anxious to get at whatever it is makes Clem look so forlornly at the blacktop in front of him. The miles seem to drag on despite Clem's excessive speed.

So what did the DA have to say after all, Clem?

Clem shoots him a warning glance, nods to the backseat. His friend's guardedness causes John to bite his nails, craving the cigarette that would not be allowed in the close quarters of the heat-blasted Lincoln. He says, there's a rest area just beyond Lake Lure. I sure could stand to stretch my legs a little.

Well, says Clem, so could I.

They pull off into a rest area by the lake and the women start toward the visitor's center for a cup of coffee while the men excuse themselves for a stroll, taking a concrete path to the lake.

There's a wind off the lake and at the end of the path they stop and look straight out over the water.

Okay Clem, what's going on?

They sure as hell don't waste much time John, executing the summary judgment.

Any idea of when the hearing will be?

Yes, says Clem. Next Tuesday.

What?

Two days from now.

Clem puts an arm around John and pulls his friend right up against him. How long we known each other John?

Bout as long as I can remember. Right when we started school I guess.

I told you at the outset of this mess I didn't want to make any promises. You remember my unfettered, impartial approach to this? I didn't want to pat you on the back with false assurances.

John grimaces, nodding slowly.

Damn it's hard to keep a professional distance here.

Just spill it Clem. I need to know. What did the DA say?

He, um... he thinks it's pretty certain to hold up John. The forfeiture.

John looks to Clem imploringly- seeking more opinions, more thoughts, more words. There aren't any.

*   *   *

On the television- football. The Redskins are losing to the Giants in a close game. Walt slouches in the recliner with waning interest. Renee is curled up next to Barbara asleep on the sofa. A vigilant Barbara forces herself awake, she can't bear the thought of her brother escaping before her parents return. A book of old photographs from their college theatre days lies at her feet. She'd flipped through the pages with Renee peering over her shoulder. She reaches for the wrinkled paperback on the end table *You Can Heal Your Life* and fans the pages, minuscule scrawling in her mother's hand at the margins. Etched in these narrow spaces are those silly names *Shoe* and *Merry* and she stares at the references to her mother's kin, there alongside the topics- children of alcoholics, painful childhood memories, unloving role models, the unloved child and self-esteem. Two names that constituted a frugal maternal lineage. Two people her memory is scarce on, two joyless grownups whose uneasy presence as a young girl she had suffered occasionally with her parents on Sunday afternoons. She thumbs through the dog-eared pages and thinks about her mother. Renee pinches her knee. I think I'm gonna head home. Barbara shivers. I was just thinking of putting a fire on. Renee picks lint off of her shirt. You want me to hang around?

Up to you, she says, secretly wishing Renee might remain here, with darkness coming on and her brother turning morose.

Renee eases herself from the chair. I gotta get up early for work tomorrow.

She slaps Barbara on the knee. I'll call you tonight.

Cool. Barbara follows her to the door, indisposed to say goodbye, takes a hasty peck on the cheek, and closes the door on the cold night beyond. When she returns to the living room, Walt is gathering up bits of kindling near the hearth. They set about building a fire and once it's going they sit cross-legged before it, the shadows cast by the flames playing across their faces.

At last Walt clears his throat and speaks.

So how long have you and Renee been, um... cozy?

Barbara stares at the licking flames around the crackling saplings. Not very long.

When did you start to-

-It's not why I left Bill. I still like men, you know.

Walt shrugs. Sure.

You know what I think, Walt? I think everyone's bisexual. Naturally. It's just a behavioral choice. It depends who you meet.

You really believe that?

Yes. I do.

Jesus Barbara.

Well it's just a theory.

Walt shrugs. So are you in love with her?

Are you in love with Cindy?

Course not.

Course not, and why? Why is that Walt? Because she left? Because it looks like the odds are pretty good she used you for her own financial gain? Wouldn't true love stand up to the test of all these things?

Well, for that matter, why'd you stop loving Bill?

People change I guess.

Well- he stabs the poker at the grate, the glowing coils- So you didn't answer my question. Are you in love with her?

Renee? I don't think so. Maybe.

There a cute guy at the bank or something?

Will you cool it with the stupid questions. Barbara drops her head to her palms, massages her temples.

They tend the fire and watch the second half of the game with the sound turned down. Barbara buries her head in a sofa cushion and falls asleep curled up next to the dog on the rug in

front of the hearth. A little while after Walt's covered her with a crocheted spread, he hears the sound of wheels on gravel outside.

*   *   *

John

My wife is overcome by emotion and she crushes my son against her, gripping him by the shoulders and pushing him out in front of her as if to verify he's not a figment of her imagination. The shaved head delayed recognition a little for me. It's as if the criminal is dressing the part, as if he's returned to us to announce a prison sentence. My wife bestows blessings and showers prayers upon the prodigal son, continuing to thank God for bringing the family together again. The dog, not usually prone to excitability, barks in every direction.

I clap my son's shoulder a few times and give it a good squeeze, walk through the kitchen past the dog to the basement, damning God as my feet fall heavy upon the steps. Damning him under my breath for bringing us together again because maybe we're not so great for each other. Because we hurt each other on a regular basis, we spoil each other rotten, we deprive each other of that which our poor souls crave most, we buy all the wrong presents, we say all the wrong things at the wrong time, we fail to cook to each other's taste, we fail in patience, we do all manner of clandestine things behind each other's backs, we leave the dog-feeding to the next person, we make a mad rush to judgment, we disappoint with our failures at social institutions like marriage, we carry emotional burdens that no one can relieve our aching minds of, we are stuck with trials and tribulations that are supposed to build character but only subject us to character assassination. And speaking of those trials and tribulations God, those constant little tests? Should any more turn up unsolicited upon my earthbound sentence as a proving ground on the road to heaven, I swear to you God when I get to heaven I'm gonna kick your ass.

Monday, Something Closer to Heaven

Barbara

You awoke this morning with a burgeoning sense of guilt and regret- it dawned on you that tomorrow is the day that marks the thirtieth anniversary of the union of the two souls who bore you into this world. There is no chance for a last-minute bid to effect the extravagant party you had considered one long month ago. Invitation cards remained buried in your desk drawer in Pennsylvania, while you set out on a passage from a kind of hell to something perhaps a little closer to heaven.

After stopping by Bacara's in Jamestown to make a dinner reservation for four tonight, you find yourself a few streets down in the county courthouse digging through dusty documents- from birth, marriage and death certificates to land records to create a true Griffin/Griffith Genealogy. There is of course, the absence of forebears on the maternal side, your mother having been folded unwittingly into the Griffiths- a woman without a history. So the clerk signed you in and you're gathering what information will help you fill out the branches of the family tree.

You start with the most obvious document. Your parents' marriage certificate. What a nice touch to enclose a copy of its public record on the thirtieth anniversary of it, along with a full-poster representation of the family tree you'll have printed over at Jed Regan's shop. Your father shrugged when you'd asked if he'd retained a copy of their marriage certificate, said he'd not seen any reason to trouble himself about a piece of paper. But you're sure he'll see it in a different light under the circumstances. From among the reams of paper tending towards discoloring, the thirty-year-old document before you bears the weight of significance, a treasure with its untarnished existence thirty years down the road from the union that was precursor to your birth. The ink has long dried on the signatures.

The date is wrong.

January 28, 1961. You read the date on the paper and do the math over and over, maybe there was a delay in executing the document? Did they go later for the certificate? Not likely. But you Barbara Griffith, came into this world on May 14, 1961 and you have your own birth certificate to prove it. You hold the parched document in your trembling hands, losing all interest in combing through any more records to create a timeline of events to outline the story. Because the timeline has altered the story you've come to believe about your parents, yourself.

*   *   *

Walt rose early, scratching himself with a sense of relief. Agreeable, penitent, he started for the bathroom with that sense of one purged of sin as he splashed warm water at his face and reached for his razor, balling up shaving cream into his palm. Three days beard stubble under that crew cut made a villain in the mirror staring back at him. Nuts and berries and little else for a few days made it so he could begin to see the shape of his ribs, leaning over the sink. He'd have to go back to the wilds for the tent and the sleeping bag. Here he is in front of the mirror he's stared at himself in for most of his life. Home again, though he senses- swiping at whiskers with a well-worn cartridge- that it will not be for long.

*   *   *

John's going the furniture restoration route, having lost enthusiasm for examining legal documents for what will come to be an administrative hearing before a judge. He's stretching some fabric over the seat of an armchair when Barbara descends the stairs.

Hold this, he says, pressing the fabric overlaying the edge of the seat while gripping a pair of shears. She places a hand to it. Harder, he says.

Well, she says after he's made the cut, I found something you've been covering up. Unless there's something I'm missing.

What's all this about?

Something I found down at the county courthouse. In the records. About tomorrow.

Tomorrow, he shrugs, pushing out dubious lips.

Have you forgotten?

No. Course not. Haven't ever in thirty years. Certainly not this one.

Have you forgotten about what made you marry?

He squints at her. I'm lost.

She's eased the pressure on the fabric. He taps her hand. Hold that thing down while I pin.

Tomorrow isn't really the big day is it? Have you managed to forget that all these years?

He lays the fabric on the workbench and adjusts the folds with a smooth of his hand. Well, I didn't think, we didn't think-

-I saw the marriage certificate. Down at the courthouse.

He plants his hands on the workbench, tapping it. Why is it so important to you. We, we've all gotten by fine all these years like this-

-I think I had the right to know the circumstances around my birth.

She paces the floor haphazardly, wringing her hands.

Barbara, sometimes what you don't know can't hurt you. I think this is one of those cases. Godammit, you were born out of love. It's not as if you were born out of wedlock, it's just-

-Would you have married if it weren't for me?

I'd say we were headed that way.

Headed that way? Had you even proposed?

I don't remember.

Don't remember!

Ssshh. I don't remember *exactly*. It's the way it pans out for a lot of folks. I just know we went on to raise you. And your brothers. We did the right thing under the circumstances.

How could you not tell me?

Jesus Barbara, when were we supposed to tell you? What for? What difference does it make?

Now I see she says, laying her head on the bannister. It's all so clear.

See what, he replies hoarsely. I just thought it better you didn't know. So did your mother.

Course *she* did, she's full of secrets. But I'd expect more from you.

Barb, I, I'm sorry.

She starts up the stairs.

He bolts over to he bottom stair and calls up to her.

Barb, please don't stay angry with me. Think what you'd do if you were in my shoes.

I don't see as you've got anything to celebrate tomorrow.
Oh yes we do.
And what's that? An obligatory marriage?
No Barb, no. A marriage and everything that came of it.

*   *   *

It's the eve on the thirtieth year of a day that has come to be known as their wedding anniversary. They pull into the gravel lot at Bacara's Family Restaurant in the station wagon. Bacara's is about the finest dining you'll find in Jamestown. It's rustic, from its weathered wood siding outside to an interior that is all wood, with a dim and cozy lounge and a large dining room.

Griffith, party of four? Barbara announces to the hostess with the reservations folder pressed to her bosom. Walter stands beside his sister, decked out in a blue sharkskin suit with a thin necktie. Barb wears a crush velvet black dress with her hair pulled up to display a string of pearls around her neck. John wears a tweed jacket and corduroys and fidgets with his tie, Ellen beside him in a plain floral print dress clutching a white purse, her eyes darting around the dark-paneled room and those loafing about nearby on leather upholstered sofas jiggling drinks in their hands. To the hostess, as she leads them to the dining room, they appear to be One Big Happy Family dressed for a special occasion. She seats them at an oak table aglow in soft candlelight. The waitress arrives with menus.

The shared experiences of a family, remembrances of the past, familiar anecdotes are trotted out to laugh at once again. But John's cheer and affability appears affected in contrast to Ellen's silence and unresponsiveness. He keeps glancing over at her to catch some tiny glimmer in her eyes at the retelling of five-year-old Barbara's going missing for hours at the county fair and then turning up at Ellen's craft booth like nothing happened after a frantic search, or Walt and his younger brother Will's chemistry experiment in the barn that ended up with a visit from the fire department.

Over dinner, the reminiscences play themselves out and at last they are returned to the bleak present. After an awkward silence, John clears his throat. Well he says, it looks like our day in court's come sooner than I thought. Tomorrow, by God.

You think it looks good? Walt asks.

We all gotta keep our chin up and hope for the best, John says not too convincingly. Life goes on, no matter what for, no matter whom with.

What are you saying daddy? Walt's eyes dart between his parents.

Just that there's the way things ought to be- John takes a swig of wine and sets the glass down for emphasis- and the way things are. There are plenty of places to live. We have our health- he raises his glass- I may lose... things around me. I might stand before the judge to hear a guilty verdict. But I haven't committed a crime. I won't flinch. They can take my land, my house, but I refuse to let them run off with my dignity.

He stabs a fork at his steak while the others remain silent, Ellen looking down and working her fork and knife at the veal.

Walt hunches his shoulders, says, I'll never forgive myself for this fucking mess.

*Walt*er, Ellen's eyebrows rise indignantly and she glances over her shoulder to see if anyone's listening.

John refills the wine glasses all around. Barbara raises her glass, clears her throat and says, I'd like to propose a toast. To momma and daddy. I remember many happy times growing up. Sometimes the memories are all I have to keep going. Thanks for giving us those happy times. May many more lay ahead for you.

Would that they could bear to raise a glass to that land of theirs, nestling them in its bosom, innocent and alluring. That promised land, that place of happy memories. The home they just might find somewhere else. Or perhaps they are fated to wander the next forty years, exiled to some barren emotional desert. Banished from their promised land, a broken promised land. The waitress comes to see about dessert. Barbara announces there's a surprise cake she will fetch from the car and the waitress leaves them smiling between themselves, the One Big Happy Family. Feast today for you never know what tomorrow may bring.

Tuesday, December 7 1991

Jamestown, Fentress County Courthouse, the Honorable Judge Gregory Ezekiel Sanders presiding.

All rise, the bailiff commands and the judge appears from the wings, bent over a cane and walking towards the bench with a hobbling gait.

Good morning, he addresses those gathered after settling himself in behind the bench and shuffling through papers. Clem had told John repeatedly that the judge was given an extensive pre-trial briefing on the matter at hand.

First up today on the docket, the judge says into the thin microphone in front of him, is the case of *United States vs. 104-acre parcel of Real Property with Residence*. Will the rightful owner of said property please stand.

John rises and speaks loud and clear. John Griffith, your honor. He raises his hand and the bailiff swears him in.

Do you have legal representation with you Mr. Griffith?

Yes your honor.

Will Mr. Griffith's attorney please identify himself to the court?

Clem rises and the judge beckons him to present his case.

You honor, Section 881a7 of the United States Code allows the civil forfeiture of any real property that is 'used, or intended to be used, in any manner or part, to commit, or to facilitate the commission of' an illegal drug transaction. The United States Courts of Appeals disagree on exactly what the government must show to prove probable cause for forfeiture of real property under section 881a7. The First, Fourth, and Eighth Circuits hold that the government must prove that the real property had a 'substantial connection' to the illegal activity. In my client's case, there clearly wasn't any illicit activity on the premises of his residence on the parcel of land in question. As stated in the transcript of the criminal case of Timothy Dawson, my client's son was indeed engaged in the activity on the tract of land in question and in fact collected a meager compensation for its use. At no point were there any drug transactions on or about the premises of Mr. Griffith's residence, nor were any of the proceeds that resulted from the illegal activity used in any way for either the purchase of that residence or improvements to it.

I believe, says the judge while riffling through a stack of papers in front of him, I have the transcript of Mr. Dawson's testimony here in the pre-trial briefs.

Now your honor, Clem continues, the Seventh Circuit, on the other hand, has rejected the substantial connection test, and instead requires the government to show only that the real property had 'more than an incidental or fortuitous connection' to the crime. Our own circuit has not expressly adopted either standard for forfeiture of real property under section 881a7. We have stated, in the context of the forfeiture, under section 881a4, of a residence used to facilitate an illegal drug transaction, that to support a forfeiture under section 881, the government must demonstrate probable cause for the belief that a substantial connection exists between the residence to be forfeited and the relevant criminal activity. We ask your consideration of the facts born out of the criminal trial testimony of Timothy Dawson in determining the proper measure of justice regarding the innocent man who sits before you who stands to lose a home that has been in his family through five generations.

They go on like this, the judge and Clem, for over an hour while John looks straight in front of him and awaits his fate.

After a long pause, the judge glances over his bifocals at John.

I have reviewed a copy of the response letter to the DEA which your counsel has provided. Is there anything you wish to add, Mr. Griffith?

John clears his throat. Your honor, I can only state clearly once again that I had neither knowledge or consent of any illegal activity on my property. These last few months have been greatly upsetting to both me and my family-

-Please keep it relevant to the civil forfeiture proceeding.

Yes your honor. I have nothing further to say.

John sits and folds his hands on the table, glancing over at Clem while Clem pats him on the arm. The judge wets a thumb and leafs through the documents before him.

Mr. Griffith, I have given this case careful consideration in light of the facts born out from the time you received notice of forfeiture regarding your assets. It is this district court's decision to deny forfeiture of the single-family residence in question. In addition this court denies forfeiture for five acres adjacent to that residence.

The judge slams the gavel. John buries his head in Clem's shoulder- shuddering.

Wednesday, April 15 1992

John

The sun is setting against a sky of red and brown hues across New Jersey's meadowlands, dipping behind the mighty oil tanks that line the flatland fields, like giant coffee cups on one giant countertop. In my son's Chevelle I skirt along the edge of this concrete landscape. Green signs loom- attached to intricate network of poles with reflective lettering indicating a means to an end- Elizabeth, the Verrazano Narrows Bridge, Holland Tunnel. The Garden State Parkway has four lanes but that doesn't help traffic any. Cars zoom past me in a constant stream, at a speed such as I've never witnessed. I'm jumpy, my eyes darting between the wide tarmac in front of me and the rear and side view mirrors. A voice in overdrive on the radio announces a blowout sale at a furniture outlet in a place called Parsippany. I've never been to this state and am just passing through. I wonder about who christened it the Garden State, and what prompted them. I try to imagine how it would have appeared to old Seamus all those years ago traveling in the opposite direction, gazing out the window of a creaky train in uniform with a gang of Union soldiers- grubby, unshaven men, most of them on their way to a certain death. Back then they'd have rolled through fields of lilies, daffodils, violets, forget-me-nots, maybe they glanced down on ripe tomatoes and corn and these signs of life in beautiful bloom perhaps served to quiet anxious minds. But for chance I may not have come to be here driving my son's Chevelle, packed to the gills with those personal effects I carry with me. The onslaught of crazy, erratic drivers makes me unsure of the odds of continuing my existence. I guess if I haven't allowed the Feds to do me in, I won't allow a few crazies behind the wheel to either. The federal government almost took my legs out from under me, right up until my house and some of its acreage were exonerated in a civil hearing. I did surprise myself with the undying will to live. What force of nature allows the homeless to wake up cold, hungry and sleepless- only to get on their feet and rummage through garbage for sustenance? At the same time what makes a high-priced law partner, or tenured professor, or self-made entrepreneur running a well-oiled machine cave to inner demons and do themselves in? I've lived and I've lost- more than some, less than others.

The decision in the district courtroom put an end to the anxiety uncertainty brings, as did Walt' sentence for cultivation of an illegal substance. The morning after the summary judgment I woke up in a house that was still mine and looked across the bed at the woman who I wasn't sure would remain my wife. We have decided that it's best to live apart for a while.

After Easter week at Mary's, I will begin a year's working residency at what is a historical landmark. My sister's practice has procured many a contact among the state's elite in culture and the arts and one of these, a fellow with a burgeoning waistline and an inclination to chuckle away under greying beard at my sister's gossipy wit is John Halloran. Big John is a professor with a PhD in American History and a member of the Historical Preservation Society. He knew of positions coming available for caretaker and restorer for residences of historical significance in Massachusetts. We dressed up both my resume and myself when I boarded a plane to spend Thanksgiving with my sister Mary and interview for these posts. In a week's time I'll wake up in a two-hundred-year-old house. I'll put the coffee on and stare across a meadow at a building that was once quarters for slaves and will now be my workshop as I restore all manner of old items for the house. I will receive a modest stipend and comfortable lodgings in return for one year, during which the place will be opened for historical tours, re-enactment. I will not be able to hang anything of a personal nature on the walls since it is not my house. I will find out what it's like to live on my own.

Ellen and I have separated, for now anyway. I don't miss the tension and the ongoing disagreements over finances, family matters and most everything else under the sun. I don't miss the castigation, the reproving looks, the fits of anger, nor assignment of blame. But I do find myself missing my wife.

Barbara's already in New York and has her apartment sorted out so that is where I am headed now to spend a day in my daughter's new life.

It's as if we've all changed our identities- we're rethinking our roles, changing our landscape, our geography. It's a wonder we haven't change our names, we are like those placed in the federal witness protection program. I should be so lucky, because

I'll probably never quite be able to shake this nagging portent of being found out unawares again for something by a government meant to protect and serve. I feel as safe with them as I would someone I'd just ratted out, after the ordeal I've been through.

Who'd have imagined a year ago I'd be driving my son's car all the way to Boston for a job commitment. I'm not one for long shots, always been for dead certainties, the serious-faced kid impatient at the next thing to do, while Mary seems to know that whatever's around the bend can wait for her to smile- at the lens, at a client, at the sky, at an ex-husband. She always smiles. That's what Will said yesterday on the telephone, and I told him I know, it could sometimes piss me off, everything to her seemed funny. But Will didn't have to hear my sister cry in a steady stream of late night phone calls when Mike left her stuck with kids and bills.

Why didn't I tell Mary straight away about that notice of forfeiture posted on our door? Why did I wait until I was certain it wouldn't hold up? My sister and I are not very close. Well that's not exactly true, what I mean is not home-town close, in the way of connecting at holidays, trading gossip, planning weddings and funerals. But I reckon over the years cards were mailed, long distance phone calls were placed. A few week-long Tennessee vacations joined my kids with their far-away cousins for a spell.

New Jersey skyline fade ye into the pit of darkness that descends upon this driver unused to the frenzy of busy highways and their travellers. Both hands squeezed on the steering wheel as I approach the George Washington Bridge. As my wife said more than once, you can take the boy out of the country but you can't take the country out of the boy. Glen Campbell sings to me on the radio *country boy you got your feet in LA but your mind's in Tennessee* as I climb this bridge with watchful eyes and scan for the next potential accident, sticking to the right lane and leaving the fast lanes to those more daring than I. Would that this wouldn't have come to pass and I might wake up and see it all as a bad dream. Would that I might have been able to remain peaceably among that which I've become accustomed to- the call of pretty birds fluttering through forests of pines, spruces, dogwood and azalea, Virginia creeper carpeting the forest floor, the flowers dancing color all around- a familiar play yet teeming with novelty. Stop it John Griffith. Pay the toll, watch the light turn from red to green. Drive on.

*   *   *

Walt's doing four months in state prison. Clem helped get a reduced sentence at his criminal trial. He has yet to exhaust the supply of paperbacks his sister brought to him. He keeps his head down, tries to keep out of way of the other inmates. He wonders what it is he'll do when there's no bed and three square meals a day. He tries to forgive himself, but he cannot. He worries about what his guilt-ridden mind might make him do besides kick himself- he might hurt himself worse. He thinks about Nashville now not with excitement but trepidation. It seems overwhelming and imposing. Perhaps he won't assimilate, will be buried in the sad anonymity of city life, hampered despite his efforts- he has a felony on his record now, on his record and his job applications.

In the meantime, he worries about funny business in the prison. Funny business like dudes picking fights out in the yard, groping him in the showers or worse. But State is way easier time to do than Federal, according to those inmates who've done Fed time. But until he's out of there, those are tenuous assurances at best. Meanwhile he's constantly watching his back, looking over his shoulder.

He worries about his mother and father, and what they'll decide regarding their future together. By the time the truth came out at his trial his mother was too drained of energy to chastise him, to pound her fists in disappointment. She hadn't punished him for his wrongdoings. None of them has, they've let him off easy, perhaps regarding the punishment of the state already too heavy a burden for him to bear. Yet he's certain he needs the punishment of others along with the punishment meted out by a penal system, so as to spare him the curse of punishing himself.

*   *   *

Barbara

It's the end of your shift waitressing at Sardi's. You report some of your tips and walk away on painful legs that will have to go that extra mile. Rehearsal tonight. One anxious audition after another led to a minor part in a small-time production of a little-known playwright. Sometimes you wonder what the hell you are doing. Like when you're on the subway and those who work in smart suits and dresses uptown fumble over you and one another and gaining a seat, spread the a copy of the Times or the Wall Street Journal on their lap. Like when you see happy couples younger than yourself stumbling arm in arm out of the revolving door of Macy's, some inside joke and a bag of shopping pressed between them. Or when you forego a night out due to lack of funds. Or when the phone rings at the flat you share with Charlotte the secretary and once again it's not for you. Or it is for you, it's your mother asking you how the money's holding out. You laugh and say what money, cradling the cordless in the crook of your neck and dancing it around an apartment too small to properly pace in. You take classes at NYU where you're enrolled in the Tisch School of the Arts Graduate Acting program. Your divorce is all but finalized and the house in Pennsylvania will be sold and the proceeds divided. You don't mind to lose the house and you need the money to enroll full-time when summer comes. You constantly remind yourself you will be alright and sometimes you actually believe it.

The last visit to Walter at the state penitentiary had you fighting back tears until you had left the bleak grey-walled innards of the penal institution. You asked if he needed more books. He merely shook his head. Back to your car, you put the key in the ignition, grasped the steering wheel and lowered your head to it. Then you just lost it. You broke down right there and shook and cried. A stocky man in a blue uniform tapped at the window and asked if you were okay. I'm fine, you said. Rolled up the window and drove off. Not a mile beyond the barbed wire gate you pulled over and lost it again. Upon groping around the glove box for Kleenexes, your hand met Renee's house key on the fluorescent green slinky-style keychain. After a quiet composed cry, shoulders shuddering, you drove off.

Meanwhile things are warming up in Manhattan, you begin to enjoy walking city streets and shopping at thrift stores. There are people bustling about in droves and they are yours to meet. There is so much to explore and many days you feel as if years have come off you since the roof caved in back there in Pennsylvania and then in Tennessee. It is springtime and Easter brings you to Boston and your aunt, your father, your brother. You called your mother in Burrville before you set out a little further north. You feel the strangeness of being with your family for the first time in years at Easter, but a gathering bittersweet nonetheless with the absence of that private woman of shifting moods that you've come a little closer to understanding. Maybe through her you'll come to understand yourself a little better. Maybe new surroundings will be just the catalyst you need for a profound change. You're out of the Box. For now, anyway.

*   *   *

Will

They told me everything.

Aunt Mary was outraged at the news. I suspect my father will have to bear the sympathetic growls of more than a few left-leaning cocktailers at my aunt's party tonight, become the subject of injustice for them to wiggle fingers at what they perceive as an oppressive authoritarian government.

Am I angry? I guess I ought to be. My anger's directed at so many targets- the federal government, the DEA, the courts, local cops, my irresponsible dim-witted older brother, Dawson, the nebulous Cindy Blum who for the record I never cared much for- and it's an anger as eternal as infinite space.

My father spilled it all to Aunt Mary last year before he flew up for Thanksgiving, out of my earshot. They didn't want to disrupt my studies. But after the holidays, they disrupted my studies only to tell me that all was not lost, having spared me the months of agonizing over losing all. I don't know if that's a good thing or a bad thing.

My father is looking forward to new surroundings, when he arrived up here he was like a bird of spring returned from a long winter, winging from branch to branch with a curiosity for all of the new landscape around him. I took him on the Freedom Trail one sunny day and we strolled from one landmark to the other and he was gaping like a kid at Christmas with each present unwrapped before his eyes- Park Street Church, King's Chapel, Quincy Market, the enormous USS Constitution. At last we went for a walk around the Boston Commons and he marveled at the panorama of all the new species of plant life, twirling around like a happy drunk behind me.

When we returned to Aunt Mary's in the late afternoon, she greeted us at the steps of the townhouse wearing canvas work gloves and gripping a trowel. She led us through the living room to the expansive kitchen and ultimately a bright sunroom at the back of the old row house- through its French doors out onto the patio to see her impeccably manicured city garden with the bright colors of forsythia, azalea, bougainvillea- flower beds surrounded by a fence covered in the greenest ivy. My father and I stood side by side on the threshold of the doors.

Look John, she said, beckoning him to a blooming garden bathed in late afternoon sun. She crouched and pointed at what I could barely discern over their shoulders as a tiny green spear jutting out of dark soil she sifted through her fingers. One of my begonia perennials, she said. The first bud of spring.

He smiled, his hands folded behind his back, peering over her shoulder.

New beginnings he said, kneeling down for a closer look while I looked on.

Make a wish, John, Aunt Mary said- her lips pursed in a smile- make a wish for your second life. Make a wish.

She crouched next to her brother- my father. I pictured them as the little kids they once were, crouching down in those woods behind the house, the smell of honeysuckle ripe among the dogwoods where they bent over to examine a cocoon on the verge of butterfly, just the way my own sister and I did one day- Barb enamored of the beauty of the transformation, I fascinated on purely scientific grounds, wanting to procure it in a pin-holed plastic tub and bring it to my microscope for closer examination. Barbara clucked her tongue, with admonishing taps at the back of my hand. *Set it free*, she scolded, *this is its moment, this is perhaps the biggest moment it will ever know, its second life*. As she returned her gaze upon the emergent butterfly her expression softened. I'd laughed uncomprehendingly at her silliness then, rolling my eyes, shaking my head at my space cadet older sister. Now, after all these years, I think I understand.

ABOUT THE AUTHOR

Ricko Donovan resides in Nashville Tennessee. When not plying his hands to a variety of stringed instruments, he types away at stories. When not raising his voice to song, he is known to tell stories. He's made some pretty cool records too.
www.rickodonovan.com

www.ingramcontent.com/pod-product-compliance
Lightning Source LLC
Chambersburg PA
CBHW031409290426
44110CB00011B/315